A **FLESH** & **BLOOD** SERIES

MEYLER

A FAMILY MEMOIR

WITH FINTAN O'TOOLE

www.**HERO**BOOKS.digital

HEROBOOKS

PUBLISHED BY HERO BOOKS
1 WOODVILLE GREEN
LUCAN
CO. DUBLIN
IRELAND

Hero Books is an imprint of Umbrella Publishing
First Published 2021

A CIP record for this book is available from the British Library

ISBN 9781910827369

Cover design and formatting: jessica@viitaladesign.com
Ebook formatting: www.ebooklaunch.com
Photographs: Inpho, *Evening Echo*, *Irish Examiner*, and the Meyler family collection

DEDICATION

To my parents Mike and Josephine, who gave me the inspiration, heart, drive and commitment to do anything I wished, and to have belief in my own ability. And to Stella, my rock, and Sarah and David, for the joy they bring to my life.

– John

To my wonderful wife Cally, and our treasured children Alanna and Brody, thank you for making my life meaningful. And to nanny and grandad Bowles, who nurtured and loved me as a young fella.

– David

CONTENTS

ACKNOWLEDGEMENTS

MY FIRST WORDS of thanks must go to my parents Mike and Josephine, who created a wonderful environment for the three of us – myself, Gerry and Carmel – to develop and grow in a loving, caring home.

A special thanks to my late brother Gerry, and my sister Carmel, for their help over the years and especially for looking after our parents in their later years. To all the Meylers in Wexford and the Bolgers in Moneenroe in Kilkenny, who helped and assisted over the years. Thank you.

Hurling has been my life and has brought unreal joy, satisfaction and massive disappointment, but I have treasured all those memories. To Our Lady's Island GAA Club, who nurtured me as a young lad; Franciscan College Gormanston for my early development; UCC for maturing me, and to St Finbarr's National Hurling and Football Club for giving me years of joy, great friendships and happiness. A special thanks to everybody in the Barrs for treasured memories.

Thanks to Wexford GAA for all their help over the years when I was a minor, under-21 and senior player, and county manager. To all the clubs I have been involved with, and special thanks to Ballinhassig and Courcey Rovers for great times, friendships and success. A big thank you too to Kerry GAA for their massive support and friendships. To the GAA family all over the country and beyond, a thank you for all your support and assistance.

To colleagues I have worked with in Murphy's Brewery, CMP, Martins Dairy, and Lee Strand, a special word of thanks for all your help. And to my current employer MTU, thank you for a rewarding life of lecturing over 30 years and affording me the honour of engaging with brilliant work colleagues.

Finally, I would like to thank Cork GAA for taking me on board in 1983 as a player, and later as a mentor and manager… and for years of joy, happiness and support. And lastly, my sincere gratitude and thanks to the people of Kilmoyley, and Kilmoyley Hurling Club, who have given me so much pride, satisfaction and happiness. Thank you all. Cill Mhaoile Abú!

John
August 2021

★★★

I WISH TO thank my wife Cally, the most important person in my life… my friend and mother of our treasured children Alanna and Brody.

To my parents John and Stella, for their love and support over the years, and to my sister Sarah for her advice and help, always. To Cally's parents Jimmy and Ann, who have helped so much through our life together.

I wish to acknowledge the support of all my schools – Beaumont NS, St Anthony's NS Ballinlough, CBC, and Bruce College, a big thank you for my education. And to Blackrock National Hurling Club and St Michael's Football Club, thank you for developing me as a young lad and preparing me for the hard knocks in later life.

To College Corinthians AFC where I started as a six-year-old… treasured memories and friendships. To Cobh Ramblers FC and Cork City FC for maturing me and preparing me for the road ahead in England.

A special thanks to all the coaches and managers throughout my career. To Roy Keane, Neil Bailey, Steve Bruce and Martin O Neill for continuing my development, and to the wonderful supporters of the Red and White. To Hull City AFC for taking me on board in 2012 and a heartfelt thanks to the Allam family, to Steve Bruce once again, Mike Phelan, Marco Silva, Leonid Slutsky and Nigel Adkins for their continued support, and to all the supporters of Hull City AFC. A massive thanks for our incredible years together in the Premiership and Europe, and our never to be forgotten FA Cup journey. My gratitude to each and every one of you.

Thank you to Reading FC, and Coventry City FC and Mark Robins, for my last few years as a professional footballer.

Finally to Ireland! My deepest sense of gratitude and appreciation for allowing me fulfil my boyhood dreams of playing and captaining my country, the greatest honour you can achieve. To my Ireland teammates, and to my Ireland managers, especially Martin and Roy. To all the Irish supporters... the Boys in Green. A massive thank you to you all.

David
August 2021

★★★

FINALLY, THANKS TO Fintan O'Toole for all his brilliant work, countless chats, zoom calls, cups of tea and scones. And to Liam Hayes of Hero Books for his vision and including our combined life stories in this 'Flesh and Blood' series. A sincere thank you to you both.

John and David
August 2021

★★★

IN THE AUTUMN of 2001, I was brought as a 15-year-old to the Kerry senior hurling final by my aunt and uncle. On a day when the rain lashed down, I saw my mother's native parish Kilmoyley win their first title in 30 years. I've often regarded the joy on show after that day as the barometer by which to judge post-match celebrations.

The winning manager of that team was John Meyler and two decades on he is still successfully coaching in north Kerry. Since then, I've been able as a sports journalist to witness his hurling work in Cork and beyond, as well as the passion and commitment he applies to every role he takes on. His son David's career is one I followed from reporting on his underage GAA career in Cork, watching from afar as he achieved so much in England and, later as a fan, as he played and captained Ireland on the international soccer stage.

Working with John and David on their sporting story has been a pleasure and a privilege. Thanks to both for their generosity, patience and honesty over many hours chatting in John's home or on Zoom calls to David. I hope they enjoyed sharing their memories as much as I did listening to them.

Thanks also to the extended Meyler family for all their support with this project. Particular thanks to Sarah Meyler for her stories of supporting her dad and brother, and David's friend Peter Kelleher for his contribution.

To Liam Hayes, the publisher of Hero Books, for first suggesting this idea, providing me with a brilliant opportunity and being of great assistance throughout.

Thanks to Denis Hurley, Niall Kelly, Declan Bogue and Jackie Cahill, for their feedback and suggestions when I started this book and later when I was trying to shape the end product. Their time was hugely appreciated.

Adrian Russell has been a huge support and help from the start when I first floated the idea of this book. Thanks to him and all the team at The42.ie, a talented group of journalists that I'm fortunate to work alongside.

Some thanks are overdue. Tony Leen, Colm O'Connor and the *Irish Examiner* sports desk, along with John McHale, John Horgan and the *Evening Echo* sports team, have all been brilliant with advice and opportunities over the years.

As always, my family were a great source of support. Paudie, Norma, Fionnuala and Ronan, thanks for your help in various ways. To my wider family as well for all your encouragement; I particularly hope the O'Sullivans enjoy the Kilmoyley stories.

Finally, to Colette and Rían, who I'm lucky to have as two big supporters in everything I do. Thanks for all your understanding and patience. It's time to give something back.

Fintan O'Toole
August 2021

PROLOGUE

Birmingham
January 5, 2011

I'M LYING ON a physio bed that has been set up in the showers of the away dressing-room at Villa Park.

My dad is on one side of me. Sunderland manager Steve Bruce is on the other.

I'm crying.

Steve has tears in his eyes; dad is welling up as well.

It's Wednesday night football in the Premier League.

My right knee is the problem, just like it was last May when I first tore my cruciate... like it will be in the future.

IT WAS MY first time playing against Aston Villa, the club I was on trial with as a teenager.

From the kick-off, I was eager to get going in midfield. Midway through the first-half the ball bounced and came toward Carlos Cuéllar, the Villa defender. He shaped to pass the ball... and I ran in, raising my leg to block it off.

Carlos dummied and moved the opposite way.

I reacted and tried to push off in that direction. But I made that split-second decision when my leg was in the air, my body already moving off and... when my knee landed... it wobbled.

I fell to the ground.

A LOT OF people said I'd rushed back; my knee wasn't strong enough and my recovery hadn't been right. I know none of those were a factor. It was just a freak moment.

It could have happened walking down a stairs... you're not paying attention, you misjudge the step... you could land and buckle your knee.

I was stretchered off and brought down the stadium tunnel by the medical staff. Dad had come down from his seat in the stand – I could hear him shouting with the security to let him into the dressing-room. They were not for budging, and it took a Sunderland official to step in to wave him through.

He came in to me, and by half-time Steve has joined him.

THERE'S A CONSTANT queue of Sunderland players, checking to see how I am. There's a lot of emotion in the air; I can see people are hurting for me.

It's 248 days since I destroyed my knee the first time, when we played Manchester United at the Stadium of Light. It's only 25 days since I made my comeback against Fulham at Craven Cottage.

It's 0-0 against Villa. The boss is trying to get the team going as they go out for the second-half.

He turns and points at me... 'Go and win it for him!'

The team does just that; Phil Bardsley scores the winner with 10 minutes left. Emile Heskey is sent-off in the second-half for Villa and their manager Gerard Houllier is under big pressure. Villa have slipped into the relegation places.

It's a good win for us, but three points can't lift my spirits.

CHRISTMAS HAD BEEN good. My family all came over from Ireland. On December 26, I realised an ambition that my nan had long held; that her grandson would get to play at Old Trafford, the home of the club she supported.

On New Year's Day, I played the full 90 minutes as we beat Blackburn 3-0.

It was a perfect home performance, the Sunderland fans were full of life. Danny Welbeck and Darren Bent scored early on, Asamoah Gyan came off the bench to get the third.

We climbed to seventh. Then, it was a brilliant Saturday afternoon, and we were heading to play Aston Villa full of energy.

A COUPLE OF nights before that game, mum asked me to bring her to the shop to get some food for the house in Sunderland.

As we were driving in the car, she told me she'd been diagnosed with breast cancer. I gripped the steering wheel tight; it nearly spun out of my hands.

She explained that she'd gone for a routine check-up back home in Cork and they'd discovered a small lump. Dad had been over to England a few times in the previous month for games but had kept it quiet, as mum had wanted to break the news to me herself.

The next day I was at the Sunderland training ground and headed straight to the club doctor. I started quizzing him about my mum's case… firing questions at him. I got upset and annoyed when he didn't give me the exact answers I wanted to hear.

He didn't have enough information to go on; he just tried to settle me down.

It was tough news to process, a really big shock.

My mind was all over the place but when we got to Villa Park on the Wednesday night, I was focused. I was always good at that, blocking out my off-field 'life' when it came to match day and just concentrating on my job on the pitch as a midfielder.

I WAS IN control of my mind in those situations, but now injury has struck again. I feel powerless.

Dad wanted to stay on with me for another week, but mum had surgery the next day. I asked him to go home to be with her and make sure she was okay. That was the priority. He flew back to Ireland after the match. (The operation went well; mum has been fine since and goes for her regular check-ups.)

But, in Sunderland, I was in the hands of the medical team again. I needed a scan on my knee, and had to get the verdict from the surgeon and to find out what the physio's rehab plan was this time.

The aftermath of my first knee injury is a blur. It was a new situation for me and I just followed the instructions to recover. Second time around is different. I'm more informed but I don't know everything… questions started creeping into my mind.

How long am I going to be out for? Six months?

Nine? Twelve?

Can I get my knee right to play Premier League football again?

Am I able, mentally, to go through all of this again?

I AM DAVID Meyler. I'm 21 years of age, and I have torn my cruciate ligament for the second time in eight months.

There are so many questions, but only one matters… I keep asking myself.

Can I come back from this?

****

John: *I left Birmingham that night just as the second-half started. I was shattered as I headed up the road in the car and turned on* BBC Radio 5 Live *to listen in. The match commentator mentioned David for about 30 seconds. 'Having done his cruciate once and to do it again, we just wish him all the best of luck now… he'll be back.' That gave me the boost I needed. Those words stuck in my head for a long time after.*

'He will be back.'

****

'Where were you when John O'Shea put the ball in the German net?'

I got asked that a lot after Ireland's captain scored the 94th minute equaliser against the world champions in Gelsenkirchen on Tuesday October 14, 2014.

Where was I?

I was on the far side of the pitch, absolutely wrecked. I'd spent 90 minutes tearing around after those German fellas; put in at right-back by Martin O'Neill to fill a gap as Seamus Coleman was out injured.

We had hung in there, were only behind 1-0 and then John took his chance in injury-time. Everyone said to me after that they couldn't see me in the celebrations on the TV after John had run away towards the Irish fans; different fellas hanging off him. I just didn't have the energy to sprint across, my tank was empty.

I jogged over and got there eventually. Jeff Hendrick turned and dragged me in for the group hug.

The final whistle sounded soon after. The German players were shell-shocked, we were just walking on air.

We go back over to salute the away section; the Ireland fans stuck over by a corner flag at the Veltins-Arena. I'll never forget walking off the pitch that night. A full house... a last minute equaliser to get us a draw... and I look up at the crowd.

I see mum and dad. There are tears in dad's eyes; he's jumping up and down, squeezing the life out of mum. After all the injuries and uncertainty and missed opportunities, it's special that they're there and able to share in that moment. Their son from Cork playing against a team that won the World Cup final three months previously in Brazil, and Ireland getting a result in the most dramatic way possible. Our emotions went through the roof.

They had a drive of over two hours after that game, heading north-west, back over the border from Germany into the Netherlands and onto Schiphol airport in Amsterdam to catch their flight home.

Over the years, dad has spent a lot of nights on the road around Ireland and England after my matches. He's covered countless miles on motorways; plenty of times when it was easy to be worried about what direction my career was going.

This time there was no worry. Just happiness and satisfaction.

That night he says the car drove itself.

A Son's Life in Football

David with the legendary Jimmy Barry Murphy (top left) after Cork regained the Liam MacCarthy Cup in 1999; and (top right) working as Maor Uisce during the Munster Minor Football Championhip final in Killarney in 2007. David and John celebrate (below) after Cork claimed the Munster Championship title in 2018.

A young man with dreams and beardless (top left) on Ireland under-21 duty in 2010 in a European qualifier against Armenia, and (top right) in action in the same game.

David's international career ended in Wroclaw in September 2018 after a friendly against Poland.

David challenges Thomas Müller in the World Cup qualifier victory against Germany in the Aviva Stadium in 2015.

With two of his heroes in the game, Roy Keane and Seamus Coleman, in training in 2014 (main) and (above) receiving some words of advice from Roy in 2017.

Tackling Nemanja Matić in a World Cup qualifier in the Aviva Stadium in 2017.

All the family together enjoying that moment after an Ireland game (top); Stella, Cally and Sarah ready to cheer on Ireland (left) and Stella and Sarah celebrating with David as Hull are promoted to the Premier League.

The family flag on tour at Euro 2016, and Martin O'Neill presents David with some of his Ireland caps.

Cally and David celebrate their wedding with family and friends, and most of all, their daughter Alanna (top).

John with Alanna and Brody (above) and Stella and John with their son and grandkids.

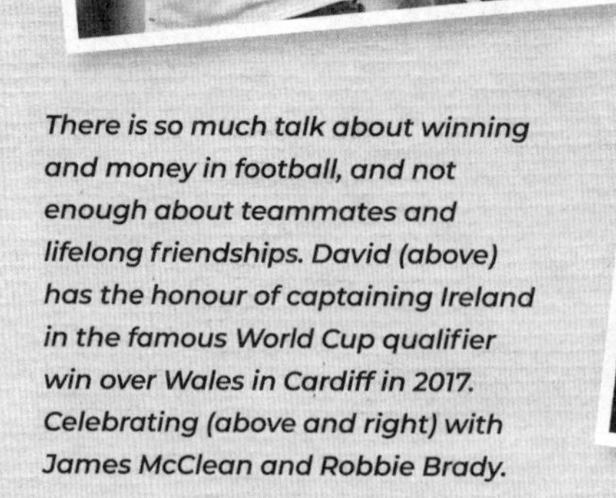

There is so much talk about winning and money in football, and not enough about teammates and lifelong friendships. David (above) has the honour of captaining Ireland in the famous World Cup qualifier win over Wales in Cardiff in 2017. Celebrating (above and right) with James McClean and Robbie Brady.

David (left) wanted to do so much more with Sunderland where he began his career in English football.

Hull became home for him, making 191 appearances, and also having the honour of playing for the club in the FA Cup final against Arsenal in 2014. Of course, there was also that 'incident' with Newcastle manager Alan Pardew the same year which became the talk of the game.

David's career in the English game ended with Reading and Coventry City.

Captaining Ireland was the greatest thrill of David's football career and here he is (left) with manager Martin O'Neill before the World Cup qualifier second-leg against Denmark in the Aviva Stadium; and (below) in action in the game.

However, losing to Denmark in that game and narrowly failing to lead Ireland to World Cup qualification is also the greatest disappointment he experienced in football.

I

Wexford Park
The Rockies
Tacumshane
College Corinthians
Gormanston
Zebo
Cork City

★★★

JOHN

BEHIND THE COUNTER of The Millhouse, our family bar in Wexford, there was a large frame on the wall with a collage of photos behind the glass.

The photos told the story of Wexford's 1956 All-Ireland senior hurling final win over Cork. Art Foley's wonder-save to stop Christy Ring. Wexford's iconic figures Nick O'Donnell and the Rackard brothers embracing Ring after he had missed out on a ninth medal. Over 83,000 people in Croke Park as captain Jim English lifted the Liam MacCarthy Cup.

Only the third All-Ireland in Wexford's history.

They've only added three more since.

I was born a month before that game and, as a child, I would study those photos every day and learn that Wexford team off by heart.

When Wexford won the All-Ireland in 1968, they came to our shop a few weeks later with the cup. Tony Doran and the Quigleys were the stars but even though I had witnessed their success, it was the 1956 team that remained seared into my brain.

Those pictures held a power over me. Not just the Wexford players, but the Cork team they defeated as well. When I started playing with St Finbarr's in 1980, I knew how big a name Tony O'Shaughnessy's is, the Cork captain.

That 1956 team was the start… the game of hurling engulfed me.

Over 60 years later, it still does.

★★★

DAVID

IN BLACKROCK, IN Cork, there was no shortage of hurling heroes growing up. The backbone of the county winning teams – the Brownes, the Cashmans, Wayne Sherlock, Brian O'Keeffe, Fergal Ryan. We loved having underage games when the seniors were training and we were wondering would they be watching.

Then we'd all get the bus down to Páirc Uí Chaoimh to see the Rockies seniors play. But my No.1 hurling hero growing up was from East Cork.

We're all glory-hunters when we're kids, so we gravitate towards one forward. Joe Deane was this five feet and six inches scoring machine. He floated around popping over points and I loved watching him. His free-taking style was distinctive, hunched low over the ball with the hurley positioned between his legs before he would lift and strike.

Joe had a yellow Cooper helmet. So I badly wanted one as well.

My helmet was a blue Mycro. I used to pester dad. He eventually sorted me a green Gola helmet. Came downstairs one morning... it was there on the island in the kitchen. That was more valuable for trading.

I managed to swap it for a yellow Cooper.

When I got to play in Semple Stadium in 2002, I'd the yellow Cooper and red jersey on a big hurling day, just like Joe Deane.

I was a slave to sporting fashion in other ways too. Adidas Predators were the kings of boots. I still have about 12 pairs in the garage. One day I want to get into management and I think I'll wear them. A good luck charm.

When we were younger, the new releases would drop in Cummins Sports in Douglas. The Manias came out around the 2002 World Cup; they cost €192. Everyone wanted them. I watched all the Cork players who had them... Seán Óg and John Gardiner for the hurlers... Colin Corkery with the white ones for the footballers.

We'd a match with St Michael's that summer. Eric Hegarty's mum drove up beforehand and handed him a pair of boots. She'd queued up; now he was wearing the Manias. I was insanely jealous. Went home after and started to make the case to dad that these boots will make me play better. He set up one of his 'challenge and reward' systems over a few games, then got me the boots. I looked the part.

They're my favourite boot of all time. When Hull played Wolves in 2017, I scored a penalty late in the game in injury-time and had those boots on. I'm retired now but if adidas put them back for resale, I'd probably buy three or four pairs anyway. I was fortunate to have the support where dad would shell out nearly €200 on a pair of boots for a 13-year-old.

Thankfully I paid him back over the years.

★★★

JOHN

HOME IS TACUMSHANE, a small village in the south-east of Ireland.

It's where I grew up close to the Wexford coast; nearby is Carnsore Point from where you look across the Irish Sea at Wales.

My father Michael was a Tacumshane local. My mother Josephine was from Kilkenny, a place called Moneenroe, near the Laois border.

My parents ran a pub, a shop, a petrol station and a farm. The business was passed down to my father in 1952 from his uncle Garry Murphy. The pub and our house were together in one building, the shop next to it with the pumps out front.

It was a busy place; a mix of local trade and passers-by on the road from Rosslare Harbour to Kilmore Quay. Tacumshane Windmill is next to the pub; built in 1846 and used to grind corn until 1961. After that it became a tourist attraction. One of my jobs as a boy was to let people in to see it.

We didn't charge a fee but I'd always get thrown sixpence or an old shilling piece after they'd been shown around.

During the summer the place would come alive. The Dublin tourists started appearing around Carne Beach and Rosslare in the caravan parks. They'd head to our pub at the weekends, lighting the place up with colour and song. For my parents in the 70s, it was a great business boost to get this annual arrival of customers.

★★★

DAVID

THE SUMMER OF 2002, I captained Cork in the Kennedy Cup. That competition is a milestone if you're developing as a young Irish footballer. *Want to get noticed?* That's the national stage to impress, with scouts dotted all over the pitches in Limerick. Talk of Ireland call-ups began.

We were young lads, who had made the grade at under-13 with Cork, but then came the next challenge. Trials with Ireland teams. There were four of us from Corinthian Boys – myself, David Bevan, Richard O'Donovan and Jamie Drennan – who would make the trip up to Dublin every few months. Teenagers trying to shine in auditions... keep our sporting dreams alive. I was the only one who wasn't capped underage. The lads all played under-15 for Ireland.

Never getting that opportunity was frustrating. There was a Dublin bubble you had to break through. A Dublin management team and a Dublin-based squad. That was just the way it was run. The best schoolboy players from around the country moved there; you bettered your case to get into the Ireland squad if you went playing in Dublin.

It has progressed now into a better situation. I'm involved with the Ireland under-17 coaching team and if young players are on the rise around the country, we'll find out about them. The best players are picked regardless of where they're from. At that age, rejection is tough to take. The lads came back home to Cork with their Ireland gear. I was that guy who went up with them and returned with nothing.

Dad used to contact the Ireland management in search of answers, but nothing came of it. I was lucky that my father didn't try and live a career through me. He'd regularly ask did I want to pursue professional football and then he worked to provide every opportunity when I'd say I did. He'd open the door and say, 'There, go walk through it!' Some fathers are pulling the young fella through the door.

We laugh about that time now.

In my life, I played for and captained the Ireland senior team.

Getting the cold shoulder at underage was all part of the journey to reach my destination.

★★★

JOHN

OUR FARM WAS on land scattered all over.

My father would draw cattle and sheep. He'd do sugar beet, corn and hay in the summer. I used to work for other farmers; we'd do 20 acres of potatoes in a day to get them ready for sale in lorry-loads to a company in Dublin. Time was also spent with my uncle Owen and aunt Lil doing the hay and shearing sheep on their farm.

My parents had a huge work ethic and they passed that on. I was put to work in the shop or the pub or the farm; it provided a great grounding in life. I met an awful lot of different personalities, between tourists and locals.

My parents never gave out to me. Their primary belief was to get up in the morning and do whatever work was needed to be done. There was no problem in me going training and playing matches; or relaxing at the weekend, having a few pints of stout or Macardles ale in the bar or, as I got older, heading to the Cedars Hotel nightclub in Rosslare on a Sunday night.

As long as the work was done, this was not a problem with my father and mother. They passed away in 2000 and '01 respectively, after a life where they had given me so much and taught me so many principles that have served me well.

THEY HAD THREE children. Gerry was born in 1953, Carmel in '54 and then I arrived two years after that. Gerry was gifted at sport, whatever he tried. His talent was incredible but he didn't have the same drive for it; his interests lay elsewhere. Big into music, he worked with a pirate station *Radio Wexford* as a DJ for a while. We were chalk and cheese... sport for me was the be-all and end-all.

Gerry went to Maynooth in 1968, but only lasted a year in the seminary. He did a degree in History and Politics, then went working with Irish Continental Line in Rosslare Harbour for years. Carmel is a nurse; she worked in Dr Steevens' Hospital in Kilmainham in Dublin. Now she lives in Limerick, and has four children all grown up.

Gerry was the one who settled at home. He took over the running of the pub in 1999 with his wife Theresa and added a restaurant. They made a brilliant job of it. When I was Wexford hurling manager in 2007 and '08, he was doing between

400 and 500 dinners a day for customers at the weekend.

I'd call out there and he wouldn't have time to chat. Mad busy.

At the time, he had plenty of staff working in a country pub but the trade changed when the recession hit. They regrouped and got going again. Then, in 2020, Covid-19 shut the doors of the pub. It was hard on him. He'd been unwell at different times and then before Christmas 2020, he went into hospital in Dublin. At the end of January 2021, he passed away.

A tough experience. My older brother had died; the whole country was in lockdown and I was making this strange journey to Wexford, having to explain at Garda checkpoints why I was on the road.

Were we close? Carmel and Gerry would probably have been closer.

Carmel spent a lot of summers down in Wexford; she was more of a homebird than me. I was busy with hurling teams, flying in and out. Then my daughter Sarah settled in Wexford in recent years and that's been the draw again for me to visit the place where I grew up.

The three of us in our family went to different boarding schools; you can lose attachments in that way. But there was a connection between us, which was strengthened later in life through sport.

When I became Cork manager, Carmel was retired. She had the free travel pass, so could hop on the train and, suddenly, I used to see her appearing at matches. She'd be there for the day out, all dressed in red.

When we won the Munster final in 2018, she was out on the pitch in Thurles with the whole family for the celebrations. It's fascinating the way that has worked out. It was brilliant to have her there.

GERRY AND CARMEL were both incredibly proud of David's football career. Gerry really followed it closely when he started playing in England. I'd get the call from him on Saturday afternoons when the team news was released... wishing me luck if David was playing, asking what was wrong if he wasn't.

Same with Ireland matches. He'd be looking for an update on the atmosphere in the stadium beforehand. David's football life had a knock-on effect on the pub in Wexford too. The lads at the bar watched the soccer matches on TV, a mini-Hull City or Sunderland supporters club forming while they drank their pints.

Gerry got me to send him photos of David in action; they'd be framed and put up in the bar. If Ireland were playing, he would remind everyone in the bar that that was his nephew on the screen. No one could doubt his family pride.

★★★

DAVID

MAYBE MY SPORTING obsession was inevitable.

My Mum Stella is a wonderful swimmer, a good golfer. She's taken up bridge in recent years; the competitiveness shows there as well.

I've just one sibling, my sister Sarah. Three years between us... she was born in 1986 and I arrived in '89. Sarah was a serious swimmer growing up. Dad still says he should have sent her off to England to a specialised swimming school because he felt she hit a ceiling in Ireland. After finishing secondary school, she went to Limerick to study to become a teacher. She's principal now in St Iberius national school in Wexford town.

Then, there is dad.

When I was younger, he bought me a pool table, an old style one that you'd see in pubs which needed the 20 pence coin slotted in.

We'd play, and he'd never let me win... the usual tears and tantrums as a child when I was beaten. Age didn't matter. There were no handouts.

It did make me practice pool non-stop. Later when I was in England, trying to make my way as a professional footballer, I was still using the lessons from those pool games. You earn everything you get. If you lose, then you need to get better.

Sport dominated my youth. I swam a bit but just wasn't a big fan of getting up at 6am to jump into a pool. There were lots of summer days spent at Douglas Golf Club. And then I'd the big three!

Hurling with Blackrock.

Gaelic football with St Michael's.

Football with College Corinthians.

I loved the variety, and the beauty was that I learned so much from each sport. Hurling taught me how to take a belt. Playing football in England, I would get clattered but could take the hit where other fellas were rolling around the field.

Gaelic football came most naturally to me. Football, or soccer as we say in Ireland, helped with my ability to think during a game, watching formations and how teams were set-up. Of the three, I feel hurling was the game I was best at.

I fully believe I'd have played for the Cork senior hurling team if I'd stuck at it. That may sound arrogant but it is a genuine belief.

COLLEGE CORINTHIANS WAS where I started playing football; my local club just up the road in Castletreasure. The team I played for won everything in Cork up through the underage ranks. The National Cup was always a step too far for us; we could never manage to beat some of the top Dublin sides.

We spent thrilling years together, full of wonder.

Richard O'Donovan, Theo Cullinane, David O'Sullivan, Steven Good, Eoghan McCarthy, Jamie Drennan... the backbone of our team. A lot of lads had trials with English clubs. Our goalkeeper David Bevan signed for Aston Villa, and had a couple of loan moves after that. Ian Turner carved out a career with Cork City and then went to Cobh Ramblers.

Barry O'Driscoll was a year younger but played with us numerous times. One of those lads gifted at sport, he was like a gazelle on the pitch with his pace. He went down another sporting path, made it with the Cork senior footballers and is still going strong at a high level with Nemo Rangers.

There was no big mystery to where I ended up playing GAA, I just followed my friends. We lived in Rochestown but used to go to school in Beaumont. All the lads in my class were playing with Blackrock in hurling and St Michael's in football. It was a no-brainer. I wanted to be playing with all my friends. Every day we'd go to my grandparents' house... Blackrock's club pitches on Church Road were just across the road. A simple decision.

In Beaumont, we were really successful at GAA but by sixth class I had changed schools to St Anthony's in Ballinlough. A bit hot-headed in the classroom, not paying enough attention, it was felt the switch would be good for me. Dad got me in, having talked to the principal Flor O'Sullivan.

I played GAA there and scored 2-2 when we reached the Sciath na Scol hurling final in 2002. I also got sent-off after cleaning a player out with a hurley as I tried to strike the ball. It wasn't intentional, but a wild enough pull meant I was gone.

It didn't tarnish my hurling record too badly as I got picked for the 'Primary Game' team to play Waterford that year, before the senior match in Semple Stadium. Noel Connors, the future Waterford defender, marked me that day, but I got a couple of goals off him.

★★★

JOHN

THE GAA IS built on the stories told of icons, stories that pass down through generations. When I was young, we had no access to video footage so I relied on word of mouth. Whatever my parents were telling me, that was the Gospel truth as far as I was concerned.

My mother had worked as manageress of Murphy Floods Hotel in Enniscorthy. When the Wexford hurlers played in the town, she told stories of how the players would come off the pitch and into the hotel, where she would feed them dinner. It built up a mystique surrounding these men.

Ned Wheeler was from Faythe Harriers, midfield on that Wexford winning team in 1956. Phil Wilson from Ballyhogue played in the same position when Wexford won the final in 1968.

The two of them worked as oil truck drivers and would call to our yard at home. More often it was Wheeler who would park up and empty the load of 400 gallons of paraffin oil into our tank. My mother would make tea with corned beef or ham sandwiches. While she was preparing the food, there was a small window of free time. *Perfect chance for a puck around in the back garden?*

Imagine this colossal figure... six feet and three inches tall, a huge man who had done it all with Wexford hurling... and him taking a break out of his day's work to hurl with me. Those few minutes were precious until my mother would rap at the window and we'd be called in.

Same story when I got to hurl with Wilson. Playing with two of my heroes left a huge imprint. My parents would make me aware if I was in the company of someone special. There was a different atmosphere if someone like Billy Rackard came into our shop or pub.

This experience made me realise the importance of having access to sporting icons. When David was playing football, he would come home and we'd head down to Mass on a Sunday morning in Rochestown. Some kids there would want his autograph afterwards. Later on the green in front of our house, he'd have a kickaround with a few young fellas who lived in the estate.

My parents knew I was mad interested in GAA. Myself and Gerry would hurl all the time in the back garden, using that 40- or 50-yard patch of grass to play in our own All-Ireland finals. My father would often drop me into Wexford Park on a Sunday. I might only be six or seven years of age but I'd stay there all day and sit on the sideline.

There'd be a couple of club matches to watch. I'd have money for an ice cream and would get a lift home from a neighbour. If it was a county match, my father would be mindful of the bigger crowds and he'd stay with me.

I don't recall seeing him play hurling; he was more into playing cricket in the local leagues in Wexford between the villages. He kept greyhounds as well, running them in track. That's how he met my mother, from going into the hotel after the racing.

He was very interested in hurling, and never critical when I started playing; always supportive. Hurleys and sliotars were always provided. Same with my mother when I started to make Wexford underage teams. On the days of training, she would come to me on the farm around 3pm.

'Stop working now. Go in, wash yourself... feed yourself and get ready for training!'

To earn my father's respect I had to play well. It taught me how to be with David, later in life; don't shower him with praise if he's been poor. Always be totally straight. My father had that honesty.

WE WERE IN the barony of Forth and Bargy in Wexford, where the small villages of Lady's Island, Tacumshane and Broadway came together to form Our Lady's Island GAA club.

Out the back of our house was a field... that's where the club trained. You'd dig into the ground in January or February, put down your goals for the year.

Two poles of wood and make a crossbar between them. Telegraph poles were used later. That was the first GAA field that I knew. We spent countless evenings there, hurling until late into the night.

★★★

DAVID

I WAS SURROUNDED by plenty of talented players growing up. Eric Hegarty was gifted at all three sports, played Cork minor football and still plays for Michael's. Declan Kelleher and Brian Ahern were excellent too.

Then there was Zebo... a famous Beaumont sporting product.

Simon is a year younger than me but we were pals growing up on the same Blackrock and St Michael's teams. He'd plenty of natural GAA talent but went off and made a name for himself in rugby with Munster and Ireland. Then off out to France for a few years to live his best life before a homecoming to Munster.

What you see with him in public is what you get in private. A lovely fella. Always bubbly and smiling. A great character. He always had that X-Factor on the pitch... in every sport. The famous flick against Wales in the Six Nations in 2013 reminded me how he just played like that naturally all his life. His ability to think on his feet in situations on a pitch was always incredible; he'd stay calm-headed when everyone was panicking.

We'd be good friends. We wouldn't speak every day, but we catch up every now and then.

ON THE FOOTBALL field, I was always a centre midfielder. My best attribute was probably winning the ball back... 'the rat' as it would be classed in midfield terms, the type who get the ball and give it off to the more creative players.

In hurling, I always wanted to play centre-forward. I wasn't the best striker off my right but I was clean off the left. I was hot-headed as a young fella. Had an argument with my dad once during a county semi-final with Blackrock. Point down and we'd a late free. I said go for goal... he said take your point. Took his advice. We won the replay.

As I got older some coaches understood I wanted to combine my sports. We were very successful with St Michael's. I'll never forget the influence of Gerry Lenihan. If I missed training, there was no problem with Gerry. He knew he could count on me. If my parents were away, he would call over to bring me to and from training.

I feel that sense of appreciation with all my coaches. John Turner and Danny Drennan with our Corinthians team, different people in Blackrock. Those younger days back in Cork, when I was switching between sports every week, gave me some of my happiest memories.

EVERYONE SEEMED TO support Man United when we were younger, so I joined Gavin Dempsey in school in supporting Liverpool. We wanted to be different.

Dad wouldn't support clubs, but he loves teams from different eras; Leeds in the 70s, Liverpool in the 80s. He bought me the old v-neck Liverpool jersey with Carlsberg emblazoned across the front.

The player I worshipped didn't play for Liverpool, yet that was never going to affect my devotion. In Cork at that time, there was a clear choice.

Roy Keane was a Cork native, Manchester United captain and Ireland's best player. *How could I not be inspired by that?* He had everything as a midfielder. An exceptional passer and goalscorer. His determination, the way he tackled and led his team.

I was never glued to watching games on TV, and preferred to watch the *Match of the Day* round-ups. But I wish I'd studied the game more; analysed players like Roy Keane properly. Later I found him really helpful when I got to work with him.

Playing in similar positions influenced my fanaticism. I captained Cork in the Kennedy Cup, just like Roy did in 1986. Every year when the team is picked, someone gets touted as the next Roy Keane.

But you'll go another hundred years and there won't be another player from Cork to match up to Roy. He's out on his own.

★★★

JOHN

MY FATHER CAME up to me after school one day. I was in sixth class in that building, just 100 yards up the road from home in Tacumshane.

'Come on, we've to go!' We were heading up the east coast to Gormanston, located in Meath and just next to Balbriggan over the border in Dublin

My mother was very friendly with the Franciscans in Wexford Town. She was a very holy woman, went to Mass every day. Gerry had gone to St Peter's College in Wexford but my mother felt I was a bit too wild. Packing me off to boarding school seemed the right call.

That's why I went to the Franciscan College in Gormanston.

My father was taking me up there to do my entrance exams. I went up for three days; we'd been told to bring our sports gear with us. Sure I thought it was brilliant; bit of exams, then the rest of the time playing hurling and football in organised matches.

I went up and enrolled there on September 1, 1969. About 450 students with 90 in first year. If you were into sport, this was the place for you.

Six GAA pitches, a 25-metre swimming pool, six handball alleys, a cinder ash running track, a gymnasium... and a nine-hole golf course. There was a big hall where we would gather on Sunday nights to watch films.

The absolute best of everything. An incredible place.

★★★

DAVID

BY THE AGE of 15, I faced questions.

What was my football ambition and how could it be fulfilled?

My good fortune was to have a father who looked at the bigger picture. Corinthians was a well-run club but dominating at your own age group creates a comfort zone. Dad felt it was time for a move. So when I was under-15, I moved to Cobh Ramblers. A bigger challenge.

The weekend schedule was intense. On a Saturday the under-15s would play at 11am, then I'd kick off with the under-17s at 2pm. Sunday morning was the under-16s, and the under-18 team that afternoon. Four games, but I was energetic and eager to play ball.

Cobh was a positive place to play. Graham Cummins was two years older but we played together underage. A traditional centre-forward with an eye for goal, he played later in England and Scotland, and shone for Cork City.

Cobh's first-team were in the League of Ireland. Sometimes you'd train with them; they were good lads. I was the young, fresh-faced kid but they didn't let me away with anything. They all wanted me to raise my standards.

Dad used to set me a challenge. The match reports would be brief in the local paper, the *Evening Echo*. To get mentioned, you needed to score a goal. Hitting the net was the challenge and €50 for every goal the proposed reward.

That prize drove me on. One weekend, I scored nine goals across four games; pushing to take free-kicks and penalties. He paid up every time but, eventually, it had to stop. The initial aim was for more recognition, now I was emptying his wallet.

Dad was asking me if I wanted to reach the top, and then mapping out what was required.

It goes back to the lesson of the pool table battles. Or when he'd send me down to the Rochestown College handball alley, where many Cork hurlers have honed their skills over the years. I would be handed a new sliotar to bang it against a wall for a few hours... before he'd see how battered it was and determine how much work I'd done. There were free-taking sessions in Church Road after he'd collect me from my nan's... 80 to 100 frees all from different angles. If I hit a target number, we'd stop at McDonalds on the way home.

There was another key person in all of this. Mum did the driving up and down to Cobh a few times a week. She'd rearrange things in her life to do that. Make sure I was eating right and all my gear was washed. Always there, always involved.

But I never felt a weight of parental pressure.

I wanted to do it and they helped steer me in the right direction.

★★★

JOHN

IN 1968, JOE Lennon lifted the Sam Maguire Cup as Down captain. It capped an amazing decade for him and the county. Their third All-Ireland win in the 60s, dominating in Ulster. He won National League and Railway Cup medals as well. That was Joe's sporting life.

His other life was in Gormanston College, working as a PE teacher and a football coach. A year after he had helped Down beat Kerry in that All-Ireland final, I walked through the doors of the school and started playing GAA soon after.

And Lennon was the man who first sparked my interest in coaching.

He was an amazing man. A deep thinker of the game, he had already written in-depth coaching manuals on gaelic football that would be studied for years to come. He would go on to become one of the first TV analysts for RTÉ's *The Sunday Game*. For us in Gormanston, there was an aura about him. Whatever he said on the pitch, we lapped it up.

Walking out onto the training pitch in runners, shorts and t-shirt, he was shaped like a top footballer. Watching him go for runs and his dedication to fitness, planted a seed in my mind. I needed to work twice as hard. I needed to always be fit.

By the time I was 15, I'd started training the junior team in Our Lady's Island and would take the running sessions.

Lennon was big into instilling discipline and the right attitude. He always wanted to be addressed as 'Sir'. He would get us fired up for games... a great motivator.

'Laddy, when you're marking a fella, the first thing you do is pull the jersey. See how he'll react.

'Give him an elbow... give him a poke. If he reacts you have him. If he doesn't, you need to think.'

'Yes... SIR!'

His sessions were excellent as well, putting miles into our legs with a mix of short sprints, long runs and endurance work. I feel so fortunate to have had that influence early in my sporting life.

There were other great people there. Fr James Groarke from Mayo was a Maths teacher and he was in charge of the football. Then we'd Fr Bob and Fr Declan doing the hurling. They were all excellent coaches and helped build us into young men.

We'd serious talent in our football team in Gormanston. We competed at the highest level of senior football. Won the Leinster finals in 1973 and '74. Then went into the All-Ireland series and lifted the Hogan Cup by beating St Jarlath's of Tuam in 1973. It's the only time Gormanston have won it; Jarlath's got their own back when they beat us in the final the year after.

★★★

DAVID

SOMETIMES, I THINK I'd love another shot at secondary school.

Just to enjoy the moments and put some work in. I went to Christian Brothers College in Cork and got in plenty of trouble. Stupid stuff, messing in class and getting thrown out. Tony McCarthy was the vice-principal; he'd be ringing dad every second week.

The principal Dr Larry Jordan knew I was sports mad. In Christians the main focus was rugby; he used to be on to me to play. They thought they could have a full-back or winger on their hands. But I'd no interest.

You couldn't escape the rugby tradition in the school, all the same. Duncan Williams, Stephen Archer and John Ryan were all in the years ahead of me; they all later played for Munster.

The games were massive occasions and I went to them all. All my classmates were playing. I did envy them their sporting routine... team meetings, having lunch together, training after school.

I was outside that bubble.

I was desperate as a teenager to be part of an elite sporting culture.

And soon enough I got my chance.

★★★

JOHN

THE GAMES IN Gormanston were 13-a-side.

I was a substitute for the first Hogan Cup final, but started the second year, stuck in corner-forward; I got a goal in the Leinster final against Knockbeg from Carlow. It steeled me for harder challenges ahead.

As a boarding school, we had quality players from all over. John Gallagher of Mayo, Cavan's Christy McCutcheon, the Reynolds' from Meath, the Dublin lads… Mickey Martin, Mark McDonald and Joe Carr. Paul McGettigan would go on to star for Donegal and later for Galway.

The star of the show was Denis 'Ogie' Moran. You knew early on that you were sharing a dressing-room with a special player.

I used to think he was a better hurler than a footballer. We won an under-14 colleges hurling final in 1969 against Brunswick St. Our first time in Croke Park. I'd always slag him in later years when we'd meet, remind him that his first time playing there was winning with us as hurlers.

His speed and skill stood out straight away. You just know when a player on the pitch is operating a few notches above everyone else. I always noticed it, the same when I started playing with Jimmy Barry-Murphy for the Barrs in hurling.

I got a kick out of seeing what Ogie went on to do. He won it all.

Within a year of battling around with us school players in the Hogan Cup, he was in with Mick O'Dwyer and the Kerry seniors, winning his first All-Ireland in 1975; and finished with eight medals, all in the same position at centre-forward.

Ogie was midfield with McGettigan and they would run games between them. When we lost the 1974 final, they scored 0-9 between them from midfield. McGettigan was a Donegal senior while he was still in school. He ended up living in Galway, played for their county team as well and got into coaching with Corofin, helping them win the All-Ireland club in 1998.

We hurled at senior B level, always able to beat schools like Birr and Callan. But when we went up to the A grade one year, we met St Kieran's and they hammered us.

I played handball with the college and ran cross-country, but football was the main game. Huge crowds went to St Ciaran's Park in Athlone for those finals with St Jarlath's; a train would be organised to bring all our schoolmates down for it. We played all over during those years... against St Finian's in Mullingar, St Peter's from Wexford, Moate College in Westmeath. Hurling and football every second week.

Food after the match, a sing-song on the bus on the way home.

I was part of a team in the sporting spotlight and loved it.

★★★

DAVID

DAMIEN RICHARDSON CAME up to me after a Cork City under-21 game in July 2007. We chatted about the match. I had played well. He praised my performance. Then came one of the most pivotal questions I was asked in my life.

'What are you doing next Monday night?'

My mind started racing.

'We're playing Sunderland... I want you to be involved. You'll get some minutes.'

The chance to play against a Premier League team. Roy Keane was their manager. Turners Cross was sold out. There was just one slight issue. A fixture clash; I had a gaelic football minor championship game with St Michael's.

Monday night football. *But where was I going to play?*

THAT JULY WAS a crazy month.

On Sunday July 1, I was in Killarney with the Cork minor footballers as we beat Kerry in the Munster final. On Sunday July 8, I played for the Cork City under-21s that beat the Kerry League in a cup game in Tralee.

On Sunday July 15, I lined out centre-forward and scored a goal as the Blackrock intermediate hurlers beat St Finbarr's in a relegation play-off in Páirc Uí Rinn. Then, to cap off the month, I'd to wrestle with this decision of where to go on Monday July 31.

It summed up the madness of the time. No 18-year-old would get away with that schedule now. I was still living the dream, getting to play three sports I loved.

I just about managed to keep them going but issues did arise.

It was my downfall with the Cork minors. I got called into a trial match down in Kinsale once and tore the whole place up, scoring a few goals.

'We're very pleased with how you've done,' said the manager Mick Evans after. 'We want to bring you into the squad. How are you fixed for Saturday?'

'Ah, I think I've a soccer match.'

That was the problem. When we won the Munster final, I was the Cork water boy in Fitzgerald Stadium. I hadn't been available enough to be picked, but packing in soccer wasn't an option.

That Cork team had serious talent. The half-forward line was Barry O'Driscoll, Ciaran Sheehan and Aidan Walsh, all future senior footballers.

Sliding doors moments. I didn't play for the Cork minor team that day and didn't play for the St Michael's minors at the end of July either.

Damien Richardson pushed me into making a choice. I knew whichever I picked, the other would be affected.

Dad asked, 'Well what do you want to do?' I was nearly hoping he'd make the decision for me. I hung my hat on going the soccer route.

Being part of the Cork City first-team squad was one attraction but the glamour of the opposition was another. And Roy Keane was in charge, his big homecoming to Cork. *Was there a chance I could get to meet him?*

I've often wondered was there a plan hatched in the background at Cork City. *Were the youth coaches worried about losing a player to GAA? Did they feel I needed some big offer to commit?*

Not everyone was happy with my decision. A few lads with St Michael's felt I'd let them down and fell out with me for a couple of years. They won that night, but lost the county semi-final later in November. I missed that due to soccer as well.

We made up. We got over it. That's part of sport.

And at least I went on to do something.

I got brought on with 10 minutes to go that night against Sunderland. A brief window to impress; I'm not sure if I even touched the ball. But still, I was sharing a pitch with Premier League stars. And I got a photo with Roy after.

I still have the photo and I showed it to Roy years later when we were together with Ireland.

'Can't believe I'm actually smiling!' That was his verdict.

He would go on to be a huge influence in my career. He signed me for Sunderland. He was one of the first people to get in touch when I suffered the cruciate injuries. Same situation when I retired.

It's stuff that people don't know about him. They see this fella ranting on a sideline or as a tough-talking pundit in a TV studio... and think... *Roy Keane.*

There's a decency at his core.

★★★

JOHN

BEING A GAA player afforded us a status in the school.

In the big hall where food was served, we got an extra potato or piece of meat with dinner. A bit of preferential treatment.

We played a lot of the schools in Dublin in those days, like Brunswick Street, O'Connell Boys and Joey's. After, we might get a mixed grill in the Castle Hotel on Parnell Square. And a few quick pints.

Back to the school after, get out the toothbrush straight away and a bit of toothpaste into your mouth... rid the smell of alcohol that would spell trouble.

The dormitories would be checked at night.

'Were you drinking today after the match?'

'No Father... I don't drink.'

Boarding school is hard; you've got to fight to stay alive at times, to look after yourself. It was challenging. If some fella took you on, you had to stand your ground. Some struggled. You'd get whipped once or twice; that was the way.

Five times down on each hand with the broomstick.

I was in with the GAA crowd and that offered a bit of protection. I grew up in a small country village; next thing I'm in with a load of lads who shared my sporting obsession. I embraced the sporting environment. I wasn't the only Wexford fella there. Bobby Rackard was there, Nicky's son. I drew up a friendship with him.

Each dormitory in the college housed about 80 lads. Everyone got a bed, a locker and a wardrobe. That was your personal space that you had to protect at all costs. If a fella stepped into your area, you had to defend yourself and hunt him out.

I used to collect stamps. My mum and dad knew about my interest; they'd ask old people coming into our shop if they'd any old letters or envelopes hanging around at home that they could give us. The stamps would be passed to me then.

One evening in Gormanston, I came back to my locker and the album was gone. That was 1972, and I was devastated.

I'd a fair collection of Irish stamps built up by then. It was never found after.

LONELINESS AND HOMESICKNESS never knocked me back.

We always loved getting out for the breaks at Easter, Christmas and summer. The countdown to the days would begin… writing down on the inside of my locker how much time was left until home called… 91 days…90…89.

I'd get the bus into Busáras and across to Connolly Station for the train home to Rosslare or Wexford, where I'd get picked up.

It was a lot of money at the time to be sent there, £160 a year. But my parents looked after it. My father would visit me the odd time; if he was in Dublin for something he'd call out. Again, he'd bring some stuff in the car.

My mother used to send up boxes of chocolate, biscuits and cake, that would keep me going. Frank O'Connor in Wexford town used to make big slabs of fruit cake. If I had it on my own I'd ration to get a week or 10 days out of it. If other lads caught hold of it, different story. I had to mind it.

There were four prefects on our dormitory… fifth years in charge to keep us quiet. I had to hand up something to them some evenings, a bribe to keep everything alright. I always looked forward to those care packages.

★★★

DAVID

I THINK PEOPLE in the football community in Cork always thought I was leaning towards GAA. Given my dad's background, it was felt I would go that way.

It is a wonderful achievement to play for Cork, but football can be your profession. That's what appealed to me, not having to combine sport with a job. That's why I was so fascinated with football.

The first approach from Cork City came in the summer of 2006. Paul Bowdren spotted me when they played Cobh. He rang dad about having a chat with us. So we met him in O'Briens' sandwich shop in Douglas Court Shopping Centre. He mapped out the path for us... paid for our sandwiches after, a good first impression.

I was eligible to play under-17 but he viewed me as a signing for the under-18s. That's what dad wanted to hear; they talked about me getting some game-time for the under-21s as well. This was a sign of taking a step up. Bowdy was brilliant for me when I was at Cork City. He'd facilitate me if I couldn't train at times. A really good guy who I kept in touch with.

When I was younger, dad would sometimes bring me to Cork City games at Turners Cross. The team of Declan Daly, John Caulfield and Patsy Freyne! As I got older, I went to fewer games but would still look out for their results. By the time I signed I was no fanatic... I wasn't at the back of The Shed every week, singing... *Cork City til I die.*

But it was still a big deal to sign for them.

When I started to train with the first-team, it was a dressing-room with big midfield names... Colin Healy and Gareth Farrelly... Joe Gamble.

In an early training session, Colin hit me a belt of a shoulder and knocked me into next week. I was coming in as this cocky 17-year-old, used to games working out easily. He forced me to understand what was required. There were times I flew into tackles with him and I think he respected that. Colin was hard on me but in the right way, so I would learn.

If training was at 9am, Colin was at the ground an hour earlier. Making sure his boots were clean, his gear was ready; he had his stretching done and organised in the gym. After training he'd do extra work on passing and finishing. Then back into the gym.

He set the bar. Colin had two bad leg breaks. You don't come back from them and play at the level he did without having something about you. I took great inspiration from him.

Joe had been at Reading; he had soaked up a lot from his time there, and was the first player to introduce me to the concept of going into the gym for activation work before training; passed on lessons about nutrition, hydration and warming up. He was built like a tank. His reading of the game was excellent. You see midfielders charging around the pitch. Joe chose when to charge and when not to charge.

When I was younger, I was more interested in the fella doing the step-overs or scoring goals. Now, I was trying to learn more about positional play. Roy Keane would later be great for advice on that. If the ball is in front of you, you've done your job. Everyone at times is so quick to press, but the higher level you go up, the better the players are and they'll pop the ball around you.

When you're running back to your own goal and the ball is gone behind you, then you know you're in trouble.

Colin and Joe guided me along. The Cork City squad went to Spain for a warm-weather training camp in February 2008. I was a few months out from my 19th birthday. At the end of the week we'd a night out in Marbella.

Everyone was having a few drinks; then Colin and Joe pulled me aside, sat me down and grilled me for 20 minutes about what I was doing.

'You've got potential but you need to straighten your head out.'

Time to cut out the outside noise. If we played on a Friday night and my buddies were going out after, I should be thinking about playing the under-21 game on the Saturday.

They displayed unbelievable faith in me; tried to steer a young player on the right path, correct my mistakes. I'll be forever grateful to them.

Maybe they saw something of themselves at that age in me; felt it was time to share the wisdom. There is a spiral effect in football. I'm involved now with Ireland under-17s. Colin O'Brien, who was at Cork City back then, was very good to me when I retired in reaching out and opening that door. A very open-minded person, who always had an interest in coaching.

And now, I find myself talking to young fellas, passing on some advice just like Colin and Joe did for me all those years ago.

GEORGE O'CALLAGHAN WAS the other Cork City player that stood out with his talent.

Georgie was a maverick.

The game came naturally to him. He'd do all sorts of tricks in training. We used to do a version of the crossbar challenge. At the old Bishopstown ground where Cork City train, there was a metal frame in the shape of goalposts that you'd walk under coming out from the dressing-rooms.

George would offer me €100 if I could hit it… and give me three balls from the centre circle. Then he'd join in after my shots and if he got it, I'd to clean his boots. I'd miss my three and then he'd bang it first go.

I was left cleaning his boots.

He was a special talent in the League of Ireland. *Could George have done more?* I think so.

He was a larger than life character and incredibly gifted.

★★★

JOHN

SPORT WAS MY big interest, but education was the core reason for being there.

There was a structure to our lives. Three and a half hours study had to be done every evening… 5.30pm to 7pm… then a break until 8pm… and back to study until 10pm. It built discipline. Every weekend between sport and study, we were kept busy. I was in the alley, on the pitch, in the study rooms. Always focused.

Maths, Irish, English, Chemistry, Biology, Latin and French… that was my timetable. They were good with the career guidance as well when we were finishing up. Chemistry and Biology were brilliant with Fr Declan, our hurling coach.

Fr Pius used to take Maths; you needed to be sharp and attentive. He'd fly through it in a minute and then wipe it off the board… and go again. There were lay teachers there as well.

Everything was structured.

Up at 7.30am to make our beds, then breakfast.

Classes from 9am to 3.30pm, then sport in the afternoon and study in the evenings. That laid the foundations for me. When I went to college in 1974, I found it easier as I had a system to stick to.

NOT EVERY STUDENT in Gormanston had the positive experience I did.

One priest was later convicted of assaulting some students. It was shocking and sad to hear. The story emerged years after we had left; it had happened around the time we were in school but we never knew anything about it.

I feel very sorry for the lads affected and what they went through.

But, I guess overall I make my impression on the place from my own personal experience. That was completely positive with the people I dealt with.

I've never regretted being sent there; I had five great years. I think everybody should go to boarding school for a few years and the army for a couple of years. That's just my view; it's not one that will sit comfortably with everyone.

But I firmly believe it builds character and resilience, crucial skills for the rest of your life. My wife doesn't agree with me. When it came to our kids, Sarah went to Regina Mundi in Douglas and she got on brilliantly. David went to Christians; that was a bit messier but he was a bit wilder.

Would boarding school have suited him? Maybe.

I made great friends in Gormanston. We don't purposely meet but if we do, we catch up. I bump into Ogie Moran at Cork-Kerry football matches. There's a couple of other lads living near me in Cork.

That's what I look back on… great matches, great players you played with… great times.

★★★

DAVID

AT THE START of fifth year, at the time I joined Cork City, I switched schools. Left Christians and moved to Bruce College, swapping Sidney Hill for St Patrick's Hill on the northside. The hope was that it would give me better focus.

Micheál Landers was the principal at Bruce. He was brilliant for facilitating my soccer commitments, particularly at the start of Leaving Cert year. School started at 8.40am. An hour later I'd drive out to Bishopstown for Cork City first-team training at 10am. We'd finish at 12-12.30pm, after a gym session.

I'd grab lunch in the Deanrock Bar in Togher, then report back to school for

2pm. They worked out a way for me to catch up; if I'd missed English or Maths, I might jump into extra classes in the afternoon where teachers were covering the same topics. School finished at 6pm and then, a few times a week, it was a drive up to Mayfield or down to Ashton School for training on the astroturf with the under-18 or under-21 sides. I wasn't an established first-team player and needed to maintain my connection to the underage teams.

Sometimes I'd go back to school for supervised study, or else head home to get stuck into the books. Next day... the cycle started all over again. Some Friday mornings I'd start off in school but if I was involved with the first-team travelling up to Dublin or Derry, I'd have to get out early.

It was tough work but I loved it.

And I could finally transport myself around, ending the dependency on my parents for lifts.

The previous summer mum and dad had gone on holidays. Sarah was in charge of the house, not that 18-year-old David was going to be told what to do there. So I made an investment.

A girl I knew, her father was selling a car. I became the proud owner of a Honda Civic saloon, 96-L-1194, for €500.

I casually mentioned it when dad rang home to see how school was going. Didn't get the thumbs up from the other end of the phone. They were not happy. So I just needed to sort it before they got back. Dad knew the owner of Canty's Garage on Anglesea Street; I'd been in with him a couple of times.

Got the car into him for a service.

Bought the parts off another of dad's buddies, who had a warehouse down near the marina.

Got Cantys to only charge me for the labour.

Played the card of being just a young lad who needed help.

Then up to some garage in Mayfield and got a big massive exhaust put on the car.

Down to Halfords, where I bought a flip out monitor.

My parents came home, and saw the car was all insured and tidied up. I must have washed it every day for three weeks straight. Eventually I won them over; they could see I was taking care of it.

And they'd a bit more free time instead of driving me around Cork.

ON SUNDAY NOVEMBER 18, 2007, I played for Cork City in a Youth League Cup final in Turners Cross.

I'd class it as the most important game I played for the club. We beat Everton 4-0... I was Man of the Match and just ran the midfield. Scored the first, and set up the fourth. Constantly involved.

Physically I was in great shape. The benefits of a full pre-season with the first-team and having people like Colin and Joe pushing me hard was starting to show. I left the pitch that night feeling like I could play another game.

Afterwards, everyone went mad celebrating. I headed up to dad; he was in his usual spot in the middle of the Donie Forde Stand. I was more reserved, felt a bit unfulfilled. We agreed I'd hit a ceiling with the under-18s. I needed more.

Two weeks later I got a taste of the higher level. Damien Richardson brought me into the senior travelling squad for the FAI Cup final. A wet and windy day at the RDS; Denis Behan hit the only goal in a win over Longford Town.

I was sat in the stand but felt a part of it, and got kitted out by Suits Distributors before the game with the rest of the lads. When Dan Murray lifted the cup, I was on the podium, jumping and roaring with all the lads.

It felt surreal to be there in the middle of the celebrations; a sign that change was coming down the tracks.

I KEPT BOTH education and football going in late-2007 but gradually my energy levels began to drop. Soon I was wrecked most days, struggling to concentrate in class if I'd had a hard training session. I was studying Maths, English, Irish, French, Business, Economics and Accounting. I was up around the 500-point mark in the October exams, then by Christmas it was 450. The decline was slow but noticeable.

Then an offer was put on the table by Cork City of a two-year first-team contract. It had been coming for a couple of months; they wanted to tie me down.

I snapped it up and they announced it in January 2008. A month of big calls. Just before the pre-exams came around, I made another one.

I dropped out of school.

With just four months to go before the Leaving Cert. Dad had noticed it was all starting to pile on top of me.

'What do you want to do?'

'I want to play football.'

He said, 'Right, that's your decision. But you can have no regrets. Don't turn around later and say you'd wish you'd done something else.'

It still annoys me a bit that I dropped out. *Could I have structured my time better? Should I have asked Cork City about missing some training sessions?* Maybe. But the workload outside of school wasn't sustainable. Leaving school was a decision made for a good reason.

Dad spoke to the people in Bruce; they were very good to deal with and wished me well.

My mother wasn't happy. She wanted me to finish school and always have the safety net of the Leaving Cert. My grandmother, my mum's mother, she definitely was adamant that I shouldn't drop out. My father said it was my decision… it was my life.

My friends were all young lads like me, wide-eyed to the world. They were thinking this is cool, not having to worry about the Leaving Cert, getting paid to play football. I was on €500 a week, living at home.

I gave my mum €50 a week for board but she did everything for me. I was the only one of my friends who had constant money coming in.

If it didn't work out after a few years at Cork City, I feel I'd have gone back to sit the Leaving again. I'm not sure I'd have drifted around the League of Ireland. I might have looked at college then, focused on a different career and maybe played Munster Senior League on the side.

But that wasn't entering my thinking at the time. I was so tunnel-visioned.

This is what I want to do. This is where I'm going.

This is it.

CORK CITY WAS never viewed as a stepping-stone to go to England. I'd only been in the squad since January and wanted to break into the team.

Alan Matthews was manager by 2008; Damien had left after the FAI Cup final win. Alan called me in that summer to say a couple of clubs had made enquiries… and Sunderland had made an offer. He was very good to deal with; never stood in my way and kept me updated throughout.

Did I want to go to England? I was conflicted.

My view was narrow-minded. Living at home with my parents, getting paid good money, hanging around with all my mates... life was great. My first-team appearances amounted to a couple of games in the Munster Senior Cup and a substitute in a few league games. My focus was on getting more game-time.

Cork City was a comfort zone that I was probably scared to step out of.

Then this Sunderland opportunity arose. I didn't have an agent; dad did everything. He looked at the bigger picture. *What's the career path?*

Cork City was in chaos off the pitch in the summer of 2008. I was lucky at my age that I was oblivious to it. For senior players who had families and mortgages, it was different. I was a teenager living at home with my parents. If I was older, I'd have been knocking on doors and looking for answers.

Cork City offered me €3,000 a week to stay. I found it tempting. Thinking... *Why would I want to go to England, when I can get that money to live at home?*

It later emerged players were only getting paid a fraction of their wages so it's hard to believe that offer was serious. Dad makes the point it was lucky I didn't accept given the uncertainty at the time.

Alan Matthews told me that Roy Keane had been over for a game in Turners Cross. Alan bumped into him and asked about the transfer.

'Wait and see!'

Typical Roy, keeping his cards close to his chest.

Then Alan called me in one morning, saying the club had accepted a bid and Sunderland would be in touch. Dad always said if the transfer was agreed, we'd sort the contract and I was going. He nudged me in the right direction.

Sunderland booked flights for the two of us to go over; then mentioned to pack enough stuff so I wouldn't have to go home.

Mum was excited about it all. The initial fear factor was gone after dropping out of school. There was a sense that this was a feasible career.

Talk of a move to England had come up before. I went to Aston Villa three or four times as a teenager. Back in Cork after, I was walking around in my Villa gear, thinking... *I'm the bees-knees.*

When I signed for Sunderland, I got more gear that I ever needed and realised you need to earn the right to wear it. Ciaran Clark was on trial with Aston Villa then as well. Years later we became roommates with Ireland.

There was talk Nottingham Forest wanted to sign me at 15; I was over and back all the time. Mum wasn't keen. At that age I was too immature. If I had gone over at that age, I'd have been back living at home by 19, thinking... *What am I going to do with my life?*

WHEN WE FLEW over and met the Sunderland chief executive Margaret Byrne, the negotiations started. A contract was put in front of us and they left the room to give us time to think about it.

I almost wanted dad to make the decision for me. I'd trust him with my life. He's one of my closest friends. He wasn't looking to cash in on a son with sporting talent. His goal was to see me achieve something.

All the previous moves, from Corinthians to Cobh Ramblers to Cork City; he got those decisions right. He always had a plan and steered me right the whole way.

Now, he might have a Masters in Business; he is a very educated man but when it comes to football negotiations, he wouldn't be the best.

Sunderland's executives came back into the room.

'Maybe we can bump it up a little there,' dad suggested, and threw out a figure.

'No, this is the offer... take it or leave it.'

'Right so, David will sign there,' dad told them.

There was no negotiating. Then we left.

We always said it's not about money. If you take care of the work on the pitch, the money follows. It was a good mindset to have.

We checked into the Marriott Hotel that night down by the seaside in Sunderland. He had a flight back first thing in the morning and I was staying.

I was asleep when he left, so he pushed a note under my door. I kept it for years.

This is it.

This is all you've ever wanted.

This is your opportunity.

UCC

Sunderland

Stella

Jordan Henderson

The Barrs

Stamford Bridge

Steve Bruce

Canon O'Brien

★★★

JOHN

VETERINARY MEDICINE IN UCD was my target all through Leaving Cert in Gormanston College. There was a local vet in Tacumshane, Dick Walsh. When I was younger he used to breeze into our yard, a whirlwind of activity. Open the boot of his car – it was packed with boxes – and he'd get to work.

My plan was to head down that same track, but it was derailed as I fell short of the points required. I needed to look elsewhere. John Costello was from Thomastown, a Kilkenny minor hurler who was in Gormanston. He mentioned he'd applied to do a Science degree in Cork. I jumped on board to follow him.

I did first year Science and flew through it. Later I realised that I could have looked into a transfer to UCD and tried to get into veterinary again. But I wasn't aware of that option at the time. If I had studied veterinary, my whole life would have been different. Instead I moved to Cork, a place I had never been to.

I landed there in the autumn of 1974 and never left.

MYSELF AND JOHN Costello started out living in digs in Togher, near the old Ardmanning Bar. Our landlady was really good but it didn't work out. We were eating her out of house and home, raiding the fridge every night we came in.

We moved into a flat in Highfield West with another fella, Paul Maguire from Dublin, who slept on the floor. One bedroom, a back kitchen and bathroom. Basic stuff. We split the £9 a week rent between us.

John moved to Galway after first year, so I fell in with another gang to share a house. All lads doing Dairy Science that I'd got to know... Jimmy Codd and Eamonn Browne from Wexford, Joe Byrne from Wicklow, and Seán Walsh, the Kerry footballer, and father of Tommy.

SPORT PROVIDED THE early gateway for settling into life in Cork. I arrived in UCC with a GAA focus but football, or soccer, soon consumed me.

We'd play games in school on Sunday evenings. My brother Gerry had started a local soccer team in Wexford... Tacumshane Albion. There was a huge passion for soccer in Wexford at the time. You played GAA in the summer, soccer in the winter. Took a field, measured it out, put up posts and nets... that was it.

Growing up I had been a Leeds fan and can still vividly recall watching them lose 2-1 to Liverpool in the 1965 FA Cup final on the BBC. Gerry was a huge Spurs fan; he would get *Goal* and *Shoot!* magazines all the time.

Myself and John Costello used to go running together; we went out to UCC's sportsgrounds at The Farm one day and saw 20 fellas training over on a pitch. There was no problem falling in with them.

It was the UCC fresher soccer team and the manager was Ger Canning. I spent plenty of time later in life chatting at hurling matches with Ger when he was working for RTÉ, but UCC soccer provided our first sporting connection. Ger was very organised and dedicated to his role; a good guy.

After a few sessions, I must have made an impression as he made me captain. We all came back in September 1975 and went into the UCC Munster Senior League team. We finished runner-up twice but just could never quite win it.

Kieran Dowd, the UCC Head of Sport, was the senior manager. He was from Northern Ireland and had all his coaching badges. A technically brilliant coach with a good tactical mind. He got involved in the UCC gaelic football team later and I started going back to the GAA. Dowd was able to manage the fixtures, so if I was with UCC football on a Saturday, there'd be a soccer game on a Sunday. It was enjoyable to combine them.

I played centre-forward in soccer; the main target man but I could score as well. I got 35 goals one season, and a hat-trick when we won the Collingwood Cup – the premier inter-varsity competition – in 1978, beating Trinity College 6-1 in the final. That put us in the shop window for the Irish Universities team, who played Scotland, Wales and the Defence Forces. Dowd was the team manager but I didn't make the cut. I was fuming; we almost fell out over it.

He picked me the following year.

We had a huge amount talent in our UCC team. Eddie Murphy was centre-half; he became MD of Ford Ireland. Michael O'Leary played later with Cobh Ramblers, and Tony Sheehan for Cork Celtic. Leo Goold played football with Cork; his son Fintan won an All-Ireland senior medal in 2010.

The other big soccer experience in UCC was the Quarry Cup, a nine-a-side tournament with each faculty represented by a team of students. The lunchtime games were held where the Boole Library is now built in the college; at that time it was a large bowl sunken into the ground. It was a natural amphitheatre, and offered a Colosseum quality to the setting as the games descended into war.

The crowd watched from above, baying for blood. It was survival of the fittest, pure machoism as opposed to skill.

GAA IN UCC kept us busy but didn't yield the same rate of success.

I loved being involved. In the summer we'd have county championship with UCC and I'd come back up from Wexford to play those games. Dad would drop me in Waterford; I'd get a bus to Cork and go play the match. Stay with one of the lads that night, then head back. Did it without question.

Back then the college was a smaller place, as opposed to the huge institution it is now of over 20,000 students. You got to know people, and sport played a huge role in developing an even wider circle of friends. The Western Star was the main cultural experience on a Saturday night. We'd head in and chat to the owner Derry Crowley over a few pints, until the big sporting names would then arrive.

All the rugby fellas trooping in after playing for UCC that day... Moss Finn, Christy Cantillon, Donal Lenihan, Jerry Holland... Garrett Fitzgerald as well, Lord have Mercy on him. A crew who became big, high-profile figures in Munster and Ireland rugby circles. They were all sound; we became friendly but we knew they were the main lads in the Star.

★★★

DAVID

I SAUNTERED INTO the changing room for the first day of training with the Sunderland reserves before the 2008-09 season started. In my own head I was the Cork lad coming over, miles ahead of the rest. *This group of fellas will be no problem.*

Jordan Henderson and Jack Colback were there on day one. Jamie Chandler too, a highly-rated England youth international at the time. I remember the goalkeeper Trevor Carson, and the striker Martyn Waghorn. And they were all miles ahead of me. That first day I was way off the pace. I walked into a squad of 22 players, but take out the couple of goalkeepers and I was ranked 19 out of 20. All these fellas were technically excellent. The standard was ridiculous.

THE BEST THING that had happened to me was training with the Cork City first-team, with Colin, Gareth and Joe showing me the way. Understanding the need to knuckle down was nothing new. I was able to properly assess the situation, then enjoy the challenge. You get more comfortable in the group and your personality starts to shine in training.

It just takes time. I was nervous after that first session though. They were competitive too, they weren't going to let some Irish lad come over and take their position. I had made my Sunderland debut back home in Turners Cross in a friendly against Cobh Ramblers that had been pre-arranged.

When I had first flown to Sunderland, I didn't bring much stuff. My dad just threw a lot of clothes into the bag and gave it to me after that friendly. He didn't want me coming home regularly; his focus was on getting me settled over there and not thinking about family or buddies around Cork.

IT WASN'T UNTIL Christmas that I came back home and that proved disastrous in a way. We finished up our reserve league on December 18, and were let off until January 1. But when I was home, the club rang; they wanted myself and Jordan to go training with the first-team. It was grand for Jordan, he was nearby.

I was in another country.

Dad was saying to get on a flight and get back over there. But they wanted us there the following morning. Jordan went in and trained; I couldn't make it over.

That Christmas, dad seemed really annoyed that I was around the house. He felt I should have stayed, toughed it out on my own and be ready if a chance came up.

It was never an issue again. I got in around the first-team afterwards, so my Christmas breaks were never as long again.

The first morning after dad had left, I went into training. After that finished, I was back in the hotel by early afternoon. *How would I fill my days?* The focus was getting somewhere to stay and getting a car.

The club helped find me an apartment. Once I got the initial help, I was off on my own. I was completely lost, a 19-year-old in a new city in the north of England. I got the apartment and rang my mother to check what I needed. Microwave, kettle, cutlery... kitchen essentials.

'Have you got a bed?' No I didn't have a bed, and had to go get one.

I got organised; sorted a TV, chased up Sky and an internet connection. A big culture shock. Mum talked me through everything... but I'd never cooked in my life. 'Mum, what food do I need?'

'Right, get yourself some chicken, put it in the freezer. Take it out and defrost it... put it in the oven and you're sorted.' I listened closely. The problem was I didn't defrost the chicken properly. I was ill for about four days; I'll never forget it.

Then I came across Nandos. That sorted me.

I WASN'T THE only Cork young lad at the club. Conor Hourihane from Bandon was there before me, and John Egan from Bishopstown joined the following year in 2009. There was only a few years between us in age so we got on well.

The day I arrived, Conor came over and introduced himself. It was a nice touch; he'd played with Douglas Hall, who were local rivals of Corinthians.

A couple years previously, when I used to train in Mayfield for Cork City teams, there was an Irish emerging talent squad based there that Colin O'Brien ran. Conor was the great prospect that a lot of people talked about.

Himself and John both made it to the Premier League, but only after leaving Sunderland and scrapping to show the fight they had in them. Conor had a long road playing at lower levels, starting from scratch with Plymouth and building himself up. I'd give them huge credit for that.

I always want to see Cork lads succeeding, and there's a layer of responsibility felt in keeping an eye out for them, having a word with coaches as to how they're going. Kevin Ball used to always rave about John at Sunderland.

John is a remarkable man, I've so much time for him. He's very adaptable, and has a great work ethic. It took him until the age of 27 to reach the Premier League but I had no fear of him when he got there.

Later, in 2012, John had a bad leg break, while out on loan at Bradford. I drove down to visit him in hospital after. Despite the pain, he was still positive and upbeat. I was so happy to see him later make it to the Premier League with Sheffield United; the same when Conor did it with Aston Villa.

There's that sense of brotherhood in English football amongst the Irish crew; we've all moved over and we're all trying to make it. With John and Conor, there was that extra element in we'd all grown up in Cork.

I think I had the easier road of the three of us. That may sound strange with my knee injuries but I didn't have to dive down to the lower leagues as a young player. You can get pigeon-holed. If you drop down to League One, you can be stuck there and the Premier League seems a million miles away.

★★★

JOHN

UCC IS WHERE I met Stella.

In the science lab one day to study, I spotted her over at a table on the far side with a couple of friends. I kept staring and walked straight into the wall. The whole place looked over and cracked up laughing. Some first impression.

But we got together. She'd a Honda 50, registration 7043HI.

We toured Cork on that bike.

She was from Cork; Beaumont Drive in Blackrock. Her mother was always brilliant to me. I lodged there for six months at one stage; I paid my way, but was so well looked after. That never changed. Stella's parents were so good when our kids Sarah and David were born. They'd mind them after school when myself and Stella were working. Sarah used to go swimming at 6am in Douglas pool; we'd drop her over and her grandad would pick her up by 8am; sort her breakfast and drop her to school.

Myself and Stella got married in 1983. Fr Declan from Gormanston did the ceremony for us in UCC. When we bought our house in Rochestown in 1986, Stella's father did huge work on it; sorted the back garden, did our first driveway... put up cupboards and shelves all over the house.

IN THE SUMMER, after college exams had finished in Cork, I would return home to Wexford. I was tipping away at club level with Our Lady's Island and began playing senior football for the Wexford District team. Our manager was as much a charismatic figure and magnetic presence back then, as he would be in the 90s when guiding Wexford to All-Ireland hurling glory.

Liam Griffin was my first introduction to the world of adult GAA. He's an amazing man. His capacity to hold a room in the palm of his hand when speaking is incredible. A truly great motivator.

Outside of training I started regularly calling to the Pier Hotel in Rosslare Harbour, which Liam owned. He'd be at the bar at night and would make time to talk to me. Our relationship prospered and those chats continued over the years. Every time I was around Wexford, I called to Rosslare to meet him. He remained a source of advice for many years.

Liam Griffin gave me an insight into how business and sport could be interlinked with ideas transferred between them. He was innovative and motivated, expanding his business group with the Ferrycarrig, Hotel Kilkenny and the Monart Spa resort. That hard work and clever thinking was brought to the teams he managed as well. That Wexford District team was moulded in his image and we won the county senior football final in 1977 against Bunclody.

Nineteen years before Wexford lifted the Liam MacCarthy Cup under his watch, I was witnessing the transformative effect Liam could have on a team. He guided us back to the final in 1978 but there was a stand-off over the date as we'd a few players away. The County Board refused to budge; there was no final played and Castletown were awarded the game.

I LOVED LIFE in Cork. Staying there at weekends during college helped. Going home was affordable but the journey was a trek.

Down to the station on Parnell Place, and the bus to Waterford; sometimes on the slower one that travelled out the coast road by An Rinn. My father might pick me up in Waterford but he had a business to run too and sometimes I was left to thumb a lift home.

I didn't mind staying put in Cork.

My weekends were busy playing or going to games. I got swept up in the massive culture of sporting success in Cork. The hurlers claimed their All-Ireland three in-a-row between 1976 and '78; the footballers had lifted Sam in 1973. Cork Hibs and Cork Celtic were successful in that decade in soccer. The rugby teams of Dolphin, Highfield, Cork Con and Sundays Well were all flying.

On Sunday afternoons I'd head to Páirc Uí Chaoimh or Flower Lodge for a game. With no car I'd walk, cycle or grab a bus.

***

DAVID

I HAD MY own Irish support network when I started at Sunderland... Graham Kavanagh, Paul McShane, Andy Reid, Daryl Murphy, Roy O'Donovan and Liam Miller. They all looked out for me. I was at the club a month and a group of them took me out for a night in Newcastle. They were all brilliant.

Andy Reid was probably the hardest on me. He had standards and would be on a young player's case 24/7; didn't want anyone to slack off. We had a run-in one day at training. Reidy had fantastic skill with a beautiful left foot. I passed him the ball, and he carved open the defence with this great pass and we got in for a goal.

I shouted over, 'Great ball, son!' He absolutely flipped at me.

'Who are you calling son?'

I was gobsmacked he went after me. I was trying to compliment him; I understood later that he took it differently, seeing me belittling him.

There was another 10 minutes of training left. We were walking in after and I was chatting to Jordan about what happened. His view was not to be bullied by him.

Then big Murph came over.

'I wouldn't take that if it were me. You can't let him speak to you like that.'

He was winding me up, and was over to Reidy doing the exact same thing.

'This young kid from Cork is mugging you off. You really going to take it?'

We'd a gym session after it, and Reidy came storming in. I gave it back to him; we were roaring at each other. There were no punches thrown, we both just lost the head. I made sure not to call him son again.

But those Irish lads were very good. Graham Kavanagh was a tough Dubliner, a good honest pro. He showed me the ropes before he then moved on to Carlisle.

They all looked out for me. They'd all been down the road of coming over from Ireland to England, and knew it could be tricky. Just all good, decent lads; no major egos. Dwight Yorke wasn't part of that group but he was a brilliant figure for the younger lads, always wanting to help us. To us he had the fame; a decade on from winning the treble with Man United, we were all a bit starstruck by him.

He'd talk to us and point out little things we needed to work on; focusing on our passing, our positioning when receiving the ball. He'd this typical West Indies personality; very relaxed and chilled, nothing really bothered him.

ALL THE IRISH lads were great, but they were a good few years older. And they had their own families to focus on. I was living in this weird bubble.

It would have been different if I was a 15-year-old thrown into that environment, trying to keep the homesickness at bay. I found Sunderland similar in size and scale to Cork; and the same working-class city where people are highly passionate about their sport.

My buddies used to come over every second week, different lads. One weekend when I got into the first-team, four of them landed. We were playing a game on the Saturday, and the lads went out on the Friday night. I told them going out to let themselves back into my house later – I'd moved from the apartment by then – just not to wake me up.

But they got into a scrap in the middle of Sunderland and one of them had his jaw broken. The following morning, I was getting up, preparing for the game and your man has strapping on his jaw... he's black and blue.

Suddenly, I'm dealing with this, instead of preparing for a game. I was young and naive. As I got older, I didn't allow such a scenario to occur; I got more selfish about my preparation before games.

I'M JUST OVER a year older than Jordan Henderson.

When I signed, there was a little pre-season tournament down the coast in Hartlepool. James McCarthy was playing for Hamilton in it; people were raving about this kid. My registration hadn't gone through so I wasn't allowed play. Jordan had a quad injury.

So we were told, 'When the game is on, you two go sit behind the dugout'.'

We just got chatting and struck up a friendship. Jordan was shy and reserved, in this bubble of wanting to be a footballer, determined not to let any other distractions interfere with that. Our relationship evolved over time; we started doing stuff together outside of training and matches.

We laugh about it now, but I used to ring Jordan in the evenings.

'What are you up to… will we go to Nandos, to the cinema after?'

'I can't, I don't have the money for it.'

'Ah come on, I'll pay for you.'

We were on different contracts, myself and the future Liverpool captain, and Premier League and Champions League winner. But I knew him when he needed a dig out for chicken and chips for his dinner, some money for popcorn and a film ticket after. We joked about those times when he got the big move to Liverpool.

Later Jordan bought the Audi off me, and Conor Hourihane bought it off Jordan. That car did the rounds. I became very good friends with his crew from school, who I'd still be friends with now.

We'd play with the reserves on a Tuesday or Wednesday night. Jordan never went out or drank but I'd go out at times with his mates, who were all in university.

That's how we became friends and over a decade on we're still close.

THERE WAS NO major meet and greet with Roy when I signed for Sunderland.

I do remember seeing him early on in my first week. It had always been drilled into me to be first for training. Coaches take notice of that. It was a Friday morning… I arrived and Roy was there.

'Morning Roy!' I was oblivious to the chain of command in soccer. You do not call a manager by his first name. He replied, 'Morning!'

He didn't go through me, but there was enough of a lingering look to suggest I'd get a pass this once but in future… it was 'Gaffer' and nothing else.

My first real experience of Roy's attitude was when we played Gateshead away in a pre-season friendly with the reserves. I knew nothing about Gateshead; it was a half hour from Sunderland, they were playing in the Conference North at the time. We played the game and lost 2-0.

Roy was due to go back to Manchester but decided to stay and watch the game with his staff. The plan was for everybody to leave from the ground after. But after we got beaten the message came through that all the players were to report to the training ground. The manager wanted to speak to us.

In the Academy of Light, there was a big TV room upstairs, which had couches scattered around the large screen. We were waiting for Roy.

He came up and ordered everyone to stand up.

We stood in a circle around him. It was my first eye-opener of what life in England was about. He spoke about the performance of the team and hammered into a lot of people. We had a mix of senior professionals playing with us younger lads. Graham Kavanagh got a fair bit of stick.

Roy had a cut off Jordan, asking him did he think he was good enough to play for the first-team. Jordan looked him straight in the eye.

'Yeah, I do!'

I'd been at Sunderland only a week or so, but he turned to look at me.

'Just because you've only just signed, don't think you can get away with that. This is serious, you need to buck yourself up.'

It was an insight to his level of expectations. If anyone thought it was a run of the mill pre-season friendly, they were wrong. Some lads crumbled under that pressure. I felt this was what it was all about; hearing from a manager who was honest and open. My dad would have had similar conversations where he'd point out flaws in my performances.

We had all played awful in the game, but Jordan made his Premier League debut a couple of months later against Chelsea. The two of us were on the bench; Jordan was brought on at half-time. Roy admired that Jordan believed in himself and that he wasn't going to shy away from a challenge.

When he gave it to me with both barrels after that Gateshead game, I just replied, 'Okay.' I had heard what he had to say!

★★★

JOHN

BY THE END of the 70s, life was starting to drift for me. Off the pitch... *What is my career path?* On the pitch... *Where is my GAA future?*

I needed a plan. At the time I was renting on Magazine Road. John O'Brien was my landlord, a Kerry native, a garda in Cork and the St Finbarr's chairman. Stone mad about football.

We were always talking about GAA. In 1978 I played for UCC against the Barrs in a championship game; John gave me a lift down to the Páirc that evening. That same year I met Stella and we started going out. Christy Ryan and John Cremin, both steeped in the Barrs culture, were part of our group of friends. Meeting them at weekends, and John O'Brien during the week, meant they all sold me on the idea of the Barrs. It became a case of why not join?

I couldn't transfer in 1979 as I was a student. After UCC, I'd gone to do a post-grad Diploma in Chemistry in NIHE. I didn't really like it and by 1980 I was back in Cork and got a job in Cork Milk Producers on Tramore Road.

That gave me a purpose, and suddenly the Barrs came back on my radar.

JOINING ST FINBARR'S at the age of 24 was a huge opportunity; moving from a junior club to a powerful senior force. I started out as a footballer but struggled initially to reach the senior standard.

One night, Con Roche and Charlie McCarthy came down near the end of football training to ask me up to join the hurlers on another pitch. They'd heard I'd played with Wexford. I jumped at the chance.

I was playing half-forward. There was a small bit of pulling and blood drawn. That set the tone. I had shown my interest and enthusiasm to those watching. When there was hurling training the next night, I was in from the start.

There was a pattern of players coming to the Barrs... Tomás Maher from Waterford, John Allen from Aghabullogue. The club were open to outsiders.

I was familiar with Cork hurling history. Midleton, Sarsfields and Na Piarsaigh came strong during the 80s but there was no doubt that it was the era of the big three from the city – the Barrs, the Glen and Blackrock. The rivalry was inescapable with the battles between the northside and southside. The tradition fascinated me.

The Barrs and the Glen match, held annually on the night of the Eucharistic procession, had thousands of people watching in the Mardyke.

Then two of them collided in 1980 in my first introduction to a county final. A few years after being one amongst the 35,000 crowd watching in the Páirc, I was a sub with a front-row seat. The build-up to a county final caught the imagination of the city. We'd meet on Sunday morning at the club and have lunch. Get the bus down to the stadium and see the crowds streaming in.

We won 1-9 to 2-4 and there was this huge out-pouring of joy after.

The Barrs had a traditional way of celebrating. Everyone got off the bus at the bottom of Barrack Street and walked the cup up the hill. Stopped at Moks for a pint and watched the bonfires lighting on the Bandon Road. Then out past the Lough to the Barrs clubhouse for the night.

On Monday morning, we met in the Bull McCabe's pub for a few pints, went to the John Barleycorn Hotel in Glanmire for lunch that afternoon and back to Togher that night. I completely bought into it and understood the significance of winning. This is what I *wanted* to be a part of.

THERE WAS A fantastic coaching culture in the Barrs.

The elder statesmen were key, like Mick Kennefick, Donie Cremin, Timmo Mullane and Jimmy O'Grady (Donal's father). Mick had captained Cork to the All-Ireland in 1943. Then came the next generation of coaches like Gerald and Charlie McCarthy, Con Roche, Seamus Looney and Charlie Cullinane. To be exposed to that level of coaching from fellas with their pockets full of All-Ireland medals was a huge plus.

I was working in CMP Dairies at the time. Charlie had his own painting company and would come by in his van to chat through the latest match. Rochy then started calling. His family trained greyhounds and he'd be looking for cottage cheese, high protein stuff, that you could feed them. We'd always start talking about how hurling was going. He was a gregarious, funny character, who had a great way for putting things. In the plant we used to make soft ice-cream to go with cones, and hard ice-cream for the blocks sold in shops. Jimmy O'Grady was a sort of gruff character, one of the Godfathers of hurling in the Barrs. He called one day and beckoned me over.

'Do you remember the match the other night when you were over the far sideline and you tried to put the ball over the bar from 70 yards? Who did you think you were?'

'I'm John Meyler.'

'No boy, you thought you were Christy Ring. He's one of the best hurlers ever and even he wouldn't have tried that shot.

'So do you not think now,' he continued, 'that it would have been better to get that ball and give it in to Jimmy Barry and he would score?'

Jimmy would leave you thinking on that… before delivering his closing line. 'By the way, give me a block of ice-cream there.'

And then the next match, if you delivered the ball in, Jimmy would come over to praise you for taking that lesson on board.

I'm a direct person. They knew I wouldn't step back from the challenge, I was going to absorb it. I tried to transfer that later to David. The messages he got from managers in England were short and sharp; he needed to quickly take in the point they were trying to get across. I was so indebted to the generosity of those men in the Barrs for taking the time to talk to me; I realised then the importance in coaching of having one-to-one chats with players.

I was blessed to land in the Barrs during a time of relentless success. I finished up with seven senior medals, five in hurling and two in football. The only year that we didn't reach a county final in either code was 1987.

After we won in Cork, the national adventures took flight. I broke into the team after the 1980 county final before the Barrs went on a run in Munster, beating Causeway from Kerry, Killeedy from Limerick and then Roscrea from Tipperary in the final.

No. 11, outside a full-forward line of Jimmy-Barry, Charlie and Eamonn Fitzpatrick; that made my life much easier. We ended up in the All-Ireland final against Ballyhale Shamrocks in May 1981. They beat us, with seven Fennelly brothers playing and three of them – Brendan, Liam and Ger – scoring their entire total of 1-15. That was the beginning of the Ballyhale dynasty.

Our schedule was intense throughout the 80s. Defeats in Cork didn't always represent the end of the road. Imokilly beat us twice in football finals, but we got to represent Cork in Munster anyway due to the rule barring divisional teams from the province.

We'd a hardcore group of around 10-to-12 dual players. Heavy pitches and long seasons made for a real slog. No downtime in December. We lost a hurling semi-final after extra-time to Patrickswell at the end of 1982, then had to beat Doonbeg in a football semi-final the week after. We drew the final with Castleisland Desmonds, the replay wasn't played until January 1983.

At least we won that game. Sometimes all the effort brought no reward. Twice in-a-row, in 1984 and '85, we lost Munster finals to Desmonds just a couple days before Christmas up in Bruff in Limerick. It was a brutal feeling.

But severe disappointments made victories all the sweeter. My best hurling experience was against Ballyhea in the 1984 county final. We were raging hot favourites after our route to the final, beating the Glen, Na Piarsaigh, Midleton and Blackrock. It was my best game in a final for the Barrs.

Near the end a free came in. I jumped up to catch the ball on the '21', turned and took half of Ballyhea with me, before burying it in the net. The *Evening Echo* photographer Eddie O'Hare later gave me three photographs of it. He'd caught the sequence of the catch, turn and strike, and celebration. A brilliant memory.

★★★

DAVID

AT THE SUNDERLAND training ground, there was a whiteboard on the wall outside the doctor's office, between the changing rooms for the first-team and the reserve team. I checked it every morning to see the training squads for that day. It wasn't unusual to go with the first-team, but generally it was if they needed cover due to injuries. Thursday was the important day. That's when tactical work is done for that weekend's game. Make the cut then and it's a sign you're closer to the first-team squad.

The start of the 2008-09 season was about adjusting to life with Sunderland. After 10 games, November began with a trip to Chelsea.

For the Thursday session before that match, myself, Jordan and Martyn Waghorn were on the first-team list on the whiteboard. Big progress. On the Friday, the squad list for the game went up.

I was heading to Stamford Bridge. Welcome to the Premier League; private flight to London that evening, coach waiting on arrival, whisked straight to the team hotel. From where I had been a few months before with Cork City, this was a world apart. I wasn't fazed about potentially playing against one of the best sides in the country. But I was worried about something.

The night before the game was time for my initiation song.

After dinner myself, Jordan and Martyn had to sing as the new lads. They did a duet of a Ne-Yo song, I went my own way. I walked into the meeting room and stepped up on a chair. Everyone's roaring and banging the tables.

I planned to sing *The Streets of New York* by The Wolfe Tones; knew the words inside out. I got through the first three lines... and then my mind went blank.

Nothing. The lads all tore strips off me. And then Andy Reid saved the day.

He's a great man for a song; he just stood up and joined in with me. Daryl Murphy did the same. It was awful but they got me through it.

I sat down, sweat dripping off me. By then Roy and the rest of the coaches had come down. Someone turned to Roy.

'Meyler's just sang.'

'Ohhhhh... has he?' Roy turned to me. 'Get back up there and sing again, so we can see it this time!' If ever there was a time that my soul left my body, that was it. Roy saw how I had frozen; he just laughed and walked off.

CHELSEA PICKED A team full of stars. Cech, Alex, Terry, Cole, Bosingwa, Mikel, Lampard, Cole, Deco, Malouda, Anelka.

This was the big time and I loved the thought of going up against these fellas. I spent the 90 minutes on the bench watching on. Martyn started up front and Jordan came on at half-time for his debut.

The game was an eye-opener. We lost 5-0. Nicolas Anelka was outstanding; he scored a hat-trick and won the Golden Boot that season. I always found him a fascinating character; he seemed to have a real edge to him. I hadn't played but still found it a huge experience. I wanted to become a regular in the first-team squad.

Then a month later, Roy Keane left the club.

IT WAS A Thursday morning in early December, two days before playing Manchester United, when word spread around the club that he'd left.

Footballers must be selfish when assessing the situation. I was only in the door a few months. *Where did I stand?* Roy had signed me and must have thought I was half-decent. I was having a sniff around the first-team, things were going positively and then, suddenly... he was gone. I didn't see it coming.

A 4-1 loss to Bolton the previous Saturday had left us in the relegation zone. A fifth defeat in six games. That form would suggest a manager was in trouble but I was young and naive. As I got older, I realised football is a tough business. There is no loyalty; it's rare people leave of their own accord.

I found it a difficult time. A fella who had put faith in me was gone. I wanted to play for Roy and I didn't get that opportunity properly until later in my career with Ireland. I didn't even have his phone number at the time to contact him and say I appreciated what he'd done.

Ricky Sbragia took over until the end of the season, a Scottish coach who had been at the club for a while. But Ricky's focus wasn't on young lads, it was about experience. He needed to survive a relegation battle and did that, despite only winning once in the last 13 games. Our North-East neighbours Newcastle and Middlesbrough went down. That Chelsea trip was my one first-team experience... I kept playing with the reserves. We won the North League and lost to Aston Villa, winners of the South League, 3-1 in a play-off.

I turned 20 that May, and had a season in England under my belt but things felt uncertain. It was all well and good having a contract but I couldn't just sit there for a couple of years, take the money and head home. I needed to play and prove myself.

Ricky left at the end of the season. In June, the new manager arrived.

★★★

JOHN

OVER THE WINTER of 1986 and the spring of '87, the Barrs got on a football run that ended in Croke Park on St Patrick's Day with the All-Ireland club final.

That season I was made captain, and I asked the chairman what extra stuff they wanted me to do?

'Nothing. Go up for the toss,' he replied. 'I'll tell you which way to play.... you play your position as normal.' No ceremony, no need for me to be thinking about big speeches to fire up the lads. That taught me a great lesson. *Just do my job.*

We played Clann na nGael in the final and I was full-back marking Tony McManus, one of Roscommon's stars, and a big scoring threat. When the first delivery came in, I grabbed ball and man; drove them both straight up the field. We'd played Castleblayney Faughs in the semi-final. They'd Nudie Hughes and Eamonn McEnaney, and we beat them after a replay down at the Páirc. McEnaney got two goals, so I vowed for the final I wasn't going to let anyone inside me. But I didn't lack support with John Cremin and Eugene Desmond either side of me, and John Kerins behind in goal.

We'd to play that day without Davy Barry. He scored 0-5 up in Castleblayney for the drawn semi-final but missed the replay with his soccer commitments for Cork City in the FAI Cup. That really annoyed me. I chased him before the final, stressed that we needed him in Croke Park but he opted to sit it out. A big pity he missed it.

It was an awful day to play football with a gale, sleet and snow blowing around Croke Park. We dug in and won 0-10 to 0-7. Clann na nGael were shattered; it was the start of four final losses in-a-row that they would suffer. Both clubs had blue jerseys so we wore white for the game to avoid a colour clash.

The week before, I gave my Barrs' blue jersey to Pat Lougheed, our coach-trainer, to bring with him. After the match, Lougher pulled out the blue jersey and I went up the steps of the Hogan Stand wearing it to collect the cup.

I wanted to reflect what all the years in the Barrs had meant to me. I felt wearing a white jersey would have been a sign of disrespect and I was duty-bound to wear the blue one. It's a gesture that I'm proud of.

THE ALL-IRELAND win was an amazing outcome after the worst day I'd had in football with the Barrs. The 1986 county senior final was against Imokilly. East Cork was a traditional hurling area but their football team still had big names like Teddy McCarthy, Conor Counihan and Denis Walsh.

I'll never understand how we lost that game. Imokilly failed to score in the first-half. We were up six points with 10 minutes left. The lead was cut to two and then, at the very end, Imokilly substitute Brian Lotty scored the goal that broke our hearts. It was a killer of a defeat but the resilience and endurance of that team helped us cope. Then we got our reward in becoming All-Ireland champions.

Sometimes there wasn't a chance to make amends. In 1990 we lost the Cork hurling final to Na Piarsaigh after a replay. I was 34 years old, heading for the exit, but came on as a sub in the second-half.

With a couple of minutes to go, Mickey Barry handpassed the sliotar into me. I was 21 yards out, and unleashed a shot. The sliotar flew high and wide, up into the crowd in the terrace. Christy Ryan was waiting inside but I hadn't passed it. The final whistle sounded soon after and Na Piarsaigh won their first title by two points. That miss haunts me in a way. If I see it while coaching, I'd pull a forward straight away. Give it to the man in the better position. *I didn't do it in a county final and look what happened.*

All those never-ending seasons of games caught up on me as osteoarthritis flared in my hips. I'd avoided injuries all through my career, never even broke a bone in my body. The flipside was near the end. I had to live on Ibuprofen tablets before a match. It was all designed to bring the pain down to a manageable level; then you were suped up and ready to go on game day. It wasn't a long-term solution.

In 1988, I pulled the plug on football. I enjoyed playing hurling more and got in a few more playing years than if I'd stayed at both. Eventually the body called a halt; 1990 was my last big senior year, and I finished up playing junior hurling.

One night, down in Ballinlough in 1993, Martin Cronin, who became known for his football with Cork and Nemo, gave me the run around in a hurling match. He was young and energetic, in stark contrast to where I was. It was time to go.

THE BEST PART of wins was always the interaction with the Barrs supporters. After county finals you were constantly approached by people thanking you for what you had done. I was blown away by the importance they attached to it. *The Barrs on top again!* They could be happy for the rest of the year.

They all worked alongside people from other clubs. The Beamish brewery on the southside and the Murphys brewery on the northside had a crossover of employees. The goal was to go to work with a smile on your face. It taught me about having respect for the older generations in a club.

Every year, the Barrs stepped up their investment in the preparation of players as we got closer to the county final. After training there was a dinner provided by the ladies committee. A bowl of soup. A main course of beef, potatoes and carrots. Apple tart and custard with a cup of tea after. Then two free drinks from the bar.

The ladies committee played a critical role in the club and were so genuine in the work they did, all with the aim of making sure we won every Sunday. We were hugely appreciative. On the last night of training, they would all be given a bouquet of flowers and a box of chocolates.

A HUGE BOND existed between those players.

Donal O'Grady was the most intelligent hurler I've ever met. I have the utmost respect for him. When I was managing Cork, Donal was my first port of call after a match. *See what his thoughts were.* He'd tell it to me straight what he felt needed to be done. Watch a game with him and he'll really hone in on specific things. A lot of that goes back to his father. Nowadays if you mention the 60s or 70s in hurling, you get labelled old school because people feel there wasn't proper coaching techniques in those days.

When Donal took over Cork in 2003, he went back to basics with the emphasis on hooking and blocking. His father Jimmy was like that… *get the essential stuff sorted first.*

'Grady' had a ruthless streak as well, a real stopper at full-back. He used to mark me in training and we'd go at it. Then after we were finished, he'd be talking about the game, analysing a specific decision I had made.

John Allen was different. A really good footballer and hurler; more of a philosopher, he worked as a schoolteacher and you could see that. Well able to get his point across, but in a different way to Grady; softer, more emotional. When John took over as Cork manager in 2005, it was a clever move to have continuation. You had good hurlers there and there was no need to break the mould. Grady kick-started it all, but John kept it going.

Gerald McCarthy retired in 1979 and then started managing the Barrs. If he hadn't retired, I wouldn't have played for the Barrs so soon. Gerald had an aura when he spoke in a dressing-room. Being a five-time All-Ireland winner and Cork captain in 1966 at the age of 21, made him an iconic figure. Gerald taught me a lot about being ultra-competitive on the field; he'd a hard as nails attitude.

One night, I was inside in Clancys pub in Cork city having a pint with Christy Ryan, and Gerald walked in. He saw us… we both looked at one another, got up and walked out. We were caught. Gerald was the boss.

You respected him. He drove the ship.

WE HAD TWO top goalkeepers in the club. Ger Cunningham was unbelievably talented, a serious shot-stopper. He had huge self-belief. People talk about modern hurling goalkeepers playing as an American football-styled quarterback with puck-outs; Cunningham was doing that in the 80s. He'd put the ball on a sixpence for you. We practiced a lot. Telling half-forwards... 'I'll see you at six o'clock before training... we'll go through the plan'.

He was really dedicated to goalkeeping, and spent a lot of time in the ball alleys in Rochestown College with Justin McCarthy. His father and mother would have been a massive influence, great to give him advice.

John Kerins in football was a milder character, a really good guy. The two lads were subs to each other but Kerinsy was more football orientated. He had a great kickout and having him in goal made my job so much easier at full-back.

John passed away from cancer at the age of 39 in 2001. Hard to make sense of it; such a tragedy. I wouldn't have known him as well as Ger. He was younger but a really lovely guy and an outstanding character.

IN MY MIND there is no question who the greatest player that the Barrs or Cork had. Jimmy Barry-Murphy. I didn't see Christy Ring play but of those I did, there's no one ahead of Jimmy. No debate.

He would make a fool out of defenders when he got the ball. The man was a genius. He was so far ahead in his thinking at times during games. We played Castlehaven once down in Bandon. Jimmy got a goal where he reacted an hour ahead of everyone else who was playing. It's like watching Lionel Messi play soccer; Jimmy had that talent which very few players have and that elevated him.

I give myself a small bit of credit for quickly sizing up the situation when I joined the Barrs. If I gave the ball to Jimmy, he'd score most of the time and that'd be my job done for the team.

I asked Gerald one day, 'What's the difference between myself and Jimmy Barry?'

'When you catch a ball,' he told me, 'You're still not turned to face the goal. When Jimmy catches, he's already turned.' Jimmy took unmerciful hammerings off defenders in those days when there was plenty skulduggery on the pitch. But he coped and was just a very nice, humble fella. The perfect teammate.

A lot of us moved onto coaching from those teams, which goes back to the structures that were in place from the older Barrs' generation. Gerald, Jimmy, Grady, Allen, Cunningham and myself were all part of Cork senior hurling management teams. I'm conscious I'm the only one that hasn't won an All-Ireland.

You could compare it to the Bootroom philosophy in Liverpool. We were taught about how to play the game and then moved into coaching to get the message across to the next generation. While I was still playing, I started helping with under-14 and under-16 hurling teams in the Barrs.

CHRISTY RYAN DIED in February 2021.

He had been struggling for a few years with illness. My brother had passed away a few weeks before. It was a really hard start to the year; two personal losses and at a time when the country was still in lockdown; there was little to do but get wrapped up in my own thoughts.

Christy was an absolute gentleman and really good to me when I started with the Barrs. Drinking buddies first around Cork and then teammates in Togher. Christy was a colossal figure for us in football, and then we were in the half-forward line in hurling. His playing record was phenomenal. Twenty county senior final appearances, winning 11 of them, and part of four All-Ireland winning teams. He played football for Cork but I felt he was better as a hurler. He worked ferociously hard but could also score.

THE SAME AFFILIATION I once had with the Barrs isn't there anymore, as other teams have come into my life. The club has gone into transition. After that golden era, the success dried up.

No hurling title since 1993. They lost a lot of football finals, but I was there when they lifted the Andy Scannell Cup again in 2018 for the first time in 33 years. I was thrilled. I met Ian Maguire after; he had been a brilliant leader of that team and I just wanted to congratulate him.

My regard for the club will always be the highest. I was welcomed by the Barrs because of how I applied myself. I didn't have the local blue blood coursing through my veins but they still accepted me as one of their own.

Did I contribute and give everything to the Barrs?

One hundred percent! No one could say that against me. And I got so much in return from everyone in the club.

★★★

DAVID

THIS WAS THE beginning of my time in football with Steve Bruce.

Myself and dad chatted in the summer of 2009 before I went back to Sunderland for pre-season. We agreed this was a crucial time. I had to start impressing if I wanted to make that breakthrough. I was always naturally fit; prided myself on that. You could pick technical faults in my game but when it came to running, I was convinced no one would beat me.

We started in July doing a lot of energy-sapping running sessions, and I was like a machine. We used a 1km track for interval running, doing a drill that would last 25 minutes with six stations... jog for so long, then the call came to go flat-out.

My goal was to stand out and I did that.

I got the call-up for the pre-season tour to Portugal. It went well. We went on to Amsterdam, playing in a mini-tournament against Benfica, Atletico Madrid and Ajax. My parents were flying in to watch the games. Steve Bruce let me know I was in the picture to play. I was excited. Then a setback. In training I got the ball, went to fire a one-two around Phil Bardsley and he dived in, ripping all my ankle ligaments. Out for six weeks. The lads went to Amsterdam. I flew back to Sunderland on my own. It was my first experience of the mental grind of injury recovery. Bruce rang with a simple message... 'Get your ankle sorted and you'll be fine'.

That spurred me on. I worked with the physio Dave Binningsley; we'd later become very close with my two serious knee injuries.

Before the start of the season, the Sunderland coaches were concerned I'd missed a good chunk of training. I was pushing and threw myself into training. Then I got clattered into my left ankle. Another six weeks out... back to injury rehab.

As the weeks passed, I needed a proper game to test my ankle. There was one arranged behind closed doors with our reserves against Doncaster Rovers. It looked a *nothing* game but it proved critical for me in winning the trust of Bruce. About half hour in, one of our young lads got cleaned out. I was one of the oldest Sunderland players and didn't like the tackle. I had a pop off the lad who went in, before the referee came over to calm things down.

THERE IS A beauty to tackling.

People think you just hurl your body at it but you have to catch someone at precisely the right time. The ball came to that same Doncaster lad.

He received it on the backfoot. I came like a train; cleaned him and the ball. A perfect tackle. The ref stopped the game, because the lad jumped up and grabbed me by the neck. Handbags stuff. The ref wanted to put us both off; he wasn't happy, this was meant to be low-key. Next thing I see Steve walking onto the pitch and he puts his arm around me. We walked off and they brought on a sub.

'Do a five-minute jog around the pitch,' Bruce told me. 'Go for an ice bath and cool off.' I wondered was I in trouble since the manager had got involved. But I'd built up a good rapport with Dave. He gave me the heads up on how Bruce had reacted to the tackle.

'He'll do for me!' Bruce had said. 'You can't put the fight in someone, but you can control it.' That was a stepping-stone for me to get into the first-team.

It didn't mean instant progression. I was in my dad's ear that maybe I needed to go on loan. But by Christmas, the Sunderland squad was hit hard by injuries. I wasn't involved for the 1-1 draw with Everton on December 26. Two days later we were away to Blackburn. This time I was in. All my family were over for the game at Ewood Park. I was tuned in that morning.... breakfast, walk, pre-match food... team meeting. I was sitting with Michael Liddle, an Ireland under-21 teammate, as the team was put up on the big screen.

I immediately looked at the subs list. Hadn't made it.

I was giving out to Michael... and then he nudged me.

'Look... you're starting!'

I looked again. David Meyler midfield with Lorik Cana and Jordan Henderson. A breakthrough at last. We got to the stadium and Bruce marched over during the warm-up.

'Just keep it simple. Don't try any Hollywood passes.

'Win the ball back... lay it off... go again!'

IT ALL FELT frantic as the game started.

After a few minutes, I ran onto a ball about 30 yards out, had a crack and it flew over the bar. Whatever nerves I had were now gone. I was up for it.

I charged into Morten Gamst Pedersen in midfield. Steven Nzonzi and Keith Andrews squared up to me. A yellow card to mark my debut.

All the details are clear in my mind. All four goals arrived in a 25-minute period in the second-half... Darren Bent put us ahead twice, Pedersen and El-Hadji Diouf equalised. Steve Bruce versus Sam Allardyce on the touchline... a draw after a mid-table scrap.

That day was a good insight into a big theme in Sunderland's season, the goalscoring of Darren Bent. The previous August he had signed for a club record fee of £10 million. If there was pressure because of that price, it didn't affect him.

He was an unbelievable finisher and worked on it relentlessly every day in training. Of the people I played with, he was similar to Robbie Keane. Obsessed with scoring goals. Benty might do nothing all game but you knew if he got a chance that he'd score. In his London twang, he'd say he wasn't there to run the channels or close people down. You hear about strikers who play the width of the box... that was Darren Bent. He finished the season with 24 goals in the Premier League, third top scorer behind Didier Drogba and Wayne Rooney.

Most people remember his famous 'beach ball' goal against Liverpool, but another one sticks out in my mind.

Third last game of the season was away to Hull. Early on, I won the ball and moved it wide to Alan Hutton. He launched in a cross, Kenwyne Jones headed it back... and Benty sticks it in the net. We were the first two running off in celebration, hugging each other... and then he turned to me.

'Bruv, you've just helped pay for my Ferrari!'

It was his 24th league goal but, more importantly, it was his 25th overall for the season. He had a bonus in his contract if he hit that milestone, and had ordered himself a Ferrari as a reward. We all knew his value to the squad. Bruce reminded us in January when we lost 2-0 to Everton and he hit the roof after.

'If it wasn't for him down there, we'd be in big trouble!' he roared while pointing at Benty. He knew how to score goals and that's not an easy trait.

I DIDN'T WANT the Blackburn game to be a one-off. Fellas were coming back from injury and suspension. I had to stay involved. I played in an FA Cup win against Barrow in early January but wanted more big time experiences. In the space of a month I got them, and received some harsh lessons.

First up was a return to Stamford Bridge. Unlike November 2008, this time I started against Chelsea. The changing room was small, so Bruce called me and Jordan into the shower area for a chat beforehand.

'Right Meyler, you're up against Frank Lampard!

'Jordan you're on Michael Ballack!

'Two wonderful players but I think we've seen the best of their careers. Ye'll be fine.' Then, after half an hour, Lampard is celebrating after scoring. We were 4-0 down.

He finished with two goals; Ballack got one. We ended up losing 7-2. It was an eye-opener to witness these fellas up close. The way they kept the ball in midfield was mesmerising. It would have been easy for Bruce to whip us off but he left us on to learn. I know we got destroyed but it was a brilliant learning experience.

YOU HAVE TO dust yourself down after a game like that. They were one of the best teams to ever play in the Premier League. Under Carlo Ancelotti, they were top of the table and won the league that year.

If people were understanding then, soon it was in short supply. In February in Fratton Park, I came on against Portsmouth. They were bottom of the table and the stakes were high. The game started positively for us. They had Ricardo Rocha sent-off. Benty scored a penalty to put us ahead. So far, so good. We went down to 10 men early in the second-half, when Lee Cattermole got a second yellow card.

Eighty-five minutes in, and I was sent on for Andy Reid. I went in left side of midfield to shore things up… *and let's head home with the three points.*

I only lasted 115 seconds. Craig Gordon hoofed a kickout towards the left wing. Steve Finnan was full-back for Portsmouth; it looked like he was going to head it but then he momentarily dropped back. I miscalculated, jumped in, leading with my forearm and caught him on the face.

Finnan got ratty, but there was no intention. I had just mistimed it; a young fella in off the bench and eager to get into the game. I turned around and the referee Kevin Friend showed me a red card.

Eighty-seventh minute, and it was 9 versus 10, with plenty of injury-time. We were hanging on. Then Aruna Dindane headed in a Portsmouth equaliser in the 95th minute… 1-1, the place went wild. A full-blown disaster for me.

By that stage I had gone off down the tunnel and Cattermole was in the changing room when I walked in.

'Oh, are we finished… did we win?'

'No, I've been sent-off.'

'YOU WHAT?!'

At that age, I had no clue of the pressure a manager might be under. That would have been a valuable three points. We finished the season 13th, clear of relegation but that was the sort of game which could have eased concerns.

Bruce came in after. It was the first time I took a proper bollocking off him. He ripped me apart but I had to take it. There was worse to follow.

Dad was at the game and we met after.

'I hope you're ready for the shitshow that's going to come now!'

That's when I understood how obsessive Sunderland fans were. The view was I'd cost the team the win. The abuse I received was outrageous. Going to the bus after the game… days later on the street… messages on Facebook and Twitter.

Horrible stuff. It was a wake-up call to see their passion spill over into absolute vitriol. I could have gone two ways but took it in my stride and vowed I'd prove that I cared for the club.

I ONLY GOT sent-off twice more in my career. Straight red against Swansea in April 2015, a double booking against Norwich in October 2017.

The Portsmouth sending-off was deserved; for the other two I was unlucky. When I tackled Swansea's Kyle Naughton, my foot hit the top of the ball, popped off, came down and I shattered his ankle.

I felt bad about it; his ankle wasn't in a good way. After I'd been sent-off I went into the shower to get changed. He had to get his ankle treated. There was a TV in the corridor. I ended up sitting next to him watching the rest of the game.

I felt awful; his ankle was swollen and he needed crutches. I was apologising and he was saying not to worry; joking he should be thankful as he'd get two weeks in Dubai.

I played a dangerous game at times, some borderline tackles. It was regularly said that if I got a yellow, my style of play would be impacted but I'd disagree with that. I wasn't an idiot, I knew when I could put in a tackle. I always felt in control.

I WAS SUSPENDED for three games after playing Portsmouth, all the time wondering how much of a price I would pay? Then Cattermole got injured the day before facing Man City. Suddenly I was back in the team.

A huge home game. It was the early days of the money flowing into Man City. Roberto Mancini was manager... Carlos Tevez up front, Vincent Kompany at the back. Shay Given was in goal.

I enjoyed the midfield battle. They started with Gareth Barry and Nigel De Jong, and brought on Patrick Vieira. Myself and Steed Malbranque dug in for the fight. It finished 1-1; a sickener as Adam Johnson levelled with a great strike in the last minute. But the game went well for me. I had a clash with Barry at one stage. I went in hard in a tackle; he jumped up and started yapping away.

'WHO YOU TACKLING LIKE THAT... YOU'RE UGLY!'

Gareth's trash-talking needed some work. My attitude was to get noticed again. The fans recognised the effort and the reception was unreal. It was hard to believe they were the same group that had been hammering me.

I was making progress and April 2010 was when it all came together. One of those perfect phases that footballers are searching for. Four games in the space of three weeks. I started them all; we won three.

FIRST UP, TOTTENHAM.

One of the best Saturday afternoons of my career. The Stadium Of Light was packed for a 3pm kick-off; the place bouncing from the start as the energy rolled off the stands and down onto the pitch. Harry Redknapp had brought Tottenham to town. He had Bale and Modric in his midfield running the show, and chasing a Champions League place. They got over that line a few weeks later, but first we knocked them back a couple of strides.

It was a crazy match. Darren Bent was fired up for it against the club he'd left the previous summer. He scored in the first minute, and then again from a penalty after a half hour. The madness started as we tried to kill the game.

Bent had another penalty before half-time saved by Heurelho Gomes. Then, into the second-half, I'm through on the right of the box and Wilson Palacios clips me. Another Bent chance for the hat-trick... another penalty miss as Gomes saves. A few minutes later Anton Ferdinand has a goal ruled out for a foul.

It looked like we were going to pay when they brought on Peter Crouch and he headed in a Modric cross with 20 minutes left. But we did finish them off, Boudewijn Zenden volleying in a screamer for a 3-1 win.

There is no better place than Sunderland on a day like that. The fans were walking on air and further good results rewarded the love they had for their club. There was no heart-stopping last day of the season; we were safe by then.

After the win at Hull to round off April, I got drug tested after the game. Dad waited for me and we drove back to Sunderland together. The journey home took four hours; at the time Hull was alien to us, we didn't have a clue where we were going. The two of us didn't care. We were on cloud nine. I was a month off my 21st birthday, into my second season in England and I felt I was starting to arrive in the Premier League.

There were just two games left in the season… against Manchester United and Wolves. And then everything changed.

★★★

JOHN

KILKENNY'S PRESENCE HAS been a recurring theme in my sporting experience, often responsible for the pain of defeat. They overshadowed my time in charge of Wexford; then were the opposition on my last day out as Cork manager.

But signs of that trend had been there long before.

MY UNDERAGE PLAYING days with Wexford brought little reward. At minor hurling, Kilkenny knocked us out of Leinster twice in-a-row. Same story at under-21 with final defeats in 1976 and '77. Football wasn't any better underage… Dublin and Kildare were too strong.

My first senior call-up came in football. Wexford got stuck in a Leinster first round battle with Carlow in 1979 that took three games to sort out. Before he became a big hurling name, George O'Connor started out as a footballer and saved Wexford with the equaliser in that first replay.

I started when we won the second replay, but we lost the quarter-final to Wicklow. I opted to commit at the time to Wexford, letting go a soccer game for the Munster Senior League against a Leinster side on the same day.

But really my focus was starting to shift elsewhere.

MY LIFE WAS in Cork. Joining St Finbarr's in 1980 made those roots stronger and I became more absorbed into their culture.

It was a world removed from the child obsessed with a photograph of Wexford's hurling heroes of 1956. Moving to boarding school in Meath at 13, and to college in Cork at 18, had changed my outlook. My passion for GAA had gone flat; it took the transfer to the Barrs to rekindle that fire within me.

Playing for the Barrs advanced my hurling. Progressing to the All-Ireland final in 1981 against Ballyhale actually resulted in a Wexford hurling call-up. It wasn't in my thinking, but Christy Kehoe from Enniscorthy was manager and he was keen to get me involved.

I played some league matches that spring. Then, in May, on the day the Barrs were defeating Scotstown in an All-Ireland football semi-final, I was down in Wexford Park, part of a team that walloped Dublin by 18 points. I wasn't totally involved; based in Cork made it hard to make every training session.

When we played Kilkenny and Offaly, I was a sub. The Leinster run ended with a defeat in the final, and my playing relationship with Wexford just petered out afterwards. The Barrs' campaigns just consumed me and became more important than lining out for Wexford. We went on a club rollercoaster between football and hurling and I didn't want to get off.

IN EARLY 1983, Jimmy O'Grady threw an idea at me. He was a Cork selector at the time. *Would I consider an inter-county transfer?*

It wasn't a notion that had crossed my mind.

I didn't have a clue what was involved. My form had been good for the Barrs; we'd completed three in-a-row in Cork in 1982. Club hurling left me content, and the county game didn't feel a big ambition I needed to realise.

Jimmy kept pushing. Making the move was straightforward. I was living and working in Cork, played my club hurling there... I just needed to sign a form.

The Cork selectors called me up in late-April for a challenge against Waterford.

Then the following week they played Wexford in Cloyne at the opening of Christy Ring Park. It was four years since Ring's death had rocked the hurling world; they were erecting a bronze statue in his homeplace and the game was to commemorate him. There was plenty of interest surrounding it.

Playing Wexford didn't faze me, even if I was going up against ex-teammates like John Conran and Martin Quigley. I went out and hurled, scored three points and was happy with my contribution. We played Kilkenny in Kilmacow in another challenge game, and I scored 1-1 there.

There was no barrier either to blending into the Cork dressing-room. The Barrs lads like Cunningham, Grady and JBM helped me integrate. I'm a reasonably open kind of man and wanted to get on with people. The lads from other clubs were approachable. Before the Wexford game, I discovered I'd no red socks in the gear-bag. No bother, Seánie O'Leary threw me over a spare pair.

HOW DO I evaluate my Cork hurling career? A missed opportunity.

In 1983 those challenge game appearances helped me get a start against Limerick in the Munster Championship. I was whipped off in the draw at the Gaelic Grounds. For the replay in Páirc Uí Chaoimh, I was gone after 25 minutes.

Marking Liam O'Donoghue, the instructions were to keep him back in his box. The game then was about commanding your square of the pitch. If your marker got on top, you were in trouble. Tomás Mulcahy came on and played well. It had to be accepted and taken on the chin. Those games just passed me by.

What caused that? I'd done well in the challenges and in training. *But in the increased heat of championship, can you cope when the temperature is turned up?* I didn't. There was a massive gap between flying high in training and performing with 40,000 people watching from the stands and terraces.

I was on the bench for the Munster final and watched Cork hockey Waterford. Then for the All-Ireland semi-final against Galway, I was dropped from the squad.

No prior warning. The harsh reality of sport.

The news was broken to everyone in the same way. We gathered in a circle in Páirc Uí Chaoimh and the 24 travelling for the Galway game were called out. I went up on the day to carry hurleys but didn't fill that role for the final, when Cork lost to Kilkenny by two points.

I felt I could have added something to the half-forward line but my view was irrelevant then. Tomás came on against Limerick and seized his chance. Finished his career with three All-Ireland medals and winning captain in 1990. Fair play to him. And my cause wasn't helped that summer by an act of complete stupidity.

I WAS WORKING in CMP and the company had a team in the Cork Shipping Soccer League. They were stuck for players one afternoon and gave me a call. I went out and played a half hour of soccer. In the middle of an inter-county hurling championship season. Pure madness, when you reflect on it.

What was I thinking? The lads at work needed a hand, I just thought I'd help. Maybe I did but it was also a stupid decision that I came to regret and paid dearly for.

Johnny Clifford was the Cork manager, and he came up the next night at training as word had got out about my soccer appearance. He tore into me about a lack of commitment. Gerald McCarthy was Barrs' manager; he rang as well about it and was very disappointed in me.

The whole Cork thing kind of fell apart for me then. I was gone from their plans as that summer progressed. We all do stupid things, I just had to accept it. There was no point protesting. It wasn't an argument I was going to win.

As a senior county manager you have to demand total commitment, there can't be any other sporting distractions. I would later understand that perfectly. In 2012 I dropped three of the Boyle brothers – Mikey, Liam and Pádraig – from the Kerry hurling squad. They'd played a soccer game for their local club Rattoo Rovers, three days before we met Carlow.

I learned one thing that summer which I passed on to David. As he climbed the ladder in England, I would cite my Cork hurling experience of 1983. When these opportunities arise, you must take them. The window to get game-time will close quickly.

BEING DROPPED BY Cork didn't end my sporting life. The Barrs was a security blanket I could wrap myself in. The punch to the gut didn't hit me as hard as if I had nothing to fall back on. I could gather myself and go again.

There were big games and challenges to face, moving between football and hurling… lifting trophies, losing finals… testing ourselves in Munster and on the All-Ireland stage.

I still fully supported Cork, knowing the players involved; and was up in Thurles at the centenary All-Ireland final and thrilled to see them win.

Over the next two years, there were some chances in challenges and the league to return as a Cork hurler. But nothing that lasted. Then the Barrs played Blackrock in a league game on a Friday night in the summer in 1986.

I went into the bar in Church Road after for a drink and Jimmy Brohan came over to me. An uncle of the Cashmans, he'd spent his life embedded in Cork hurling, playing corner-back in 1956 against the Wexford team I had idolised growing up.

Now he was a Cork selector. We chatted away for a few minutes.

'What are you doing tomorrow?' asked Jimmy.

I was working. He mentioned Cork were playing Offaly in a challenge in the afternoon in Thurles. The team bus was leaving in the morning.

'Jimmy, I'll be there. I'll drive myself up and see ye there at two o'clock.'

I did a few hours in CMP in the morning, got into the car and drove off to the match. Cork only had 17 players and two of them were goalkeepers. So I was starting... and got 1-3 off Pat Delaney. I was delighted with myself. A big opportunity... this time I took it. And with that, I was back in.

BY SEPTEMBER I was on the bench for the All-Ireland final win over Galway. I didn't play that day or in the semi-final against Antrim. But I was involved and I felt a part of it. There was a bit of uncertainty who'd make the squad at the time. John Hodgins and Dermot McCurtain had torn their cruciates. Teddy McCarthy went on holidays and missed the Antrim match.

We were coming down home on the train from Dublin after that game. I was sitting in a booth with Jimmy Barry, Dr Con Murphy and Johnny Clifford.

Johnny turned to me, 'Can you excuse us here? We want to have a chat.'

I moved away from them. But I was half-listening in to what they were saying and it turned out they were picking the team for the All-Ireland.

It came to a debate over the half-forward line and I was edging over, trying to hear. Teddy was mentioned. It was gas. He was sunning himself abroad on holidays while the rest of us were heading back to Cork. Teddy came back refreshed, started and made his championship debut, and Cork won the All-Ireland.

I loved being a part of the occasion for the whole weekend. The Cork lads were very focused beforehand; then just overpowered Galway when the match started. The homecoming on the Monday was special. Stopping the train at Charleville and Mallow on the way down... getting off at Kent Station, boarding the bus that came down McCurtain Street before turning at Paddy Barry's corner.

You're not sure what sight will hit you until this sea of red appears as you look down to the city. People packed on the roadside at every corner, roaring their heads off.

Up on the open-top bus, I tried to take it all in and was just left with the sense of gratitude that achievement brings.

IN LATE-1985 I had played a league game with Cork up in Limerick. And hurled well that day and scored 1-2. I had travelled up in the car, with Canon Michael O'Brien in front, and Jimmy and Ger Cunningham. The Canon's buddy Tom Buttimer from Lehenaghmore drove us. A great group to be with.

Coming home, we said we'd stop in Buttevant for a pint in O'Neills Bar. As we spilled out of the car, the Canon called me over on the main street.

'Meyler, well done today!

'Stick with me now... I'm going to make you great!'

That was the Canon, a master psychologist and supreme motivator. He was an incredible man. I played under him for a while in UCC and then we were opposing managers later in life. I got on really well with the Canon.

He was a good man. Quick witted too; he enjoyed that interaction with players. He had this presence about him.

At the time, priests carried huge weight in society.

Before the 1986 All-Ireland final he said Mass in The Burlington Hotel; the room was packed, everyone hanging on his every word. I was brought up in a tradition where the priest carried huge importance.

I still go to Mass every day. Coming out of the hotel after hearing one of his sermons, you'd be fit to take on the world.

I MADE ONE more appearance for Cork after the 1986 All-Ireland. An Oireachtas match against Wexford, but the condition of my hip meant county hurling was no longer possible.

I got an All-Ireland senior medal. I'd like to have won it by getting 30 seconds on the pitch but at least I was there. I accept I won it as a sub and that devalues it in some people's eyes. I don't care. Chances had been missed beforehand but I got an opportunity to redeem myself.

I cherish that medal.

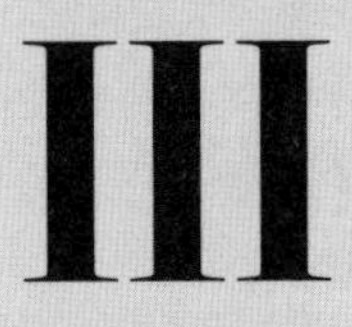

III

Under-19s
Roy
Oman
Gelsenkirchen
Banna Strand
Kerry
Christy Ring Cup

★★★

DAVID

IRELAND RECOGNITION EVENTUALLY arrived in March 2008.

On a Tuesday night I played in Waterford against France in an under-19 international. It had been a long wait. First-team status with Cork City had validated me in a way and helped ensure the call was made. You have to show you're at a certain level to get in the team. That you deserve your spot.

I came on as a second-half substitute. Moussa Sissoko and Morgan Schneiderlin were future Premier League names in that French midfield, but it was Gabriel Obertan who ripped us apart. He scored a couple of lovely goals that night and the following year Man United signed him.

Once I made the under-19 squad, I felt I had to leave a lasting mark. Seán McCaffrey was the manager and I wanted him to remember me that week. Dad used to say whatever time team events are, be there way before everyone else.

We ate with the French team, in one big massive conference room in a Waterford hotel. Breakfast was at 9am, I was sitting at the table by 8am. Seán was the second person down. I'd always be there waiting and we'd chat away.

For team meetings I made sure to be there 45 minutes early. I'd leave whoever I was rooming with and get in there before the video analyst was setting up. I had waited, coped with the underage rejection, but now I was prepared and ready.

We had a meeting in Cork before the second game against France a few days later. Seán put the team up. I was starting in Turners Cross. The news left me a little dazed. He called me out in that distinctive Monaghan accent.

'David, why are you starting?'

'Eh... because you picked me.'

'No, it's because you're a good player. That's why you're starting.'

That was the validation from someone I had respect for and looked up to. It stuck with me for a long time. I really enjoyed playing for Seán. He passed away in late-2017. He had a big impact on people with small gestures, was loved and respected by players, and just one of the good fellas.

THE DESPERATION TO play for Ireland was always there. I think it's there for everyone in the country growing up with a football interest; the national team is the goal. There is a photo at home where I'm in my USA 94 kit, but World Cup 2002 is the first big international tournament that registered with me.

Roy Keane was at the peak of his powers then. Everything he did for club and country was huge news.

Saipan is a national obsession and I think it always will be. The fascination lies in the unknown. Ireland lost in the last 16 on penalties and haven't been back to a World Cup since. *How far would we have gone if Roy was there?* At the time he was in the top five midfielders in the world... Ireland's captain and best player.

I've never talked about it with Roy. Being honest, you wouldn't know if it's a topic he's interested in revisiting.

PLAYING IRELAND UNDER-19 was great, but stepping up to under-21 football was a total different kettle of fish. I'd a new manager, was fighting with older fellas for game-time and my own background had changed as I'd joined Sunderland.

My first under-21 cap is cool to reflect on.

In February 2009, Ireland played Germany in Turners Cross. Playing in my hometown was great with all my family at the game. Being the local lad playing is cool, but you need to perform.

I came in late to the starting team after James McCarthy got injured, and we drew 1-1. Germany had a class team; they later won the Euro under-21s that summer. Kevin-Prince Boateng was their household name, playing with Spurs at the time, and he ran the midfield. But Manuel Neuer, Jerome Boateng and Sami

Khedira quickly became the stars. The following year the three of them were in the World Cup semi-final against Spain in South Africa. In 2014 they were all involved as Germany won it in Brazil.

That was the beauty of international football. I enjoyed measuring myself against players and tracking where they went after. We beat Spain the following month, 2-1 in Waterford. Dani Parejo, with Real Madrid then, was their player tipped to go all the way. César Azpilicueta and Jordi Alba were two that jump out from that Spain team. We didn't have much success at under-21 with Don Givens, no major tournament qualification. I did strike up some great friendships in that team, however. Seamus Coleman started right-back that night against Spain.

I watched his debut for Everton later that year against Benfica, a 5-0 loss in the Europa League. He played left-back and was all over the place. A tough start. But his strength of character has always been there. I'd describe him as the stereotypical corner-back in GAA. Flaking into someone before the ref throws in the ball. I know he played centre-back for Killybegs, I imagine he was horrible to mark. He was raw starting out in football but matured and developed into such a good full-back.

IN MAY 2010 I tore my cruciate on a Sunday afternoon against Man United.

On the Friday my agent had rung to say I was going to get named in the next Ireland squad for the upcoming friendlies against Paraguay and Algeria. When my knee went, it was one of those thoughts that flashed across my mind soon after. The Ireland dream was on hold. I was the first of our group to get called up but then had to watch the lads all my age all break into the squad. I was as excited as everyone else before Ireland played in Euro 2012.

The country got caught up in the hype. There was so much hope in Ireland but it was all wiped away by the results. They got pumped by an exceptional Spain team, with Croatia and Italy winning either side of that. I felt that team was at a turning point and opportunities would open up in the squad.

We played Swansea away with Sunderland in September. That morning in the hotel, Martin O'Neill came up to me. Good news, I made the Ireland senior squad. I was trying to take it in. Two and a half years waiting for this chance. John O'Shea was sitting next to me; it was good to have another Irish player there.

He was congratulating me but also reassuring. That was John, always cool, level-headed and looking out for people. Ten days later I was making my senior debut for Ireland. Playing Oman at Craven Cottage isn't the stuff of dreams but the setting and opposition didn't bother me. This was a lifetime's ambition. We won 4-1; Robbie Brady made his debut as well and marked it with a goal.

It felt a proper debut, the full 90 minutes from the start instead of a token few at the end. I was pumped afterwards. Kept thinking... *Don't be one and done.* The single cap wonders that no one ever hears of again. I was determined to achieve more.

I LOVED SENIOR international football from the start.

People knock smaller countries, like Oman and Gibraltar. But I always felt I was facing the best available players from that country. As proud a moment for them, as it was for us. It never became a chore hopping on a plane and heading to Dublin. It shouldn't be and if it ever does, you should get out. We have a lot of fellas nowadays who are English with Irish heritage but I feel the majority of them do love it. When I looked at the squads I was in, there were no real bad eggs.

Ciaran Clark is a great example. He was born in England, his mother is from Leitrim and his father's family come from Donegal. He's fully into it, you couldn't doubt his passion for Ireland. Some lads don't buy into it. Take Irish football's high-profile departures of Jack Grealish and Declan Rice. I know Declan well. He made the call to declare for England in February 2019. The previous summer we'd played together twice against Turkey and France.

I always felt in my heart he was gone. Taking that long to decide his future was a bad sign for Ireland. I think he was buying himself enough time to play well with West Ham, establish himself and see could he get into the England squad. I don't doubt that he had affection for Ireland but his loyalties lay with England. It was his decision. I fully respected it and wished him all the best.

Identity is a complex topic but I think if you get any senior cap, you shouldn't be able to change your mind afterwards. People ask me about my son, and if he ends up playing football? He'd be eligible to play for Scotland through his grandfather, Ireland through me and England through my wife. *Who should he play for?* If he's talented enough, it's his decision.

Everything was spot on when Declan was with Ireland. He trained well, applied himself correctly in games. But then England came up and his mind started to wander. The whole mess dragged on. Once he made his decision and left, there was no point for Irish football in wasting time thinking about it.

TRAPATTONI'S TIME IN charge of Ireland didn't end well. The buzz before the Euros was well gone and we didn't have a good crack at reaching the World Cup in Brazil. I was in and out of squads; sitting on the bench in October 2012 when Germany ripped us apart 6-1; Özil, Reus and Kroos running riot.

Minutes were hard to come by under Trapattoni. Between my debut and when he left as Ireland manager, I got three more caps. Substitute appearances against the Faroe Islands, Greece and Spain. Combined, it was less than 30 minutes.

I didn't have much interaction with him. I think he did rate me because he put me in the squad but he was very stuck in his ways in general and changed little. He didn't have a lot of English so communicating to get feedback was an issue. Marco Tardelli had a better grasp of it.

With Trapattoni, I wasn't focused on him leaving but then when he did, you start to wonder who'll come in as Ireland manager.

When Martin O'Neill replaced him, I was really excited. We'd worked together at Sunderland, so there was a connection. Dad was wary; he felt Martin didn't play me then and nothing would change with Ireland.

I looked at it differently. My fitness levels were now high, my knee was good. I was a regular with Hull; in that 2013-14 season I played 30 times in the Premier League and 27 were from the start. The chemistry was right, I was sure the international opportunities would come.

If 2013 was frustrating with Ireland, 2014 turned in my favour. We'd had a long season with Hull reaching the FA Cup final. A week later we played Turkey in Dublin; a week after that was Italy in London; then Costa Rica and Portugal on a USA tour.

You hear stories of players drained from club activities and having no enthusiasm. That wasn't my attitude. I was never an Ireland regular in my career so my hunger to play always stayed high.

When I was injured, I used to stare sort of longingly at Ireland squad announcements. When fit, I wasn't turning down the chance. Every squad I was available for, bar Martin's first two, I was in. If there was a game and I was injured,

I'd travel anyway, be in and around the hotel and squad. I had this real need to be a part of it.

BY AUTUMN 2014, it was time for the serious business.

No more friendlies, the Euro qualifiers were the main tests. The road to France began for us in Tbilisi, and Aiden McGeady dug it out with a magic winner against Georgia. In October we had two games in four days against Gibraltar and Germany. Seamus was out injured. That posed an issue. Martin floated the idea with me of playing right-back just before the Gibraltar game. I was happy to do a job.

It was one of those nights you feel fortunate Robbie Keane is in your team. He had scored a hat-trick by the 18th minute; that settled any nerves I had about an unfamiliar position. It was an easy game to play and we won 7-0.

That was the trial. Playing at home against Gibraltar is one thing. Playing away against the World Cup winners was another. We flew to Germany to play on a Tuesday night in Gelsenkirchen. Martin pulled me aside on the morning of the game.

'You're okay to play right-back again tonight, yeah?'

It was as casual as that.

Martin displayed great faith in me. He could have found someone else. He knew I wasn't going to set the world alight but that I would pour my heart and soul into it. At Sunderland I lined out a couple of times at centre-half for Martin. I think he knew I'd slot into a gap and give him everything. Adrenaline helps get you through it.

As do great teammates.

I was so lucky. Jon Walters played right wing and John O'Shea was right side centre-half. People say I played solidly but it was all down to them. Sheasy shouting all night.

'LEFT!'

'RIGHT!'

'PUSH UP!'

'DROP BACK!'

He talked me through the game. Walters covered anytime I was in bother, that engine of his motoring all night long.

Germany had special players. Bellarabi was left wing, Kroos controlled everything in the middle. Draxler started and Podolski came on. Müller and Götze were always dangerous.

At one stage they all piled over to my wing, popping one-twos around me. It was almost hypnotising to see up close.

I didn't feel over-awed though. You have to cherish the moment and live in it. Rise to the challenge, make sure the game will not pass you by. At one stage Podolski slipped in and shaped to shoot. I'd played against him, he'd scored twice for Arsenal against Hull the previous April.

I dived at the ball and he volleyed the side of my head. *Don't be the one that messes up here...* that was my aim. We couldn't hold out and Kroos put them ahead 1-0 with 20 minutes left.

Then, into the 93rd minute and McGeady takes the ball near the corner flag and rolls it back to Wes Hoolahan. I was a few yards away as a passing option but there's no way I was getting the ball. These are the situations Wes takes control of, whipping in crosses.

He pumped it too long and it was only later the realisation hit of how well Jeff Hendrick did; following the flight of the ball, swivelling and sending it back across the box. Then it's all about John O'Shea on his 100th cap having the drive to get ahead of Mats Hummels, put out his right leg and score one of Irish football's most famous goals.

It's the greatest equaliser I've ever been part of on the pitch. The mad joy of the team celebrating, the happiness when we all got to the dressing-room, and the emotion at seeing my parents after.

I'm in the middle of it all. No Ireland underage career to speak of, waiting until 2008 for an international debut... until 2012 for a first senior cap.

Then, this magical night in Gelsenkirchen.

It showed the value of sticking at it. I'm a firm believer that your mind is an amazing thing if you set it towards a goal. You just need to figure out your levels of desire and determination.

I'd been knocking on the door for Ireland for so long and, that night, it felt I had forced my way through.

★★★

JOHN

WHEN THE FINAL whistle sounded in Walsh Park on May 23, 1993, I turned to the rest of the Kerry management team on the sideline. A few words of thanks and slaps on the back after a job well done. We started thinking about Tipperary in a fortnight, discussing our plans to get back training on Tuesday night.

I walked off the pitch, through the tunnel and into the dressing-room. It was like entering a different world. That small room was full of jubilant Kerry hurling people. Liam Cotter, the vice-chairman of the County Board with a primary role for developing hurling, was hammering home the point of what we had achieved.

Sixty-seven years. We'd broken that long wait for Kerry to win a game in the Munster Hurling Championship. Liam started singing the *Rose Of Tralee*, everyone was high on life.

There were no TV cameras that day, no video footage exists of the game. RTÉ Radio cut their sports broadcast to go live to our dressing-room to sample the post-match mood. It is a day of hurling folklore, that exists in the memories of those that were there.

Kerry 4-13 Waterford 3-13.

We had produced one of the greatest shocks in hurling history.

IT WAS A long way from Banna Beach

That's where we gathered for my first session as Kerry manager on a Sunday morning in the autumn of 1992. I rocked up full of enthusiasm. I'd been told Banna was a great place to train; once the tide was out, the sand and the dunes behind would be perfect for putting miles in the legs.

Five Kerry players turned up that first morning.

I was shocked. I was coming from a culture in St Finbarrs where full attendance at training was expected. This was a disastrous way to start.

Eddie Murphy, one of the selectors, turned to me.

'Don't worry John. There wasn't many here to greet Roger Casement either in 1916.' That cut the ice and got a good laugh. But I was still troubled by the way this had all began. *Where did we go from here?*

My immersion in Kerry hurling came about through a work move. In 1992 I started in Tralee with Lee Strand, as their dairy processing plant was moving to Ballymullen outside the town.

It only lasted six months before I returned to Cork, but it opened key doors in my life. I went for lunch every day in the Grand Hotel in Tralee and would bump into the Kerry footballers. I'd been in Gormanston with Ogie Moran and in UCC with Seán Walsh, then got to know Ger Power, Bomber Liston and Mikey Sheehy.

Tony O'Keeffe was there most days, the principal of the Green in Tralee and also secretary of the Kerry County Board. He'd been in Maynooth with my brother Gerry. GAA always sparked the conversation; the lads were interested in how the hurling was going in Cork.

Tony asked me one day would I meet himself and Seán Kelly, the County Board chairman, in Ballygarry Hotel, on the way into Tralee. They got straight to it in the meeting. The offer was there to become Kerry senior manager. I was interested straight away.

Stella was very supportive. Sarah was six and David was three at the time; we juggled things and made it work. Sometimes, I'd pack them into the car and bring them to training. Fill them up with chocolate and a fizzy drink for the journey down, and they'd fall asleep on the way home. Stella's parents, grandad Michael and granny Mary were also brilliant; never an issue in dropping the kids over.

At 36 years old, loads of people said I was mad.

EDDIE MURPHY, MAURICE Leahy, JP Hickey and PJ McIntyre came on board as selectors. Eddie and myself were in UCC together. His father was the great Cork hurling figure, Willie 'Long Puck' Murphy. Eddie worked in Tralee and hurled with Austin Stacks.

Maurice was from Causeway, a very respected hurling figure. His brother DJ was corner-forward on the team. Myself and Maurice had marked each other in the 1980 Munster Club Championship, the Barrs playing Causeway. PJ was an Offaly native, who had hurled for his county, and was now based in Kenmare. Then JP was from Crotta O'Neills. We all hit it off.

A good spread of people who knew Kerry hurling inside out.

After the no-shows for that early beach session, we sat down, went through every Kerry club and every player who could lift a hurley.

That was a core principle for me; make sure training numbers are high and that will breed confidence. After about a week, nearly everyone was turning up.

We trained hard. Back then you didn't have a choice of facilities, you took what you could get. Ballyheigue's pitch only had lights on one side so we trained on that half; nights with the rain and wind whipping in from the Atlantic.

Bill Kennedy owned an equestrian centre in Ballyard in Tralee, which we used for indoor running and hurling. Before we'd start, everyone would take down the horse fences and we'd put them back up after we were finished. The rain would lash off the galvanised roof but we were dry and it was effective for us.

Kevin Kehilly and Noel Collins both worked in Cork RTC. They'd trained Cork hurling teams and had sports qualifications from Loughborough University. I tapped into their expertise and got fitness programmes for the Kerry lads. Kehilly came down a few times; we packed in sessions to get the lads fitter, and always made sure to head into Kirby's Brogue Inn after to feed them.

I HAD NO prior concept of the passion within North Kerry hurling, but quickly discovered the fire for the game that burned within them.

Numbers were an issue. You had your solid core but when you needed more competition for places, the players weren't there. Still, they were a committed bunch of fellas. A good mix from the hurling heartland in the north, a few from the south in Kilgarvan and Kenmare, and then others like Seán O'Shea, brother of future Kerry manager Pat, from Dr Crokes in Killarney.

League hurling was in the old-style format, beginning in October. We hurled out of Division Two, winning six of our seven games, before losing a quarter-final to Tipperary by nine points. That spring of 1993 brought small signs of progress but the target was Waterford in championship.

We hit the challenge game circuit.

We got some hammerings; the lads would go away deflated and it'd be hard to pick them up at training the following Tuesday night. But you'd get the buzz going again and we were constantly learning.

Len Gaynor and Ger Loughnane were brilliant to us. Clare didn't turn their noses up at a challenge against Kerry. Maybe they recognised the struggle of a county trying to climb up the hurling ladder. If Clare were down in Killarney for a weekend, they would train in the morning and I'd Fitzgerald Stadium available; so they'd jump at the opportunity to play us.

Eddie went down to see Waterford play and returned optimistic after his scouting mission. The mood was positive. We stayed in a hotel near Dungarvan the night before. As I drove past Kent Station en route, the Cork team were coming out after winning the league final that day in Thurles. I slowed down to chat to Ger Cunningham; he sensed we'd a big chance.

On the Sunday morning, we took the team to the beach in Clonea for a puck-around. We bumped into Babs Keating; he was down for the weekend and Tipperary were playing the winners.

'Ye'll beat them today!' he shouted over, as he walked past us.

All little boosts of confidence. I felt good heading to Waterford city on the bus.

There wasn't really a dress-code back then, the way teams now wear matching gear. Our lads turned up with their bags and hurleys; next thing I see the Waterford fellas in their suits with proper blazers and ties, getting photographs taken.

I couldn't believe this sideshow happening before a game. It annoyed me.

Three years before Liverpool walked out at Wembley before the FA Cup final in their white suits, Waterford made their own fashion statement.

But on the day it all just clicked for us. We were up a point at half-time, then came the Waterford push and they hit the front, 3-11 to 2-8.

And then things fell our way. Joe Walsh kicked home a goal. Jerry O'Sullivan came on and struck two points. DJ Leahy hit a shot over from near the corner flag, then mishit a free late on and it ended up in the net.

We were three points up, and under siege at the finish but we survived.

LIAM COTTER GOT the party atmosphere going after. He told great stories about sport, politics and life. Cotter wasn't from a hurling club but he did so much for us.

'Whatever you want Meyler, you'll have!'

Kerry hurling is mainly a pocket in the north of a mad football county. But once you're producing the goods, you'll get everything you want. That day in Walsh Park, we had put Kerry hurling on the map.

Afterwards, Cotter brought me outside to a supporters' bus that Ned Horgan from Kilmoyley had organised. I talked to everyone, shook hands with them all.

Seeing the emotion on their faces and hearing it in their voices, you could sense something big had happened.

This day would be remembered.

I got back to Cork about 9pm and went up to Moks on Bandon Road for a couple of pints. Met the regular Barrs crew.

'Ye beat Waterford today.'

'We did.'

That was it. No wild celebration. Back down to earth.

Now when I look back and take in the significance of the first win since 1926, it stands out more. But, back then, I woke up Monday and it was less than a fortnight before we faced Tipperary. We needed to knuckle down.

A Munster hurling semi-final was a big deal. We stayed in the Glen of Aherlow Hotel the night before and there was plenty of excitement.

I was searching for a performance but Tipperary will always turn the screw if they get a chance. We might have held our own in the league in Killarney but the roof collapsed on us at Semple Stadium. Tipperary put 4-21 on us and breezed to victory.

WE NEVER REALLY pushed on after 1993. That's where the lack of playing numbers tells as you try to freshen things up.

There were too many hard luck stories in the league. In 1994 we lost to Offaly by a point, Clare by four and Kilkenny by three; couldn't get over the line. When we played Clare in the championship, I was hopeful but in truth we were slipping and they were coming. Ger Loughnane had started his revolution with Clare. Their hurling and fitness levels had exploded, they were far too good.

In October 1995, we did beat them. It was a Saturday evening in Tralee, a month after they had become the biggest story in hurling by ending their 81-year wait for the All-Ireland. The celebrations were still in full swing. Loughnane was bringing a team of household names to town. We fired the Kerry lads up for it and won 3-7 to 1-8. The conditions for those games before Christmas suited underdogs like us, slowing down the game.

That Kerry team in 1995 remained a solid unit but was in need of fresh blood. My problem was, the team wasn't moving on under my direction. I had done all I could. By the end of 1996 it was time for someone else to take it on.

SEAMUS MCINTYRE WAS corner-back on that team; a hard, old-school defender who fought his corner. Tough as nails.

In that 1993 league quarter-final against Tipperary, he was part of a full-back line that held the heavyweight trio of Fox, English and Bonnar to a combined total of 0-4. It was a fair achievement.

Seamus worked as a garda in Cork city. He used to travel with me down to Kerry training and I got to know him well on those journeys. I had a real warmth for their family, with his father PJ a selector.

In the early hours of a Sunday morning in April 2001, Seamus and another garda, George Rice, who was from Kilgarvan in Kerry, died in a road accident. It was a huge shock.

Seamus had all the qualities you wanted in a hurling defender but, more importantly, he was a lovely fella. He was only 29. It was incredibly sad; it rocked his home town of Kenmare. Every time I drive on the North Ring Road in Cork city, just across the road from the fire station, I look at that spot as I'm passing by and I think of Seamus.

THEY SAY NEVER go back to a managerial job, but I'd no reluctance when Kerry came calling again at the end of 2009. I was still in tune with Kerry hurling from working with Kilmoyley and had helped the Kerry under-21s win the All-Ireland B final in 2009. We won three in-a-row at that level. When we won in 2010, we had Paul Geaney wing-forward. I'd remind Paul of that when he's starring for the Kerry footballers; his first All-Ireland medal arrived as a hurler in Semple Stadium.

Plenty had changed. Before as Kerry manager, I did it all but this was a new era and I needed to delegate. The competition structure was different. Kerry were gone from the Munster Championship, and the Christy Ring Cup was the main show in town.

Leaving Munster had been the wrong move, it's the level you learn most at. We lost the Christy Ring Cup final in 2010 and then won it in '11. That team was on the rise and should have gone into the Munster Championship in 2012.

It was a disaster that we didn't. I pushed hard for it but everybody said we needed to win the Christy Ring again.

Could the players survive in the heat of the Munster Championship? If they couldn't, that's fine. But we wouldn't know unless the chance was given.

I felt we had proved ourselves and I had displayed my ambition for the group. Joe O'Connor was a lecturer in Tralee, who we got in as trainer. He rightly got rave reviews for his All-Ireland-winning work later in Clare and Limerick. Joe would have got the Kerry hurlers in shape for the 2012 Munster Championship. Frank Flannery from Cork was the hurling coach, he made it a really good set-up.

We added to our squad. Transfers were possible for fellas based in Kerry or who had family links. I looked out for candidates to inject us with extra impetus.

Bernard Rochford had been goalkeeping understudy to Donal Óg Cusack in Cork. Willie O'Dwyer was a winner with Kilkenny and I had seen him put 2-3 past my Wexford team in the 2007 All-Ireland semi-final.

They were both working in Kerry and had finished up with their home counties. I met them separately, sketched out my hurling vision and invited them in. Rochford joined first, and Willie came later.

WE LOST TO Kildare in 2012, a game I would rather blank from my memory. It was the biggest low in my time with the county and I quit in the aftermath. Our Christy Ring Cup title defence had gone up in smoke and after three seasons I was done. Maybe as a group we didn't recover from the setback of not being accepted into Munster. That was a crushing disappointment.

I GOT A great kick out of the 2011 Christy Ring Cup final. I was raging the year before. A Westmeath player threw the ball in injury-time, we got no free and they went on to hit the winning point.

The hurt of 2010 drove us on in 2011. We cruised through games. The test came in the semi-final up in Down and we passed it by a point. Then we hit top speed against Wicklow and dismantled them by 13 points.

It was a Bank Holiday weekend. I went home that night and headed to Kerry on the Monday morning. The craic was mighty. We started off in Causeway at 11am and hit different pubs around north Kerry for the day.

I loved that day; looking around at this united group, drinking pints, sharing stories... and the satisfaction of having won a cup in Croke Park after months of hard work. They deserved to be classed as a Munster hurling team in 2012.

It's a massive regret they didn't get that chance.

IV

Man United

Cruciate Club

Semple Stadium

Steve Bruce

John Considine

John O'Shea

Strikes

Martin O'Neill

★★★

DAVID

THERE IS A before and after story in my career, and it hinges on one day... May 2, 2010.

Second last game of the Premier League season with Sunderland. My first time playing Manchester United and the excitement was high.

Only two years since they'd won the Champions League in Moscow and they still had a team of stars. The football-mad youngster in me couldn't wait to have a go at playing against Scholes, Giggs and Rooney.

Just before the half-hour mark, Nani put them ahead. Then just after the half-hour mark, the ball broke to Patrice Evra. I charged towards him. He leaned across and I got knocked off my stride. That's when my knee buckled; went into spasm and felt momentarily numb. The pain was bearable. *Take a couple minutes, get to the sideline, shake it off... and go again.*

The medics came rushing in; the Sunderland physio Pete Brand and the doctor Glen Rae. They examined my knee. They instantly diagnosed a damaged cruciate and a stretcher was needed

I was taken off and into a physio room, looking at the bag of ice covering my knee. A few of the Sunderland subs came in to see how I was; Steve Bruce popped his head in at half-time. The team still had a game to play. That had to be the focus; no room for sentimentality.

I was alone with my thoughts. The career-turning nature of that day didn't register at the time. I couldn't compute this was a long-term injury, even though I could hear the 'cruciate talk' and that a scan was needed.

Only when I later met the surgeon did the bad news really hit home.

IT WAS A Bank Holiday weekend in England, so the scan results didn't come back until Tuesday. They sketched out the mess my knee was in.

All the ligaments... cruciate, lateral, medial... were destroyed.

Bone ripped from my kneecap. The bicep femoris tendon that connects the hamstring to the knee had been snapped off.

The initial thinking was that my career was done. *Get set for retirement.*

The world had seemed to be at my feet with first-team appearances; the offer by Sunderland of a new five-year contract and speculation I was going to get an Ireland senior call-up. One tackle later, and I'm facing the prospect of my playing days being over. *What the hell is going to happen now?*

★★★

JOHN

ON A SUNDAY afternoon in the middle of July 2002, I walked out of Semple Stadium. Headed down to the square in Thurles in the sweltering heat, moved through the crowds and made my way into a pub on the left corner. I had Bertie Óg Murphy, Teddy Owens, PJ Murphy and Pat McDonnell for a company. We ordered pints and there wasn't a word said between us as we drank them. We were the Cork senior hurling management and had just watched Galway cruise past our team. The dream of summer glory was over.

A month before, we'd played Waterford in our first game in Munster; bad start. The rain poured down, we conceded a soft goal when Tony Browne hit a shot from distance, then Ken McGrath scored a late point and we lost by one.

It was the first year of the All-Ireland qualifiers so there was a safety net. We took our chance in beating Limerick, but that result papered over the cracks and Galway punished us. Our third trip to Thurles was the end of a horrible summer. We were beaten men staring into our pint glasses, uncertain where were we going next. The mood on the bus journey home was desperate.

And that winter things did not improve.

★★★

DAVID

BY THE END of that week, I went under the knife to repair the damage. The surgeon was Dr Steve Bollen, based in Bradford. He had an arrogant attitude in talking about his work. I didn't mind that. He bragged he was the best and said he could fix me. He was worried if I'd do the necessary rehab to recover. I was worried he'd do the surgery properly.

We disagreed but I stressed that I'd do what I was told.

The operation was at 9am in Bradford, about two hours from where I lived. Sunderland put on a driver for me; the plan was I would be collected at 6.30am. Having to fast from midnight, I wolfed down a big dinner at five minutes to 12 to ease off the hunger in the morning.

Then I slept-in. Dick was my chauffeur for the day, a lovely man who had to bang my door down for about 20 minutes to waken me up. When we landed, the surgeon was standing outside with his scrubs and gloves on, shouting... 'Come on!' Dave Binningsley was the physio assigned to my recovery. He watched the surgery so he'd be there when I woke up. He told me later that when the surgeon finished stitching up, he took his gloves off, and went 'JORDAN'... mimicking a basketball shot as he tossed them into the bin.

But he was delighted with how the work went. It would be 18 months before I was back in football due to the extent of the injury I had suffered.

I did the sums in my head. That was all of the 2010-11 season gone. I'd turn 22 in May 2011; figured I'd aim to back for a full pre-season after that summer. Every players starts that 'game' when they get injured. *How much time can I knock off this?* Everyone's looking for cuts. *Maybe I could shave another six months off... get it down to a year!*

It was a testament to Steve Bruce how he acted after. I was back at the training ground on crutches and he came to see me.

'We'll give you the contract... there's no problem.'

I'd wondered were they going to back out? Those doubts were natural when the suggestion was made that I should retire. So, I was very grateful to him for pushing that through and the club for looking after me. It put my mind at ease.

The rehab plan was to work in 12-week blocks and return for a check-up after each. I needed to do everything in my power to get back.

★★★

JOHN

MY CORK COACHING journey began on a happier note, starting out with an underage team in the late-90s and moving up through the years with that group. John Considine became minor manager in 2000 and drafted me in as a selector. We lost the All-Ireland final that year to Galway but turned the tables 12 months later against the same team, coming back from a Munster final loss.

If you measure minor teams around their future achievements, then that 2001 bunch was one of the great Cork sides. John Gardiner at centre-back. A pair of Kieran Murphys in the forward line... 'Fraggy' and 'Hero'.... Martin Coleman, Cian O'Connor, Shane Murphy and Kevin Hartnett... and they all became Cork seniors. Brian Murphy was there in 2000, a truly outstanding defender.

You could build a team around Gardiner at the heart of your defence. I got to know him better when he went to CIT and his leadership really surfaced; a hard defender that I knew was going to hurl senior. In that 2001 All-Ireland final, he gave an exhibition. Fraggy was a typical corner-forward, a goal-poacher; scored a hat-trick against Kilkenny and one against Galway in the big games.

It's funny but I nearly think more about the lads who left after... Setanta Ó hAilpín played Aussie Rules, Tomás O'Leary had huge success with Munster rugby. He was dabbling in schools rugby at the time in Christians, even though he was steeped in hurling with his father Seánie.

Setanta's departure was more sudden. The appeal of professional sport doesn't need an explanation but I would have loved if Setanta stayed with Cork. Teams would have been built around him, he could have shaped a different future.

THAT AUTUMN I was driving to train Kilmoyley when Frank Murphy, the Cork secretary, rang me. I stopped the car and pulled in. The board were meeting soon to make their 2002 plans and he offered me the minor job. Considine had left as manager along with the other selectors.

I found that decision difficult to handle after our success and was wary of starting afresh. The under-21 team felt a perfect fit, given I'd worked with recent minor teams, but Frank said that was role was filled.

Then he mentioned there was a vacancy for a senior selector. The board chose who filled those roles at the time. I threw my hat into the ring and soon he came back to confirm Bertie Óg as manager... with PJ, Pat, myself... and Frank, the Blackrock nomination as county champions.

Looking back I made the wrong decision. I should have taken the minor job; shouldn't have stepped up to senior. It was too soon.

★★★

DAVID

JOHN O'SHEA HAD been centre-half for Manchester United in the game and had come to see me after in the physio room that day. We had a five-minute chat; he wished me all the best. I'd never met him before. It was an older Waterford lad checking in with a young Cork fella, but really how many opposition players would have done that? I'm not sure it would have crossed my mind straight after a match.

John went out of his way to meet me, it was a really nice gesture. We didn't know at the time we'd become Sunderland teammates a year later or go on to have experiences together with Ireland. John is the best sort of person you could aspire to be, with the type of standards by which he lives his life.

When himself and Wes Brown joined Sunderland in July 2011, I was doing rehab for my second cruciate on the day they had their medical at the training ground. At the start I was almost in awe of them, these multi-Premier League winners that were suddenly in our dressing-room. Training with them every day, you got to see their high standards and understand why they'd lasted so long at

Manchester United. For all the profile the sport had given them, they were just normal, hard-working lads.

AFTER I TORE the cruciate, I got another call of support. It was a surprise to hear the voice on the other end.

'David, it's Roy here.'

I grew up admiring Roy Keane so much, and here he was being generous with his time and kind with his words. He talked about knuckling down for rehab, trusting the surgeon and physio… not to get side-tracked from the target I was aiming for… not to fall out of the team circle and… not to wake up one morning feeling sorry for myself and fall behind.

Roy also got in touch just to see how I was? He helped realign my thinking. He understood from his own injury experiences and knew the thoughts that could consume someone's mind at that time. His view was if he could recover, I could. That message helped shape my attitude. Roy is someone you listen to.

THE INNOCENCE OF youth. It helped that I was 21 when I tore my cruciate and didn't have another care in the world. Contrast that to when I had shoulder surgery a week before my wife had a C-section when Brody was born. In the hospital the midwife turned to me but I wasn't able to hold him; my arm was in a sling. At 29, married with two children, there was a lot more going on during that injury recovery.

When I was younger facing rehab, I was more carefree. And not engulfed by doubt. I had that bit of fearlessness.

What do I need to do to get back? This was another obstacle in my way to playing in the Premier League. Injury can cause mental health struggles but I was fortunate it didn't get on top of me.

I kept in touch with the first-team; always kept 10.30am-12pm free so I could watch the lads train and not feel isolated from the group. I went to all the home games and any away fixtures that were within two hours. The club was happy to facilitate that.

I did my cruciate in May, then Frazier Campbell did his in August. As bleak as it sounds, maybe there was an element of fortune in that. We were in it together. In a freak occurrence, we both did two cruciates back-to-back. During tough days in rehab, there was someone to lean on for support and drive one another on.

We also had Dave. When you're injured, the physio becomes your best friend. He's now first-team physio at Man United; we still speak regularly.

I had a massive metal brace on my knee after the operation and needed to do some work in the swimming pool to get my muscles moving. It took me an hour to take my first step. I couldn't bring myself to put my weight on the leg. I had a complete mental block. Dave was great, he didn't push me, told me to do it in my own time. All that help was great but it mainly comes down to the individual's attitude and I didn't see any reason why I couldn't get back.

Johnny Small was a friend of Jordan Henderson's. He was in a university course that didn't interest him much and was happy to help out any way he could. I couldn't drive for three months so I got him insured on my car. He drove me anywhere I needed to go around Sunderland. His mother Julie cooked dinners for me; she washed my clothes. The amount that his mum, and his dad Duncan, and that family did for me was incredible.

★★★

JOHN

JOINING UP WITH the Cork seniors meant operating at the top of the hurling tree, a team who had been All-Ireland champions a few years before. It felt a privilege.

The players were searching for something. Bertie Óg looked an ideal manager because he had won All-Ireland under-21s with the core of that team. The basis for a strong relationship. We got to work that winter in the gym in Na Piarsiagh and running around the tunnels of Páirc Uí Chaoimh. We made a positive start to the league.

But from the start, there was an undercurrent that left me uneasy. The longer the season went on, the more you could feel the tension. In every squad, there will be some unhappiness. Not everyone gets picked on the team, not everyone plays well, not every result is positive. But the sense of dissatisfaction that hung in the background in Cork that year was different.

It should have been thrashed out internally, but we didn't do that. We soldiered on in the blind hope things would work themselves out and issues were swept under the carpet. But the mistrust between players and management remained and never truly went away. Then it exploded into full view for the whole world to see at the end of the year.

As a management team, we should have been more up-front in tackling these things head-on. Sometimes I'm seen as too brutish in that way. That's come against me in hurling; being too straight can offend people.

But the feeling is unmistakable in a squad when something is off.

And in 2002 there was something definitely not right in Cork hurling.

PROBLEMS SURFACED THROUGHOUT that year.

On St Patrick's weekend, we trekked the length of the country; played Derry in Swatragh in a league game. The trip was a nightmare. That week I told Bertie Óg I was caught to make training due to college lectures, but would meet the group in Cork Airport the morning of the game.

He said we were travelling by bus the day before; the flights were deemed too expensive. I was stunned. That was a time before motorways in Ireland… driving from Cork to Derry to play a game was a disaster. Given the unhappiness in the camp, I knew this would make things worse.

I made that case to Bertie Óg but his hands were tied, it wasn't his call. We stopped in Tullamore for food, then headed up to stay at a hotel in Monaghan. We got lost en route. A few fellas had travel sickness, so we had to make roadside stops.

We beat Derry but Niall McCarthy got split in the face. He was treated by medics at the match and was heading to hospital, when it was decided to go back to Cork and have him fixed up the following day. Niall was on the bus all the way home trying to control this bleeding wound. The optics were terrible.

We ended up reaching the league final in May against Kilkenny in Thurles. We lost the game by a point but the post-match talk was dominated by the pre-match protest.

In the parade some players rolled down their socks and wore their jerseys outside their shorts. It was a show of solidarity with the Gaelic Players Association, who were looking for better conditions for players from the GAA. The GPA became a hot topic in 2002 as their influence started to grow.

Players should be treated right and a representative body is a good idea if it's done for the right reasons. But the timing didn't sit well with me in that approach before a game. Arguing about what way to wear your socks was petty and a lack of respect to Cork hurling. There were legitimate grievances but that gesture was a distraction. The focus should have been on the league final.

The training gear for the squad arrived late that season. I had to hand out t-shirts in Mitchelstown one day before going to Semple Stadium. Halfway between Cork and Thurles, you're giving lads tops to put on before playing in the championship. Not a day I reflect on with personal pride. It was totally wrong to the players and our fault as management that the situation had developed.

When I took over as Cork senior manager in 2017, I swore there would be no repeat of that mistake. Seánie Barry was in charge of logistics and we straight away made sure the players got the gear in November with no delays.

If there is an incident that has hung over me from that time, it is a comment made to Mark Landers in the week of the league final.

I told him to… take a good look around Páirc Uí Chaoimh because he wouldn't see it again. That's the quote in isolation that most people focus on without applying the context. The banter at the coalface of inter-county teams is relentless. Some of it is hard-hitting and has a spiky edge, more is light-humoured.

We were at the City End of the stadium; a line of players getting ready to do sprints at training. Comments were flying around. I threw that remark to Landers, then the usual back and forth followed. It's not like I led him out to the middle of the pitch on his own to issue a warning. No one was shy in saying their piece.

You take it and give back as good as you get. I was well able for that. That's part of the sporting environment. I still talk away to Mark and have no problem with him.

THE HOPE THAT things would come good for championship never materialised. By the end of the summer there were whispers and rumours all around Cork. It didn't paint a good picture. I don't like gossip but it was inescapable; everywhere I went, people were throwing different stories at me.

It all fell apart as the year dragged on. Bertie Óg was gone as manager in September. My attitude then was to redouble my efforts for 2003 and not have a repeat of the year we had endured. I didn't get that opportunity.

On the last Friday in November, the Cork hurlers announced they were withdrawing their services. No players on the squad.

A couple of days later, Frank asked me down to Páirc Uí Chaoimh, and let me know that Pat and PJ had stepped down. He wasn't taking up the Blackrock nomination.

I'll never forget his next words.

'John, you're on your own!'

Sound, Frank.

'There's a form there... you can sign it to resign.'

I wasn't going to resign, I felt I'd done nothing wrong.

There were mistakes made on both sides that year. A breakdown in communication. An absence of trust that poured more petrol on the fire. I blame the board for not sitting everybody down and thrashing things out. There were strong characters. It wasn't straightforward but that could all have been harnessed into a positive; then arrive at the best solution for Cork hurling. That's all I wanted.

Yet, suddenly, from a five-man management team, I was left alone. Last man standing.

When I left that day, the stadium was alive with activity, a strange occurrence for a December day. RTÉ were setting up cameras outside. There were crisis meetings going on upstairs. I kept my head down, hopped into the car and headed home. Only one option left.

Fall on my sword. Let Frank know my decision later on.

At a County Board meeting the following Tuesday night. it was officially announced. We were finished as Cork senior hurling selectors. I was raging over the whole situation.

Frank was in the spotlight then as Cork's hurling row was playing out before the sporting world in the run up to Christmas. We've always got on well, myself and Frank. I met him first as a referee in the 80s when I played with the Barrs. One of the great administrators in the GAA. His influence or power in Cork never bothered me; you need people in roles of authority and that can create envy. If you look at his track record of success, Frank has done a huge amount for Cork GAA over a long time. Cork hurling slipped back because the proper work wasn't put in. He was involved in that, as were a lot of other people when the coaching structures were not right.

I've also had more rows with Frank than anybody. Every manager states their case and that's bound to lead to arguments at times with County Board people.

In 2018, for instance, Cork were invited to the Fenway Hurling Classic in Boston. We'd chatted before the trip.

'Frank, that's brilliant. We're going to Boston for five days... that's paid for.

'Now... we're also going to stay in Boston for another five days,' I continued. 'That's for the two Munsters we've won in 2017 and '18.'

'Oh right, John,' Frank replied. 'Now normally Cork go on a holiday when they win an All-Ireland... and we've won none!'

'Well Frank, we were only a hair's breadth away from reaching the final two years in-a-row. We won two Munsters and the holiday would be a sign of respect to the players... for their effort.'

'Certainly... and who's going to pay for that?' Frank replied.

'You're paying for it Frank... and you're coming with us as well. My man Seánie will be down tomorrow to discuss the logistics.'

I got my way in the end.

We all went off and had a brilliant trip. I wouldn't say a bad word about Frank. We've got on great but you have to fight your corner with him, like anyone would with a boss when they want something and must justify their rationale.

★★★

DAVID

AS MUCH AS I was determined to return, there was naturally doubt about whether I would be the same player again? In a way I never was. I lost a yard of pace; I was a lot quicker when I was younger. I tailored my game, though I loved tackling; the art of it. As I got older, I just needed to learn to read the game. Pick up pockets of space and look to intercept passes. Get a better grasp of what would make me a good defensive midfielder instead of playing off the cuff.

After a summer of hard work, I was buzzing for the 2010-11 season. Around September I felt I was moving better. Bruce and the physio did point out I was running lopsided, not putting proper weight through my leg, but I corrected that. Physios and doctors were happy.

It was just a matter of ticking the boxes... non-contact training, contact training, a reserve game... then try to get into the first-team. I was known for my tackling but the club fined me £50 every time I went in for a slide-tackle at training. They wanted me to stay on my feet as I recovered, so Bruce came up with that fine system.

It had been a positive start to the season for the club. We were in the top six on Christmas Day. A 5-1 defeat away to Newcastle was a disaster but results like beating Chelsea 3-0 at Stamford Bridge were huge.

I played some reserve games in November and then the first-team came calling. A start in mid-December away to Fulham. I didn't feel great beforehand.

Reserve games are nothing fixtures, this was the Premier League. Fulham players rightly had no regard for the state of my fitness. They were there to beat us. *How would I cope in that environment?*

I played just under an hour and survived.

Asamoah Gyan replaced me, our big-money signing who had starred for Ghana in the World Cup. We drew 0-0 and two weeks later, I got to realise my nan's target of playing at Old Trafford.

I'm not into the element of hatred amongst football fans. I grew up a Liverpool fan and understand the heated rivalry with Manchester United but I still admired the club. Playing in their stadium was a big deal. My nan loved Alex Ferguson and his older team with Bruce and Pallister at the back.

We lost 2-0 but it still felt like a significant day.

BY JANUARY 2011 I was back in a familiar place. In Bradford, with a busted knee, to see Steve Bollen. He quickly pointed out the recurrence was no reflection on his initial surgery work. I accepted that.

After that night in Villa Park, I had moments thinking my knee didn't feel as bad as the first time. There was a slight cruciate tear, the right knee again. It needed surgery but it wasn't snapped. The surgeon's original work had been so good that it didn't all come apart and he was confident that I'd be okay.

Back to rehab work with Dave.

I had greater insight into what was required but the frustration was deeper.

All the exercises you do are new the first time, but feel repetitive the second time. I'd always say to someone who's done their knee that the sooner you can accept this is a long journey, the sooner you will get back playing. Dwelling on why it happened, as natural as that is, won't help you one bit. The work has to be done.

After Liverpool won the Champions League final in 2019, I was at the after-party and got talking to Alex Oxlade-Chamberlain. I made a point of congratulating him, not on the victory but on having made it back into the squad, a year after he'd damaged his knee so badly against Roma.

There is a sort of 'Cruciate Club', a sense of brotherhood amongst those who endure the injury. There we were on one of the biggest nights of his career, trading war stories on injuries.

2011 WAS A year of change.

That summer we went on holiday in Marbella, seven lads in a big apartment. Before heading to the beach one morning, Jordan asked me to wait on.

'I think Liverpool want to sign me.'

'WHAT?!'

It was a mad, surreal morning. He ended up cutting short the holiday and heading home early.

I was delighted for him and sad to see him go as well. He was a fella I clicked with from the start at Sunderland. He helped me settle in and I became friends with all his buddies. His father looked after me.

When I bought my house in Cottingham outside Hull, Brian Henderson viewed it first for me. We'd just got promoted and I was away that summer when these houses came on the market. Brian's not an auctioneer but was just someone I could trust. Not a problem for Brian, he drove down and sorted everything.

Brian was there the day Jordan signed and Kenny Dalglish asked how I was recovering from my injury. He mentioned they were interested in buying the two of us together. A good few years later, I briefly talked to Kenny about it. It's a waste of energy to think about that. No one knows if it was realistic.

I feel really happy for Jordan at how he's taken his opportunity. A decade at Anfield... first-choice midfielder... captain... Champions League winner... Premier League champions.

He'll go down as a legend at the club and I got to witness the start of it; the excitement as he waited in Spain that morning to get a call from his agent to confirm that one of the biggest clubs in the world wanted him.

THE OTHER BIG departure came in November.

Steve Bruce was sacked. I was gutted. The man had done so much for me. Steve was very clever when I was injured. In April 2011 he put me on the bench for an away game at Birmingham City. We both knew deep down I was nowhere near ready to play, but it was his way of recognising the hard work that was being put in.

A show of support I appreciated.

As I edged back to fitness in the 2011-12 season, I got a few runs as a sub under Steve. Then after we lost 2-1 at home to bottom of the table Wigan, he was out the door. That was Wednesday and by Saturday Martin O'Neill had taken over.

Dad rang me straight away. We'd both watched his work with Celtic and he thought this was a brilliant fit; a manager who'd make me a better midfielder.

The problem was the gap between our respective needs. Martin couldn't accommodate a midfielder easing back to fitness. The pressure was on instantly to get results. People later reckoned I was in trouble when Martin was appointed Ireland manager as he hadn't played me at Sunderland. There was more to it, to do with my fitness, and not a simple fact that Martin didn't rate me.

I understood, but was getting frustrated at playing reserve football as 2011 ended. If you've tasted the Premier League, it is a serious comedown. *A Tuesday playing somewhere like the rugby pitch at Widnes in awful weather?* More grim than glamour.

We played Man United at that time; I scored in a 6-3 win at the Eppleton Colliery Welfare Ground outside Sunderland. All our young lads were raving before about their midfielder Paul Pogba. If I was a bit dubious then about the next big thing tag, I was in no doubt after the game. That 18-year-old was destined to be a top midfielder.

THAT SEASON WAS a write-off in my development. I continued to stall in the autumn of 2012. Martin was desperate for me to stay at the club. I put in about 10 requests for a loan move, as I wanted games with the view to coming back stronger. He turned them all down.

'No, I need you around the place!'

That was a brilliant thing to hear but it didn't change my situation. I eventually wore him down and he agreed I could go out for two months in November 2012. Five or six other clubs made enquiries but Steve Bruce had taken over at Hull and they wanted me. It was Alex Bruce who got in touch first; I'd met him a couple of times through Lee Cattermole, and he gave me an idea of the club. Then I chatted to Steve about it.

Dad was uncertain about this voluntary drop down a division.

But I went for it for two reasons.

Steve Bruce was manager and he vowed we'd get promoted. I trusted him and wanted to be a part of it. That was one good reason!

The second? Hull were fourth in the table at the time I joined on loan and had a good Irish group at the club. It was time to make the move.

★★★

JOHN

MY SPIRITS WERE low after resigning as a Cork hurling selector in 2002. The personal disappointment was rooted in how everything had unravelled to such an extent.

Separating hurling life and home life is something I've always tried to do. Family might get the worst of my moods for a day or two, but Stella is tough. She helps me move on; herself and the kids are very good to me.

Maybe there was an innocence in my thinking that the problems could be sorted. The core belief was that Cork hurling was bigger than anybody – players, management and board. It was the only thing that truly mattered and was the biggest long-term victim. Cork hurling lost more than any individual involved. I saw that later in life when David played for Hull. There was conflict between the owner and the fans, and the club ended up the biggest loser.

My last act after I was turfed out was to make another call to Frank.

'There's only one man to take over here and that's Grady.'

I had a huge insight into Donal O'Grady from my time with the Barrs and

Cork. He was the ideal person for the job, with his hurling intelligence and ability to command total respect after such an unsettling time.

I'm sure he had been considered as a candidate but have no idea if my suggestion played a role in the decision process. It's not something I've discussed with Grady. Our relationship doesn't involve him ringing me for advice; I'm the one that needs to call him.

I didn't care about what emotional pain I felt or any blame I was receiving for my role in the whole mess. I cared that Cork hurling was suffering. Grady was the best manager Cork could appoint and that had to be made known.

After we left, Cork's progress didn't surprise me. The players felt they had been right and they backed up their course of action by winning All-Irelands. I take my hat off to them for that. They'd the right man in charge in Grady and later with John Allen taking over. I was glad for the two lads. Ger Cunningham should have got it in 2007 for the continuity that would have been maintained.

The players going back on strike again was a disaster. That whole time set Cork hurling back, creating so much division and resentment in the county. When people remember that hurling era for Cork, the strikes will taint those memories. The All-Ireland wins were great but there is a cloud. It's sad, but true.

The whole experience didn't leave me with scars and twist my mind into bitterness against hurling. After all the strikes, a lot of people I knew refused to go to see Cork hurl again until those players had left. I never stopped attending matches. Any job I was asked to do with a county team, I did it. My support for Cork hurling never wavered. I have an ability to move on in life after a chapter closes. I fell out with people over those events but they don't affect or concern me. They wouldn't be on my Christmas card list. I'm sure I'm not on theirs either.

I still have a brilliant relationship with some of the players, especially those I had at minor level. I coached Cork teams with Fraggy since, and meet Ronan Curran regularly. Him and a few Barrs lads became part of our lunchtime crew in the Tennis Village in Cork. Myself and Curran would argue so much that we'd have a debate over the time of day but we'd always be in touch.

Leaving in the manner I did as Cork selector was not a nice feeling. It still hurts. We all move on. You get a job in Cork hurling, playing or managing, you try and leave it in a better position than how you found it.

None of us did that in 2002.

Hull City

Premier League

Paul McShane's Rice Pudding

Liverpool

Alan Pardew

Wembley Stadium

David Beckham

★★★

DAVID

I FLEW TO Marbella at the end of the 2012-13 season. I had a few days to kill before reporting for Ireland duty, so myself and Kelogs – my best friend Peter Kelleher – took off to the sun.

We were in a restaurant one day when the Championship play-off semi-final came on TV... Watford against Leicester. The end of the game was absolutely wild. Anthony Knockaert missed a penalty for Leicester in injury-time... Watford went straight downfield and Troy Deeney scored the winner to send them to Wembley.

Pitch invasion... pure mayhem!

Looking at that madness I was glad to be watching on. The previous week had been crazy enough; last day league drama. It's the outcome TV executives and viewers are craving. Late goals, permutations, fans smiling and in tears. The hype machine is stirred into overdrive as the promotion and relegation storylines play out.

The final day with Hull City that year packed in the type of drama that I'm not sure will be surpassed. We should have had a relaxing end to the season, but we won none of our last four games. We took over 5,000 fans to Barnsley with plans for a promotion party and lost 2-0 to a team fighting relegation.

It came down to the last Saturday afternoon.

We were second and playing Cardiff, a point ahead of Watford who faced Leeds.

Half-time.

We're drawing 0-0.

Watford were drawing 1-1.

And the madness kicked in.

My good friend Frazier Campbell put Cardiff ahead; it looked like we were bottling it. Then our German striker Nick Proschwitz made it 1-1.

Five minutes later Paul McShane put us in front.

Deep into injury-time, we were hanging on to that lead when they went down to 10 men. A couple of minutes later, I got ahead of the defender in the box and… foul!

Penalty!

Some fans thought the referee has blown for full-time and raced onto the pitch; it took a few minutes to clear them off before Proschwitz struck the penalty.

Saved!

Cardiff booted the rebound down the pitch and won a throw-in. Aron Gunnarsson has a ridiculous long throw; he hurt England with Iceland in Euro 2016, and this time he hurled it into our box.

Goalmouth scramble!

Hand-ball… and Cardiff got a 95th minute penalty. Nicky Maynard scored.

2-2.

Full-time.

Our heads were melted; screaming for the Watford scoreline, then discovering there'd been a big delay at Vicarage Road. Watford had to change their goalkeeper just before the game, then the replacement went off injured and they'd to bring in a youngster.

Dream stuff for Sky Sports. They whack a camera into the KC Stadium tunnel where our players have all raced in to watch the Watford-Leeds game. Lads are screaming for it to be over; I had stayed in the changing room with the staff until the final whistle sounded, then I had sprinted out to join my dad and Kelogs.

It's a long wait. Fifteen minutes for the result. The entire stadium is on edge. A Watford goal and we're in trouble.

Then the roar came… an eruption of noise as the news filtered through. Leeds had scored, Ross McCormack chipping the goalkeeper. Soon it's confirmed. We're promoted… just as Steve Bruce had promised the previous November when he rang and asked me to come to Hull.

And I'm with dad when this rollercoaster of a day comes to a halt. We're hugging and there's tears of joy as we realise we're heading to the Premier League.

It was all we'd ever wanted, and we were together when it happened.

THE HULL CITY squad I joined was filled with players that had enjoyed brief tastes of Premier League football. They wanted that experience regularly. It was the unspoken goal driving us all on.

The squad was filled with strong characters and they formed a tight-knit bunch. Paul McShane and Robbie Brady both lived in James Chester's house. That was the group I slotted into.

Every Friday before a home game, a group of us would hang out at Chester's house. Paul McShane would cook dinner. Usually it was a good chicken, rice and vegetables combo; he'd like to experiment in the kitchen, and the likes of me requesting plain meals would annoy him. We'd a nice routine. Eat dinner... watch the Championship game that was live on TV... and then have Paul's rice pudding for dessert with coffee.

Those nights are some of my best memories in football, all hanging out and having a laugh. That group spirit translated to match day and I appreciated the importance of that atmosphere when I met with the exact opposite later at Reading. We always did stuff together at Hull; midweek cinema trips or meeting up after a Saturday game.

That core of players acted as our engine on the pitch but also monitored the dressing-room. The better relationship you have with players, the more honest you can be. There was no whispering around corners; we'd bawl each other out if needed. No one had hidden agendas. We were all there for the same thing. It was a special group.

The first of my 191 games with Hull was away to Cardiff City on November 10, 2012. We lost 2-1 but the setback wasn't serious. Soon I was playing regularly. My knee felt good. With every match I played, I felt stronger and was in a great headspace. The confidence was sky high in the squad.

That December we won five times; I started every game and scored three times. My first goal as a senior pro in England arrived against Watford. Corry Evans took a shot that Manuel Almunia saved, sending the ball looping up into the air.

I saw the empty goal, jumped to head it and the roar went up. Scoring when your team wins is the biggest adrenaline rush. I repeated it against Huddersfield and Leeds, victories in local battles that sent the spirits of our fans soaring.

Bruce didn't want me to head back to Sunderland. Dad was happy I was playing the whole time. I felt it was a 50-50 call. Hull was a special group but part of me relished the challenge to go back and fight for a place at Sunderland.

Ultimately the decision was made for me. Sunderland were looking to sign a Senegalese midfielder, Alfred N'Diaye, and were happy to sell me as part of their plans. One in and one out, that's how transfer windows work.

Finalising the deal was complicated. After the loan period finished, I was told to go back to Sunderland first. Then my agent Neil Fewings called to say... 'Head to Hull'. Another call... the fee couldn't be agreed... and I needed to return to Sunderland.

Up and down, driving on the A19 motorway.

Eventually it got done. I made the move on Tuesday January 8, 2013, the same day as Robbie Brady permanently signed.

Neil was great in sorting everything. He looked after Jordan first and that opened the door for me to get him as my agent. When I signed for Hull, there was a stand-off as I'd a salary figure in my head. There was a difference of a thousand quid in the offer and Neil stuck in there for me to negotiate it. Every time I've really needed him, he's looked after me.

What I achieved with Hull, I'd love to have done with Sunderland, the club that had given me my break in England.

But the decision was made. The loan move provided a taste of life with Hull and it felt good. Nothing changed when the move became permanent; the Hull players knew what they were getting and it was just about maintaining that form. By May we'd hit the target of top two in the table and I felt a strong part of that.

THE BEAUTY OF promotion is that the buzz lasts all summer long. When the fixture list came out, we started our season at the beginning of the second Jose Mourinho era. I played midfield against another Chelsea team loaded with talent... Lampard, De Bruyne, Hazard, Oscar and Torres. Lampard missed a penalty but then scored an outrageous free-kick. We lost 2-0 but had steadied after a rocky opening.

The 2013-14 season was a pivotal one. After all the injury struggles and hardship, I became a Premier League regular; played 40 times for Hull, 30 of those in the league with 27 starts.

At 24 years old I felt more established, but I had to rise to a challenge. Signings are inevitable after promotion. In the summer of 2013, we signed two midfielders from Spurs, Jake Livermore and Tom Huddlestone. Two proven players who had been capped by England.

We often played three in the middle, so there was a spot up for grabs. That December our system clicked. Huddlestone sat deeper, I played more on the right and Jake was to the left. Jake's dad used to chat with my dad, he loved how we combined together.

We complemented each other, as myself and Jake did the running for Tom. He'd joke that he was the master in midfield holding two dogs and he'd set us off at the start. We didn't like that analogy, but it was pretty accurate. Jake had more in his locker, I was focused on my specific strengths. Cover the pitch, win the ball and lay it off to Tom to spray.

I didn't need the headlines, I just needed to play and the team to succeed. It was the start of a strong midfield relationship.

Our dressing-room remained strong, even though there were new personalities added to the mix. Curtis Davies and Allan McGregor also joined and slotted straight in. And Ahmed Elmohamady, who was on loan the season before, joined permanently.

In January, Bruce targeted strikers and he brought in Shane Long and the Croatian Nikica Jelavić. They were important signings. Jelavić finished our top Premier League scorer with five goals; Shane got four. We needed help and they freshened us up.

Shane was a familiar figure from Ireland squads. He brought the Irish crew up to five... myself, Paul, Brady, Stephen Quinn and Longy. That dynamic was great, we were all honest in our approach. Shane moved to Southampton the following August but he had fitted into the Hull mindset and worked hard.

Our group attitude kept us up that year.

The Fulham game was key at the end of April. They were 19th and fighting for their lives, and we were down 2-0. Then Jelavić and Longy both scored in the last 15 minutes to secure the draw.

We lost our last three games but we knew then we were okay and safe from relegation.

NOT EVERY SIGNING worked out. Hatem Ben Arfa moved on loan in September 2014. A five-time Ligue 1 winner, he had a big reputation.

His move was a disaster. The day he signed he turned up with his own camera crew, said he might make a documentary; wanted to record everything. We couldn't understand that attitude.

Hatem was so gifted that he wanted everyone to bow down to him. He was a phenomenal player but he didn't care. Myself and Quinny got wound up one day, had a full blown argument with the coaches over the way Hatem trained. It started to filter back to Bruce that he was becoming a problem.

If he performed in games, we might have let it slide. We played Man United at Old Trafford in November. He started and was subbed off after 35 minutes. He sat in the changing-room at half-time; Bruce was going mad and he just started laughing at him.

That was the end. He went back to Newcastle and they eventually released him. He joined Nice and the following season in France scored 17 goals as they finished 4th to qualify for Europe. We saw none of that form.

STEVE BRUCE IS a really good man-manager. He could assess what the team needed. At the end of November, we lost to Crystal Palace but were still allowed our pre-arranged Christmas party. We flew to Dublin that night; out on the Sunday in Temple Bar with Monday off.

Back to work on Tuesday, we felt refreshed and knuckled down. Next up was Liverpool at home.

The day before the game, Bruce asked me was I ready to play? I nodded.

'You'd better be clean-shaven then!'

I went home and got rid of the beard. I didn't understand his motivation but took no chances.

He told me years later that they'd an FA Cup final with Man United and as they boarded the bus, Ferguson had demanded to know why one player wasn't clean-shaven? That player was a bag of nerves but the incident stopped him getting overawed by the game. I didn't think I was nervous like that, yet it felt like a little trick by Bruce to distract me from thinking too much about facing Suarez, Gerrard and Sterling on the Sunday.

Liverpool pushed hard for the title that season.

They only lost six games, but one of them was to us. The match was a dream. I set up Livermore for the first, scored the second and we won 3-1. Afterwards, I had this superstition for a while about shaving before every game.

It was my first time playing Liverpool, the club I grew up supporting, but I didn't get caught up in that sideshow; the emotion was parked. Jordan got the ball at one stage and I nailed him. He moaned at me for a few weeks after as he'd damaged his ankle. But we're all professional. Once the whistle is blown, no one cares who they know.

That Liverpool game was a reminder of how special Hull home games could be. The place was alive.

And I produced a moment that contributed to that.

In the 72nd minute, there was a scramble for the ball and it broke to the edge of the box. I whacked in a shot. Blocked, but I got a second chance from the rebound.

I took a touch with my right, and moved to my left… steadied for a moment. And pulled the trigger again. Often, I'm so focused on technique using my left foot, that I lose balance. As I shot, I fell over and it was only hearing the screams a second later that confirmed the ball was in the back of the net. I got up, and ran around in a state of shock.

First Premier League goal… we were in front 2-1.

IT WAS ONE of the best days.

The second arrived later that month against Man United.

Sometime later, I was at Liverpool visiting Jordan. He'd training so I went in to watch and he sent me upstairs to the canteen for breakfast. Brendan Rodgers walked in and did a double-take when he saw me; then came over to say hello and sat down for a chat.

He brought up that game against us, and marked it as a turning point in their season. All the talk later was how the title challenge came apart in the loss to Chelsea, when Steven Gerrard slipped, and the draw with Crystal Palace. But Rodgers went back to their defeat to us; that was the type of game they couldn't afford to lose if they were to become champions.

I ALWAYS FELT comfortable in front of goal. Clearcut chances didn't come often but when they did, I didn't panic. I always felt I could outsmart the goalkeeper. That's a key part of it.

Goalscoring was not central to my game, but I hit four that season, all significant. Two in the league and two in the FA Cup. Steve Bruce would point out it'd be great if I could score in the regular matches instead of saving them for the big games.

In the FA quarter-final that year against Sunderland, I came inside on my left when the expectancy would have been I'd hit with my right. I had blocked down Lee Cattermole, the pitch opened up and after sprinting from my own box, I just needed to keep my head. In the semi-final against Sheffield United, I shot high to the net as the goalkeeper dived low. I felt composed in those situations. I ended up taking penalties in my last season with Hull for that reason.

Cup runs are a great distraction. That spring, it felt like a release from the pressure of trying to avoid relegation. We felt confident playing Sunderland after doing the double over them in the league.

The semi-final against Sheffield United at Wembley was bigger. A crazy game to play in. Eight goals; the first-half shambolic. Yannick Sagbo put us in front, but we were complacent against a League One team and Sheffield hit two to go ahead. Steve Bruce said nothing at the break, but Curtis Davies went berserk, grabbing players, throwing fellas against the wall… the whole lot. He was captain, screaming about the importance of getting to an FA Cup final.

We took over in the second-half. Matty Fryatt, Quinny and Huddlestone all scored… 4-2 up by the 67th minute and we were cruising. They scored in the 90th minute… 4-3. A little doubt started to creep in… 71,820 people watching on.

I passed to Matty, and went again.

He hit it wide to Elmohamady. I could hear Bruce roaring.

'TAKE IT TO THE CORNER!

'TAKE IT TO THE F***ING CORNER!'

But I'd run on. Their defence was stretched; I'd a clear path to goal. If it was anyone else on that pitch other than Elmo, they wouldn't have made that pass. I scream and he puts me in; took a touch with my left, chose where to put it with my right.

TV commentator: *That'll do it. A fifth goal for Hull City, who are heading to their first ever FA Cup final.*

WHAT THE HELL is Alan Pardew doing?

That's the first thought that entered my head.

We're losing 3-1 to Newcastle. The ball goes out over the touchline. I race to get it. Pardew goes to put his foot on the ball and then pulls it away.

That annoys me; we start shouting at each other. Then I think he felt we were going head-to-head. He makes a move forward. It's not a proper headbutt, but I'm not happy. Elmo tries to calm me down.

Loads of players wade in.

The referee Kevin Friend gives me a yellow for retaliation and Pardew is sent to the stand; later he gets slapped with a seven-game ban.

Newcastle end up winning 4-1 and afterwards that's the biggest talking point; we'd been pumped at home.

But the Pardew story explodes and the impact still lingers. During lockdown in 2020 when all of sport was shut down, I was reminded of it on TV one day.

Ten Most Bizarre Moments In Premier League History.

It makes the cut.

It was a weird time. Steve and my dad both said the same thing after… stay away from the media. Everyone tried to get me for an interview, to hear my side of the story. It was a long time before I spoke about it.

I didn't care too much. He hadn't hurt me or knocked me over. That would have been embarrassing; at least I stood my ground. The loss concerned me more as we headed on international break with Ireland. Everyone there wanted to talk about it.

Pardew wouldn't be the most liked figure, and there were plenty of suggestions I should have hit back. But I never thought that was the wisest move.

On the Monday after, I got a phone call. The police wanted to discuss the incident.

I hung up.

They tried again… I hung up again.

I was convinced it was one of the Hull lads winding me up. The club secretary rang and said it was a serious call; the police needed to know if I wanted to press charges. I'd no interest going down that road.

Pardew never apologised in person or contacted me himself after. It was bad form that he didn't just ring me to clear the air and admit he'd lost his cool for a moment.

The club received some token letter which he'd signed, but I never looked at it.

We played Crystal Palace later when he was their manager. In the tunnel before the match, I went to shake his hand and kept looking at him. He shook my hand, said nothing and just turned away.

He'll never forget me for the rest of his life after that incident. He had the opportunity that day to say, 'Sorry about all that'. *Just acknowledge it.*

But he didn't and that was his call.

THE 1996 FINAL is my first memory of the FA Cup... Eric Cantona hitting the late winner, the Liverpool players in their white suits. It is a special competition and I had a chance to win it in 2014.

But first I was fearful I might miss it.

After playing Man United a couple weeks earlier, I was accused of stamping on Adnan Januzaj. It turned into a big storm but I hadn't meant to stamp on him. Steve Bruce fought tooth and nail that it wasn't intentional. A three-match ban would have meant I'd miss the final. He left me out for a game against Everton, shielded me from the attention.

There was a pile-on from United fans but I stayed clear of that and escaped any suspension.

The build-up to the cup final in Hull was huge; this enormous sporting occasion that the whole city bought into. We got the train to London the night before and went to our hotel. The mood was relaxed; a few of us played Fifa that night, and I felt good the next morning going for a walk.

My pre-match meal plan was Weetabix in morning, then later... chicken, pasta and bolognese sauce. That day I was one of the last to queue... there was no chicken left. I was giving out that all the food was gone... the fitness coach got stressed out but it didn't matter much in the end. My reaction was just a sign of big-game nerves.

Upstairs to get ready and put on the cup final suit.

Ushered onto a bus.

As we turned up Wembley Way, it was two hours before kick-off with only a bunch of fans there. Later the pubs would spill out the thousands going to the game.

We arrived, and after a while Bruce brought in a guest to the changing room... David Beckham. It was a genius move. Beckham came in, just popped around the room to meet everyone. It was a good distraction.

Some of the lads who didn't make the squad grabbed him for selfies.

Every game in that cup run, we'd been above the team we were facing in the league. We always felt we should win. The difference now was the opposition. With Arsenal, we said we *could* win.

We were so well drilled; knew exactly what we were doing. We lined up in tunnel together. Arsenal came out in dribs and drabs, lads hadn't their laces tied... were slow putting their shirts on. A few high-fived the referee.

Not sure they're tuned in.

We were staring out at that pitch and waiting for that first whistle. That's why the game started the way it did.

Firstly, Quinny arrows a corner to Tom at the edges of the box. He fires a shot in at pace and Chester just diverts it to the far corner of the net.

Then a cross comes in from deep and I almost get ahead of Bacary Sagna to head it, but it flies just past us. Quinny makes space and stands up a cross. Alex Bruce gets a header in; hits the post and Curtis smashes in the rebound.

Eight minutes gone in the FA Cup final. We're winning 2-0 because two of our three centre-halves have scored. *What's happening?*

WE'D BEEN HERE before. It's not the first time Chester has scored in the fourth minute that season; same story at home to Man United back in December. The class of Man United told that day as they won 3-2.

And the class of Arsenal also eventually told.

If we'd survived until half-time with that 2-0 lead, I feel I'd have got my hands on that trophy after the game. But Santi Cazorla put a free-kick in the top corner... 2-1 at the break. We needed another goal but didn't want to commit too many forward. There was danger in their team everywhere you looked... Arteta, Ramsey, Cazorla, Özil, Podolski and Giroud all starting.

Koscielny scores and it goes to extra-time.

I could sense trouble. Our bodies are tired now, our minds just hoping we get to penalties. They throw on Rosicky and Wilshere. *We're wrecked.* It's the only game I've ever got cramp in. Running down the wing after over 110 minutes, with 16km in the bank… my left calf locks. If it had gone to a shootout, I'm not sure I'd have had the energy for the walk from the centre circle to size up the kick.

It didn't get that far. Ramsey buries the third goal and Arsenal are ahead. We've poured our heart and soul into it but that's the winner.

Straight after game, I got drug tested. Drained and dehydrated, I just couldn't give the testers the sample they wanted so we could all go home.

The game kicked off at 5pm. There was a post-match event organised for players and families at 8.30pm; I didn't get there until two and a half hours later. My family were waiting but I was so frustrated after the day, I didn't want to go to the party and just went straight to my room. Dad came up to me.

Be with the rest of the lads. No point wallowing on your own. That was his message!

ALL MY BUDDIES landed at the hotel, the gang from Cork I grew up with… all wearing Hull shirts they'd put on for the day. We sorted entry for them all.

Niall Quinn was there, he's good mates with Bruce. He came over to our Irish group, sat down and had a few pints. The lads were desperate to get Niall to sing. He joined in a couple of times when the lads started.

And it actually turned into a nice night, with plenty of people around to help ease the disappointment of the loss

I was heartbroken at the time but can now appreciate the incredible occasion it was. If we'd lost to Sheffield United, I'd have lived with that regret for the rest of my life. Against Arsenal, we gave it everything but just came up short facing a good team.

Dad used to reflect a lot then over how far I'd come. From being trapped in a tunnel trying to get my knee right, that was the season I moved into the light.

FA Cup run.

Goals against big teams.

Constant games.

Staying in the Premier League.

A great adventure from start to finish.

VI

North Kerry

Kilmoyley

Neilus Flynn Cup

Catherine O'Sullivan's spaghetti bolognese

Shane Brick

An Tóchar Bán

★★★

JOHN

EARLY IN JUNE 2000, I got a call from Joe Walsh. Joe had played for me with Kerry, full-forward on that team that shocked Waterford, a solid fella who put his heart and soul into hurling. He was a hardcore Kilmoyley man and they were opening their new pitch in Lerrig on the Bank Holiday Sunday.

Their senior side were playing a challenge against Sixmilebridge from Clare; the undercard before the main event of the Kerry and Galway senior footballers facing off, just a few months before they would later contest the All-Ireland final.

Joe wanted me to come down for the day to give himself, Pete Young, Joe Walsh (Ardrahan) and Gerard O'Sullivan a dig out with the Kilmoyley team. That was the initial plan; just stand on the line to take in the match and see what happens. Afterwards, the Kilmoyley lads were chatting about their plans that week for the team and I just said I'd be back for training… Tuesday night.

That was the start of it.

And over 20 years later, I am still heading down there to help out a hurling community that my link with refuses to break.

IT'S ABOUT A two-hour spin for me from home in Rochestown to Kilmoyley's pitch in north Kerry. I leave Cork and point the car west… past Ballincollig, through Macroom… and then roll over the county boundary.

Onto Killarney and Tralee… north from there… into the village of Ardfert where I take a right... then a left at Lerrig Cross, and the pitch swings into view on my right. This is hurling country.

If taking the senior job in 1992 was the start of my love affair with Kerry hurling, then my time with Kilmoyley has deepened that bond.

Kilmoyley are one of eight senior hurling clubs; the pitches of the other seven are all less than 10 miles away. The parishes live side-by-side. The games are charged with emotion in the stands and on the pitch, and the outcomes carry huge meaning. Everyone wants to be there on county final day in Austin Stack Park in Tralee every autumn and get their hands on the Neilus Flynn Cup.

Kilmoyley had to endure a long period without landing that title. They won it in 1971 before their famine kicked in and a lot of good players couldn't get their hands on a medal. My first season there wasn't successful; we got knocked out by Ballyheigue in the quarter-final. I couldn't find fault with the set-up in the club but I quickly realised we had started out too late that year.

In 2001, there was no delay, I got down to work with them in February. That September we won the Kerry Senior Championship final, smashing down the barrier that had existed for 30 years, and that was the start of a magical four in-a-row. I stayed on for two more years but Ballyduff defeated us both times.

By the end of 2006 I had taken over Wexford, but Kilmoyley has proved impossible to turn my back on. I looked after the minor team in 2009, got back involved with the seniors as we won in 2015 and, after my time with Cork ended, took over again to win a sixth Kerry final with them in 2020. I just love it down there. There's no pretensions from anyone involved. People don't talk around corners, they say it straight. You get an awful lot of sham at county level; fellas swanning around who think they have a lot of experience but they haven't really and have just jumped on a bandwagon.

Club is different; it is a genuine form of hurling and Kilmoyley epitomise that perfectly in my view. There's the Lerrig Stores shop, the church in Kilmoyley, the pub An Tochar Bán across the road and the hurling pitch in between. That's their area and that's their life.

The people are fantastic to deal with. Ned Horgan, who has a meat distribution business locally, would often pull in before training and straight away hand into my car a few packets of rashers and sausages.

The Regans are a superb hurling family; Padraig and Micheál and Big Jim were playing when I started, and their parents were two brilliant characters full of chat and stories. The two O'Leary brothers, Willie and Michael, played for the club down through the years. Willie had a butcher's shop in Ballyheigue and he was a fierce man for coursing.

He was club president up until he died in May 2021. Even as the years passed on, he'd never miss a training session. His wife Therese would bring him along every evening and they'd sit in the car behind the goal. I'd always call over when we were coming off the pitch and chat for a few minutes about how the players were going.

Seán Murnane was the chairman for about 10 years, a huge character and an absolutely brilliant clubman. The Bull McCabe of Kilmoyley with his white beard and a gruff way about him. You'd have it out with him regularly but his heart was always in the right place. He challenged me as a manager but he always cared greatly.

After training, everyone would pile into the clubroom and sit down. The kettle was boiled and cups of tea lashed out. A different person was in charge of food each night; it might be a tray of sandwiches made at home or a pot of spaghetti bolognese from Catherine O'Sullivan, whose husband Mike was a club sponsor with his business, Flahertys Hardware.

THE FOUR IN-A-ROW team truly kick-started my relationship with the club. That breakthrough on the last day of September in 2001 was a special moment.

Reaching the county final was a big deal but the mood amongst the players was good and they didn't get overawed by the occasion.

Fr Maurice Brick was the uncle of Shane, Ian and Billy, who were playing. I got him to say Mass in the meeting-room at the club pitch that Sunday morning. His sermon was like a motivational speech; fellas were fired up walking out the door, their chests pumping and tuned in for what lay ahead.

It was a desperate day in Tralee, torrential rain and driving wind. Horrendous conditions for hurling and the game turned into a savage battle against Ballyheigue. We were up by seven at half-time but they came charging back at us in the second-half. Shane Brick rocketed home a penalty at a key stage, yet Ballyheigue drew level late on.

Then five minutes into injury-time, Ollie Diggins popped up with the most famous point in the club's history. A one-point win.

The emotion came pouring out of every Kilmoyley person present as they jumped out of the stand and terraces to get onto the pitch. I hadn't stopped to think about the significance of a potential win beforehand; I was so wrapped up in planning for the game.

'It isn't just a monkey off our backs… it's the whole of Dublin Zoo!' as Christy Walsh put it afterwards. Christy had soldiered a long time; his brother Joe was goalkeeper-selector and they were lads you'd be thrilled for. It had been hard-earned. We put in the extra effort from the start of 2001, got the players really fit and drove up the level of commitment.

We trained a lot on the beach in Banna; that's where the punishment took place by running the lads up the sand dunes. I returned to where I'd started out with Kerry in 1992 but there was no issue with numbers this time. Everyone turned up and once they started winning, they kept coming back. Lixnaw were beaten in the finals of 2002 and '03, then Causeway in '04. It was the first four in-a-row in Kerry senior hurling since Causeway (1979-82).

We used to travel all over Munster for challenge games. We'd fix a match for somewhere in Limerick or Tipperary on a Tuesday night; fellas would get lost driving around the countryside. There's no problem now in dropping a location pin into the WhatsApp group but back then the first task was everyone landing into the right dressing-room.

There was a Munster club league on the go as well in the early 2000s. When you've a small number of clubs in a county and you're playing each other four or five times a year, teams can become trapped in a stale cycle. That was a great initiative by the Munster Council.

Playing outside the Kerry border freed up our lads. I pushed the team hard and wanted to test them against strong sides. We played the Barrs, Blackrock and Na Piarsaigh from Cork. We toured around Limerick going up against Patrickswell, Ballybrown and Na Piarsaigh.

I PUT A Kilmoyley minor team into the city league in Cork in 2009. The Seandun Divisional Board gave us the green light. We played nine matches and nine times the lads came up on a bus. You'd try to get teams to come halfway but they wouldn't. That's the backbone of the current Kilmoyley senior team; that competition did a lot for their development.

I often thought about trying to get Kilmoyley into the Cork Senior League, like some of the Carlow teams who play in Kilkenny. It's about trying to promote hurling. Some people want to help and some people don't; they say we're in the way.

A lot of clubs wouldn't travel down to Kilmoyley for senior challenge games either, so we'd go to them; a two-hour trek up the road. I felt it was a sign they didn't rate us. That hasn't changed and I don't think it ever will because it's a *hurling team* from Kerry. That often hurts me, that the lads are not respected, that they're branded second-class citizens of the sport.

But the players never complained about the travel. We'd got over the line after 30 years; they just looked to me and asked what else do you need? They were a really good crop of fellas who were mad to play. And one shone brightest of all.

SHANE BRICK WAS the best hurler I came across in my years with Kerry. He had natural hurling skill; he was a brilliant athlete at centre-forward that you could launch puck-outs down upon and he had an eye for a goal.

But it was his ability to deliver in pressure-cooker atmospheres, the pattern of standing up when it mattered most that set him apart. His free-taking was top-class, and he thrived in taking on those shots.

Out of those four county final wins, he won the Man of the Match award three times. He scored 1-5, 1-6, 1-4 and 2-6 in those games. Brick was our Henry Shefflin, the leader of our attack.

He was often approached to go somewhere that people thought was bigger and better. There was talk at one stage that Limerick were after him. He was in Cork teaching in Ballinlough, so naturally clubs around the city went looking for him. But he's passionate about Kilmoyley and that outweighed everything else. His father was involved, his brother Billy and his cousin Ian were central players. Just like Christy Walsh kept coming back to Kerry from Kilkenny, Brick did the same.

I probably got Brick at the right time. Kilmoyley won in 2001 and took off just as he was coming into his prime. There was the incentive of success to help him stay loyal to Kilmoyley, to keep travelling down from Cork. He finished his playing career with Tracton in Cork, the local club where he had settled but only after giving his best years to Kilmoyley.

Becoming the champions of Kerry was one thing, but announcing ourselves further afield was the step that I really wanted us to take.

WE HAD FOUR cracks at the Munster Senior Club Championship. The draw pitted us twice against Blackrock, and twice against Toomevara. I often wondered at the fact we never got drawn against someone different from Clare, Limerick or Waterford. Getting past those teams was a massive hurdle.

Blackrock were really good at the time. You're talking about a team backboned by Wayne Sherlock, the Brownes and Fergal Ryan. Top Cork players. Then Toomevara had all the Dunne brothers with Tipperary and they were very strong.

In 2001, we played Blackrock in the field in Lerrig and lost by eight points. In 2003, we went up to Thurles and gave Toomevara a fright in the first-half but they pulled away to win by eight.

In between came the big chance. We played Blackrock in Páirc Uí Chaoimh in November 2002. With a few minutes left we were down by two points after Brick fired a 20-yard free to the net and our tails were up. But Blackrock weathered the storm and got two late points, seeing them over the line by 2-13 to 1-12.

Afterwards we were sick with regret. Brick was immense, Man of the Match with 1-10 yet we couldn't get enough scores from elsewhere. We'd started slowly and conceded 1-1. Maurice Murnane hit a rocket off the crossbar in the first-half. But the main bone of contention was Brick scoring a goal in the first-half that was ruled out. The referee said the sliotar had been thrown to him in the build-up, but bizarrely still gave us the free which to this day still doesn't make any sense.

THE LAST GO we had at senior level was in 2004. We were at home and Seán Murnane said to me the week before that he'd let the grass grow on the pitch.

'Ah Seán... you can't be doing that!'

On the day the pitch was heavy and the grass long. It was something different but it didn't do us much good. Toomevara hit 5-19 and beat us out the gate. Diarmuid Kirwan was refereeing the game and he reported us after to the Munster Council.

That was it. It often annoyed me they pulled Kerry out of the Munster club senior after and into the intermediate. We still can't win at that grade, losing to Wolfe Tones of Clare in 2015 when I was involved.

I constantly questioned what could we have done differently in training, in how we set up or instilled belief to the players. *How could we close the gap?*

Looking back now the four in-a-row was an incredible time. High stakes matches and massive victories. I'd have loved to have won a Munster club game; that's just my attitude, always craving something else and thinking of the ones that got away.

And there was one memorable day, in 2003, when we won the Munster Senior League. We beat Castlelyons in the quarter-final, Cloyne in the semi-final and Na Piarsaigh in the final; three clubs packed with Cork hurlers.

The final against Na Piarsaigh was in Fitzgerald Stadium. Weeshie Fogarty was providing updates that Saturday but Radio Kerry cut across near the end for him to do live commentary of the last five minutes when they got word something historic was on the verge of happening.

Much like Walsh Park in 1993, there is a mystique about the game as there's no video footage of it. It's not every day a Kerry team beats a Cork one in a Munster hurling final but it happened that November Saturday in Killarney.

WINNING DEVELOPS A deep trust between a manager and players. I built it up with that Kilmoyley group and we still have it.

You can see the legacy of that team's success. Kilmoyley have won nine titles in the last 20 years, which is a strong return. At underage the numbers aren't huge. The under-16 and minor teams are joined up with Crotta O'Neills; the emphasis then is on picking up one or two every year to join the seniors and ensure they don't get lost.

The 2009 panel that won the county, there was a pile of lads that emigrated after. The Youngs, the McCarthys, the Sheehys, sets of brothers that were forced to leave. But the club coped and moved on.

Bringing in outside coaches has served them well. Anthony Daly won a couple of county titles, Fergie O'Loughlin from Clare and Leo O'Connor from Limerick were also there. The Kilmoyley hurling brand is well-known which is a positive. A trust has always existed between all the Kilmoyley managers that come in. There's a great grá there for the club as distinct to doing it for themselves.

Daly rang me when he took charge and the one simple message I gave him was that it was 'county or nothing' now for them every year. In their eyes the drought was over and it was time to keep drinking. The club has grown to demand success. There's a different Kilmoyley group there now, but the core principles remain the same. 2020 was a tough year as the pandemic ripped up our plans yet I could see their resilience and commitment remained intact.

Midfielder Paudie O'Connor texted me one night that he was in trouble to get off the farm and make training in time... 'Sorry John, the cows are being a bit uncooperative tonight with me'.

Hard to argue with that.

But Paudie still fits in hurling, just as another farmer Daniel Collins does. When the players had to train on their own, Collins would send in a photo of himself to the group after doing a gym session at 5am before he went working on the family farm with his father Gerald. They're both Kerry hurlers as well; Collins has won a Joe McDonagh Cup All Star. Not many top hurlers are milking 150 cows and still starring in Croke Park.

Work takes Tom Murnane around the country, putting up electrical poles. He was based in Clare for a good bit but he stayed tipping away at the hurling and would train with Clarecastle through our connection with Fergie O'Loughlin. That's the type of honesty in the squad. It'd be easy at times to park the hurling but playing for Kilmoyley is a way of life they will not give up. And they're getting their rewards in still landing county titles.

SEPTEMBER 2020 WAS the sixth time I was involved for that moment of championship glory. It was a beautiful sunny day in Tralee for that final and we had a brilliant one-point win over Causeway. It was the strangest year to be a manager with all the challenges Covid-19 presented but the players still developed and bought in.

A few years back some lads from Dingle, a football-mad area with no hurling club, started to play with Kilmoyley. Matthew Flaherty has played senior football for Kerry and won All-Ireland medals in Croke Park but he has huge interest in hurling with his family background in Clare. The football ended early for him in 2020 and he joined us for the hurling, a massive help at midfield. He took huge pride in being the first player from his west Kerry area to get a county senior hurling medal. A couple of weeks after the game he took the cup back home, sending me photos of the silverware at the picturesque coastal spots around Slea Head.

Seeing all those reactions reminded me how two decades on, the significance of these victories has not been diluted for the club.

The slagging always comes thick and fast down there. They'd be saying I was 'nothing' before I went to Kilmoyley and they made the name of John Meyler as a hurling manager. I'd cut back that they were stuck until I came down and got them winning counties.

One night in that summer of 2020, the secretary John Nolan called me over and said there was a new addition to the photos on the wall in the clubhouse. A group of players and other members had gathered around as they brought me in.

Ellie Morgan lives 300 yards down the road from the club; she works as a nurse but is also a sketch artist. The club gave her a few pictures to work with and there was the result... a portrait sketched of me, framed with the green and gold Kilmoyley crest in the bottom right corner. Now it's up on the wall of the front room at home in Rochestown.

It was a really nice personal touch. They'd be a mighty club for that. When I was Cork manager, they always asked me down on the Tuesday night after our year had ended. It was like a form of therapy after the devastation in Croke Park the previous Sunday, losing against Limerick and Kilkenny, and seeing All-Ireland dreams shattered.

But instead of sitting at home in Cork, replaying the defeat over in my mind, I could drive to north Kerry. I have my favourite coffee pitstop just outside Tralee and, on summer afternoons, I will head to Banna Strand. A walk on the beach followed by a swim in the sea... dive around in the waves for 10 minutes and when I come out of the water, I'm energised ahead of the evening.

When I get to the pitch for training, I can unwind in a place where no one is going to pester me over a match the previous weekend, and I get to work with a group of willing people.

It's the only job in hurling I've ever totally enjoyed. No matter how bad things got, I always wanted to keep coming back to Kilmoyley. It feels like home.

VII

Martin O'Neill

Euro 2016

Angry Roy

Regretful Me

★★★

DAVID

MARTIN O'NEILL CLEARED his throat and prepared to speak. *It all comes down to this announcement.* Thirteen days out from Ireland's Euro 2016 opener against Sweden and finally we will find out who's going to France.

Seems fitting in a way that I'm in a dressing-room at Turners Cross. The biggest moment in my international career and the news will be broken to me at my local stadium.

We've just lost 2-1 to Belarus, before a sell-out crowd in the sunshine for the last warm-up game. I haven't played well and now the fear of rejection is growing. I'm either packing my bags to head to Versailles, or I've got the summer off. And if I do miss out, it's not like there's an instant chance to make amends. Major tournaments don't come around often for Ireland; a lot of our greatest players never went to a European Championships. It's quiet in the room as the tension hangs in the air.

From the night we beat Bosnia in the play-off the previous November, I've been thinking about this moment. Anyone could have sat down then and written out the 17 or 18 bankers to make it. Then you debate for the remaining seats on the plane. *Who's in and who's out?*

If you're Seamus Coleman or Robbie Brady, you've just got to stay fit and be sharp when the summer comes around. For the rest of us, it's different. Four players for two midfield places… myself, Harry Arter, Stephen Quinn and Darron Gibson. I don't want to be a hard luck story.

On the Saturday, Ireland had played Holland. Harry was excellent alongside Quinny. He hadn't played in the qualifiers but, suddenly, he's got a foot in the door and could make the squad.

At the same time I was in Wembley, celebrating Hull's promotion to the Premier League after the play-off final. Up until six in the morning, on the beer with my family, friends and teammates. Then, an early flight to Cork to meet with the Irish squad.

Martin played me that Monday against Belarus in midfield with Darron. I was all over the place; probably the worst game I've had in an Ireland shirt. Roy had a go at me after in private about my performance. *They needed more.* It's justified... I was off the pace.

MARTIN HAS THE list in his hand.

'Right lads!' He rattles through the names. You've got to concentrate. Sitting... head down... hands on knees. You're hanging on his every word, just waiting to hear your name called. Then... 'David Meyler'.

That's it... I'm in.

It's a moment for celebration but you must check yourself. There are lads who haven't made it. Myself and Quinn are selected. Harry, who has picked up an injury, and Darron miss out. It's hard on them.

The most heartbreaking omission is David Forde. He'd played in four qualifiers; the goalkeeper for the draw in Germany. Now he is out! That's how tough it is. We're all grown men. You have to take it. But it's dog-eat-dog.

It's me or you. *I'm going to make sure it's me.* That's professional sport. People don't want to admit it, but it's a very cruel business.

I leave after and meet dad outside.

ANOTHER SQUAD ANNOUNCEMENT many years before comes to mind. In 2002 I got asked to captain the Cork Kennedy Cup team in Limerick. A huge deal for a 13-year-old. Then the 20-player squad was read out for the tournament... 'David Meyler' is not called out.

The lads who hadn't made the cut were politely asked to leave. I headed over to the car and told dad I wasn't in the squad despite the captaincy invite.

Turned out it was just a big mistake. The coach read the list wrong. I got called back, but that five-minute wait wasn't enjoyable. Now the stakes are higher. 'Are you going?' asks dad.

'Yeah.'

'Well, thank God for that!' By his reaction, I can tell he wasn't confident either.

AFTER THE DRAW with Germany in 2014, we headed to Glasgow in November with a bounce in our step. Celtic Park was a ground I loved and had sampled the atmosphere on Celtic's big European nights. I was desperate to play but spent the game on the bench. Quinny and Robbie were brought on in midfield.

The worst thing was we lost 1-0. Martin went bananas over the goal we conceded; I lost count of the amount of meetings we had afterwards about that game.

There was an edge to the mood in the crowd that night; felt like it could kick off at any stage. It only needed one moment to light the fuse, and Scotland provided it with their goal. Shaun Maloney took a short corner, played a one-two with Scott Brown before curling a shot into the far corner in the 75th minute. It was a lovely finish but Aiden McGeady came off the back post. If he stays there, he blocks the shot. Martin was raging; not doing the basics at set-pieces had cost us. The result was a proper kick in the teeth.

The year ended on a nice note. Four days later, Martin called me in at the team hotel in Dublin. He was making me captain for the friendly against the USA. He told me it was because of the job I'd done for him in Germany.

The personal honour was huge but my reaction was low-key. That was deliberate. I only told dad. It all goes back to the Ireland under-21s when we played Turkey once in Cork, and I got taken off at half-time after one of the worst games of my career. Before the game I must have sorted 60 people with tickets. Even that morning and lunchtime, I was racing around, thinking... *This is great... I'm in Cork, I'm playing for Ireland... who wants tickets?*

Just let me know, I'll sort you. Everyone came to watch me play and I was hauled off before the second-half started. Dad hit the roof after. Ever since, I just sort him, mum and Sarah. *Let them look after everyone else.*

SO, CAPTAINING IRELAND wasn't my focus; performing in the game was. It went brilliantly. We won 4-1. Robbie Brady scored a cracker of a free-kick to round it off.

And after, I could reflect on the captaincy role, the trust Martin placed in me when he could very easily have made someone like Shay Given captain that night. It's difficult to describe the emotion of it and that feeling swelled further when I got to captain Ireland in the qualifiers a few years after.

Mary O'Brien, who worked with the FAI, got me the pennant from the USA game. I'm not sure was she meant to but Mary appreciated the small details. A lovely touch; it's at home now in Cork in a frame with the armband and the jersey from that night.

SIMPLE INSTRUCTIONS. STEPHEN Ward is coming off injured.

Go in and shore up that midfield.

Keep it steady, stay with the runners. I'm nodding and listening to Martin on the sideline.

October 2015.

0-0 against Germany... 69 minutes. *And I'm in.* Seconds later, Germany win the ball in their box and try to counter-attack. Marco Reus makes a run... John O'Shea gets a foot in and the ball rolls loose to me. Quick thought... *Am I getting pressed?*

Think I'll send it back to Randolph.

I turn as Randolph boots it and watch on. Shane Long is lightning quick. The ball hits his left shin and falls perfectly as he's gone past the German defence.

He blasts it past Neuer... 70 minutes and it's 1-0. There's a split second pause and a huge roar erupts. *He's scored! We're beating Germany! This is unbelievable*!

And then I wonder how we're going to hold on? Drawing or losing to Germany in the last 20 minutes is different to this. Now we've got something to protect and that creates a greater fear. *Don't be the one that makes a mistake.*

That same thought is on everyone's mind. We're under siege and everyone's shouting.

'COME IN!'

'PUSH!'

'PRESS!'

'DROP!'

Goalkeeper, back four and midfield all need to be in line and switched on.

Germany have enough talent without us making it easy for them.

Seventy-seven minutes.

Kroos and Özil work it on the wing. I'm keeping an eye to my left on Thomas Müller. Then Hector gets to the byline and drags it back. Reus and O'Shea go for it but they both miss the ball. I'm caught by surprise, stick out my left leg and it rolls past me towards Müller. I fall and can only sit in the box watching him.

A second frozen in time. Müller has the chance to pick his spot; this outstanding player who has scored 30 goals for Germany and 10 in the World Cup. He side-foots it and I turn to watch the ball fly past the post; relief rushing through my body as I realise... *He's missed.*

Got away with it. But I can hear Martin and Roy roaring at me.

I'm hungry and alert for the rest of the game. This is my chance after those games sitting on the bench in Glasgow and Faro and Dublin. *We must not concede.* Germany have all the possession but there's no way through; the final whistle blasts. We have beaten the world champions and secured a play-off for the Euros.

Later, at the team hotel in Malahide, we have a few pints and try to make sense of it. My phone is going off the wall. From family to some fella in the middle of nowhere in Australia that you went to school with, everyone is messaging... everyone has watched the game and everyone is celebrating the win.

Fairytale stuff.

REGRETS. THEY DON'T haunt me from Euro 2016 but they are there.

I didn't get any game time. Only four of the squad didn't play and two were goalkeepers – myself, Cyrus Christie, Shay and Kieren Westwood. There was an opportunity after the Belgium game to force my way in. I didn't do enough.

It's easier said than done with the games coming thick and fast, but I should have done more in training.

We were at the team base in Versailles after a session one day and I headed back to my room. A few hours downtime, I sat there with the PlayStation, headset on, talking to my friends. All the players stayed on the one floor and the doors were left on the latch. I heard a rumble at the door and called out... 'IT'S OPEN'

I turn and next thing I just see Roy standing there. Jump up. Whip off the headset. Drop the controller.

Roy is frustrated with the way I'd trained. We were preparing to play Belgium and he wanted to see more; for me to push myself.

He was right. Roy was reminding me not to get comfortable. I had almost slipped into the mindset of an Irish fan away at the Euros, just there to enjoy the ride. That may sound harsh, but it is the truth.

Hindsight is a beautiful thing. I had put so much into making the squad, that getting to France felt like an achievement. Working to get my hamstring right in April, pushing for the play-offs and that Irish squad spot in May. I realised those goals, but in June I forgot to set another target.

When the tournament started, I was just glad to be in that 23-man bubble. Being involved is something I'll always look back on with great pride but if we'd reached the 2018 World Cup, my mindset would have been completely different.

At the Euros I was happy to be there and before I knew it, it was all over. The moments were still special; I loved being an eyewitness. Wes striking the ball sweetly in Paris against Sweden after Seamus had clipped the ball across. Taking on France in Lyon and going in front. Bordeaux was awful, Belgium hammering us out the gate, but that meant Lille ended up being a night of total euphoria.

Sitting on the bench at the Stade Pierre-Mauroy, when Wes misses the chance and thinking... *That's it. Pack up and go home.* Then he picks up the ball, puts it on a sixpence and Robbie heads it in. Absolute magic.

I ran so far onto the pitch in celebration after the goal, I should nearly have got a cap.

We were always capable of digging out a result when it mattered. A goal for Ireland like that lifts the country to a state of sporting happiness that rarely comes around. The mood in the dressing-room after was electric. For a tournament everyone has their friends and family there, that adds to the emotion.

We had all grown up on tales of Euro 88 and Italia 90. Now we were all together, experiencing an Irish international football night that would not be forgotten.

OFTEN, INJURED IRELAND players will not go to home games.

It's a personal choice. They'll stay in England with their clubs and get treatment. I preferred to be there, let the Ireland management know that I wanted to be with the squad. A throwback to my Sunderland days after damaging my cruciate. It helped mentally to be there, as tough as it was not being available.

In November 2015, In the week building up to our Euro play-off against Bosnia, I collided with Marc Wilson in training. Innocuous enough but I paid a price… Grade 2 tear of the medial ligament in my right knee and I was out for the two legs. I watched the first game on the Friday night in the East Village Bar at home in Douglas, as the lads drew 1-1 in the fog in Zenica with Robbie scoring. Then, straight to Dublin before the second-leg on the Monday night.

I used to always find myself in the snack room of the team hotel the night before games. Bowl of cereal, slice of toast or cup of tea before bed. Martin would often be there and we'd get chatting. For that Bosnia second-leg I wasn't playing and so, in no rush to get some sleep, we sat and talked for the bones of an hour.

I always had great conversations with Martin about football. Those were the best times. There was a perception that Martin constantly harked back to his playing days. He did it occasionally. You can only reflect on your own football journey. Martin was a two-time European Cup winner, played in the 1982 World Cup when Northern Ireland beat Spain. If you can't draw on those experiences, what can you draw on?

As a boy, I was a huge Celtic fan and Martin managed that team I idolised with Larsson, Lennon and Petrov. I signed up to The Huddle Group, a supporters' club. Birthday and Christmas cards would come through the letterbox in Cork with Martin's signature on them. He'd laugh when I brought that up and recall the Celtic secretary giving him a pile of cards to scribble his name on.

He had fascinating stories about the Leicester City side in the 90s, and the Aston Villa team later. People forget footballers start out as fans. I loved listening to all that.

He was nervous about the Bosnia game, mindful of their star names Eden Dżeko and Miralem Pjanić. I felt the lads looked good and sharp; told him not to worry, we were going to win. I even predicted the right scoreline… 2-0.

After the match ended and Jon Walters had scored the key goals, I hobbled down to the side of the pitch on crutches, my right knee in a brace. Martin was hugging all his staff. He spotted me… I hug him and he says, 'You were right!'

On the pitch for the lap of honour and in the dressing-room after, is as happy as I have felt in football. We had done it.

Cork Institute of Technology

MBA

Brian Corcoran

Michael Fennelly

Ballinhassig

Courcey Rovers

★★★

JOHN

WHEN I LEFT Tralee in late 1992 after working with Lee Strand Dairies, it was for something different in Cork. A position had opened up as GAA officer in Cork RTC in their campus in Bishopstown, with the aim to promote Gaelic Games amongst students.

I jumped at the chance. It gave me a foot in the door in the college.

Lecturing was something I wanted to pursue and, over time, I went down that road full-time. Three decades later, I'm still there.

OVER TIME, IT has changed, become the Cork Institute of Technology in 1998, and rebranded to Munster Technological University in 2021. For all the growth, it has remained a place where I have been able to marry my interests in lecturing and sport.

In 1993, I started my MBA and completed it part-time over the next four years. That paved the way for part-time lecturing before I got a permanent role, later focusing on business strategy.

It is a wonderful place to support people with a passion in sport. I had day and night lectures, which meant my hours were flexible. Managing GAA teams could fit around that. When David moved to England, I would slip off over to see him play. I'd travel over and back for a midweek match, without missing work or people even realising I had gone.

There was a lot of goodwill from everyone in CIT towards sport. Damien Courtney, my boss in Applied Social Studies; Paul Mahony, the Head of Adult Education; Dr Barry O'Connor, the president; and Brendan Goggin, the registrar.

They were very supportive when I took manager roles, even the time-consuming ones with the Cork and Wexford seniors. That employer-backing is critical. Dr O'Connor would mention it at conferrings for students, when I was in charge of Cork. They were proud of people furthering themselves in sport, and within the college they saw the value in developing the sporting facilities. The complex of pitches there now is top class.

Keith Ricken, Liam Hodnett, Eamonn Cashel and Jerry Forde were all great GAA people, working in various roles in the college. Keith came in as the GAA officer when I went lecturing and did a great job. When I started, my focus was on the senior football and hurling; get things off the ground. Keith developed GAA there in a broader way, bringing in ladies football and camogie, and introducing more teams.

WHEN WE STARTED, the college was in Division Two in football and hurling with Kevin Kehily and Noel Collins doing the coaching; soon we qualified for Division One. By 1993, we were competing in the Fitzgibbon Cup and Sigerson Cup.

I later took the hurling team, enjoyed the coaching and we were blessed with some great people from the start.

Brian Corcoran was the biggest Cork name early on. A star in both codes. Most mornings around 11am I'd watch him go past my office to get a can of 7-Up and a Mars bar from a vending machine. He was a quiet, calm fella, doing a degree in Computing. A super hurler. In 1992 he was a teenager who won Hurler of the Year playing for Cork, and inspired Erin's Own to win their first senior county. He was just fantastic to watch.

Others came from outside Cork. Eugene O'Neill from Tipperary, Pat O'Neill and Philly Larkin from Kilkenny. Big Pat was a huge character, one of the best hurlers I ever came across. I'd still be friendly with Philly and his father Fan, who used to come to Cork to watch Philly's college games. Any time I go to Nowlan Park, I'd always look out for Fan.

There was no pretension about Kilkenny hurlers. No matter how many All-

Irelands they were winning, they remained grounded. They had a deep love for hurling and their lives revolved around it. Same with the lads later on I had in the Fitzgibbon Cup… Jackie Tyrrell, Michael Fennelly and Taggy Fogarty.

They were really good to CIT. We started putting teams into the Cork Senior Championships and the Kilkenny lads always played.

In 2004, CIT won their first Cork senior hurling game against a Newtownshandrum team that had won the All-Ireland club final that March. John Murphy of Carrickshock was full-back and Michael Fennelly started midfield.

I'm proud of those Kilkenny lads. If we meet, they thank me for what I did even if I feel it should be the other way around. That's the type of people they are. I get huge enjoyment out of seeing their hurling progress after college. If I had 0.1% input into their development, that's very satisfying.

In the Fresher team, Jackie didn't set the world alight. But he stuck at it. He kept himself within the Kilkenny circle and his patience was rewarded. I wasn't surprised with Jackie's development; he always possessed the right character.

Michael Fennelly was a really good hurler for CIT, not a superstar then, but turned up for everything. No excuses. He took his game to another level later on. In my playing days, Frank Cummins was that hurler driving through the middle like a train; Fennelly had the same power-packed style for Kilkenny.

The key was timing. Michael knew when to run at the defence and that's why he got so many scores.

I HAD BEEN embedded in UCC as a player, but my job with CIT was soon all that mattered. The rivalry between the Cork colleges was intense. UCC were too strong in the 90s with Joe Deane, Seánie McGrath and the Enright brothers.

There was a lot of slagging at the time about the Techies playing a bunch of plumbers, plasterers and electricians.

'Lads, great of ye to get the day off work to come hurling in the Mardyke,' was the greeting from a Cork hurling individual one day.

By 2003 we had a brilliant team. Martin Coleman in goal, Brian Murphy, Jackie and Ronan Curran in the backs. John Gardiner midfield. Taggy Fogarty and Fraggy Murphy were our two corner-forwards.

We travelled across to the Mardyke for the Fitzgibbon Cup semi-final that year. We took our preparation up a notch and stayed the previous night in the

Rochestown Park Hotel. I just felt we needed to do it, get all the lads out of their college houses and have them together, focused on the game.

The first Cork hurling strike had happened that previous winter. Bertie Óg Murphy stepped down as Cork manager; I did as selector.

Now Bertie Óg was in charge of UCC and I was with CIT.

It was a hard-hitting game, hell for leather stuff before a massive crowd. Gardiner, Taggy and Garvan McCarthy got the key goals and we won 3-6 to 0-8.

It was a really satisfying win but Waterford IT beat us in the final soon after, so that colours the memory. Their strength was crazy, it was a roll-call of county stars... Paul Curran, JJ Delaney, Ollie Moran, Mick Jacob and Setanta Ó hAilpín.

That day in the Ragg in Tipperary was the closest we got to winning the Fitzgibbon Cup. I really enjoyed coaching in CIT but craved the final win that refused to come. CIT kept knocking on the hurling door but couldn't get through. They did win the Sigerson in football though in 2009, which was fantastic to see; a serious team packed with lads who won All-Ireland medals for Cork.

I BUILT RELATIONSHIPS with CIT, and that helped open doors for me around the country. Two of the most rewarding experiences were in the south-east of Cork... and two clubs. Ballinhassig and Courcey Rovers are about 13 miles apart and both are madly passionate hurling areas. They were in the same divisional area in Cork, in Carrigdhoun, and shared the same relentless ambition to win a county intermediate title and get up to senior.

I loved working with both clubs. The Ballinhassig journey lasted two seasons, 2005 and '06, while I was with Courceys for four years beginning in 2011. In my first year I hit the jackpot with both, and won county finals to help each become senior hurling clubs. In 2006, Ballinhassig also made it to the All-Ireland intermediate final where they lost by a goal.

Different Ballinhassing families, the O'Sullivans, the Colemans and the Dineens, had their kids studying in CIT and playing hurling. That naturally sparked a relationship.

John O'Sullivan, the father of the lads, was chairman of the club and he approached me at the end of 2004 about coming on board. It was just a short spin down the road.

I bumped into Brendan Murphy from Courceys in late 2010 in Páirc Uí Rinn one night at a match. He says, 'What are you doing hurling-wise next year? Sure you might come down, sort us out and try to win a county'. His lads had gone to CIT so I knew him through the college. That's how the conversation started.

The stories of the two clubs mirrored each other in the struggle to make that breakthrough. Ballinhassig came up from junior in 2002, having previously lost two finals. Courceys had been defeated twice in intermediate finals in 2004 and '08.

I didn't have the magic touch to cure any perceived underachievement. But Kilmoyley had taught me that instilling belief and getting the fitness base right were critically important.

I would chat to older people in the clubs to get the details on the prior setbacks. Ignoring those previous losses would have been a huge mistake. *What caused those defeats?*

In my job, I view myself as an interactive lecturer. The Socratic questioning technique is one I would lean on heavily, whereby you give students leading questions that are designed to get them to arrive at a logical conclusion. I would transfer that to players in a team. *Why did they lose previous county finals? Examine that game, tell me where it went wrong.*

Juggling jobs wasn't an issue. I managed Kilmoyley at the same time as Ballinhassig. Then Courceys overlapped with Kerry and Carlow. It's not a problem. You map out the week... one night here and one night there. There's also the chance to constantly learn. If a training session doesn't go well with one crowd, you plan it better the next night.

BOTH HELD THEIR own at senior level. There were a couple of big results against traditional senior sides... Ballinhassig beat Na Piarsaigh in 2006, and Courceys defeated Blackrock in 2012. The step up was a challenge but they were competitive.

I loved my time with both clubs. I still have a relationship with people from there. The success helped most of all in building trust. Winning a county title together forms a bond that won't be broken.

Harry Maguire
Planes, Boats and Rental Cars
Celtic
McDonalds and More McDonalds
Relegation Scrapping
Penos
Lee Cattermole
Land Of My Fathers

★★★

DAVID

WHEN WE LANDED home after the Euros in 2016, I got off in Dublin airport and headed through passport control. Then a BMW came to the runway and spun me over to the Ryanair flight to Portugal that was kept waiting for me.

Cally booked our family holiday that summer, but I hadn't checked the dates. So when we reached the last 16, I knew I'd to miss the start. After we lost to France, the next day we headed to Ireland as the management were keen for everyone to fly home together.

Someone in the FAI organised the logistics of my trip.

Finally, I got on the plane for Portugal and everyone's staring at the entrance, annoyed and wondering who was delaying the start of their holidays. Luckily, enough people had watched the Euros, so there was a cheer when I boarded. The mood improved, I sat down and we headed off. It was a great trip.

After the play-off final and the summer in France, I needed the break.

Especially with the shock I was hit with when we got back. On July 22, Steve Bruce quit as Hull manager. It was a massive personal blow for me. Steve gave me my debut at Sunderland and had brought me to Hull.

I'd describe Steve as my 'father figure' in football, Martin is like my 'father-in-law' and Roy is my 'uncle'. I've been very fortunate to have had long relationships with these three people. We'd been on a successful journey at Hull but now it had ended abruptly and the future looked uncertain.

I knew Steve wasn't happy with matters behind the scenes. Frustration was building up. You could tell by his demeanour. After the final win at Wembley, he wasn't in the heart of the celebrations; he seemed restrained.

I've never spoken to Steve about the problems. The Allam family owned the club. I know Steve had a fantastic relationship with the father, Assem and a difficult relationship with his son Ehab. I think Ehab had raised questions over the money spent on signings that didn't work out. As we headed to the Premier League, Steve was naturally looking to strengthen his squad. Ehab was getting more involved. The atmosphere at the club changed.

Compared to our previous promotion in 2013, when we bounced into the new season full of enthusiasm, now there was so much upheaval.

A sorry state of affairs all round.

HARRY MAGUIRE AND Andy Robertson weren't high profile signings. They arrived on the same day at Hull in July 2014; costing around £6 million between them. Harry had been with Sheffield United in League One. Andy was up in Scotland with Dundee United.

It was a stepping-stone for them to bigger things.

Harry becomes Man United captain, reaches a World Cup semi-final and a Euro final with England. Andy wins the Premier League and Champions League with Liverpool, and helps Scotland reach an international tournament again.

That big time would come later. When they arrived in Hull they still had to make that jump. When Andy signed I knew he had great potential. I felt he could reach a top six club but never saw him going on to be one of the best left-backs in the world. I imagine he's surprised himself a bit. He's taken off like a rocket.

Harry had played against us in the FA Cup semi-final that year. He was the exact same defender then. Now, I feel he has more pressure on his shoulders and is subject to more scrutiny. Any small error is analysed in depth. That comes with the territory when he's playing for a club of that stature. I knew Harry would establish himself in the Premier League but becoming the world's most expensive defender? *Didn't see that coming either.*

Steve Bruce was good in his transfer business. He spotted the right characters. He made sure there were very few toxic influences in the dressing-room that might destabilise the squad.

★★★

JOHN

IN A WAY, I would be mad jealous of my son

David played soccer for 13 years in England and got paid for it. I would have loved the opportunity to play hurling for 13 years and get paid for it. To have sport at the centre of your life, being rewarded financially as a result and to then retire after with the support of a lovely family. I am proud of what David has done

He moved to England in July 2008 and retired from playing there in August 2019. Over that time, I travelled over to be at 85%-to-90% of the games he played. He always knew I would be at his games. I would message to say I wanted one ticket; a handful of times I needed more if I had someone with me. David always sorted that out. Stella often came to games and she made a trip out of it for a few days. Sarah came on other occasions, but I mostly went on my own.

I was happy to make that journey over and back in a day, sticking to my routine. For Saturday 3pm kick-offs, the alarm went off at home at 5am; *get up and go to Cork airport.* I flew most often to Manchester; it was two hours from Hull for home games and within easy reach of plenty of other venues around north-west England for away games.

Pick up the car at the airport I'd hired the previous week and away I went. Premier League games with Hull sometimes meant flights to London and a jump on the Underground to reach a stadium. If I needed more flight options, I would drive to Dublin on a Saturday morning and could be heading over to Leeds-Bradford or Newcastle.

Landing at the stadium meant a chance to park up and catch up on some sleep in the car. Team buses arrived around 2pm and I'd always be there to salute David. Head to the ticket office at every ground, pick up the envelope left for me under his name and then go in to take my seat for the match. I was very organised, constantly checking the match schedules for Sunderland or later Hull, and working out my plans a few weeks in advance.

The success of the trips hinged on how the match went for David. In 2015, Hull were away to Brighton in the Championship. David started poorly in midfield and was taken off after half an hour. The red card in Fratton Park after coming on against Portsmouth in 2010 was another day to forget. But those low moments were rare. His effort levels and application were consistently good, his performances were worth travelling to witness.

Some people thought I was mad. But my presence over there was not to pressurise him or criticise him. I wanted to be there for David. We always met after the match, chatted for a few minutes. I'd ask him did he need anything and then would throw in a couple comments about the game.

SOME DAYS WERE destined never to be forgotten. When Hull were at home to Liverpool in December 2013, I brought a buddy over with me, Colin Harris. He'd hurled for me when I was manager of Kerry and Kilmoyley.

Colin was a big Liverpool fan. He'd picked out that game once Hull got promoted to the Premier League and booked his place as my travel companion.

The stadium was full and rocking from the start that day. We were sitting behind the goal when David scored at the opposite end to put Hull ahead during the second-half. The place erupted and the fans sang all the way to the end of the 3-1 victory. Everyone was on a high after when we went into the players' lounge. Colin was a bit sore seeing Liverpool lose but he soon got over it. David gave him Jordan Henderson's jersey as they'd swapped after the match.

I loved that hour after the game, moving around this place I had special access to, mingling with Premier League stars and the Hull staff for the match post-mortem over a sandwich and cup of tea.

There was a big Irish contingent at Hull and we got to know all their families. Stephen Quinn's brothers were regulars, the same with Paul McShane's family. Robbie Brady's dad and his brother. They weren't all there as much as me but we became a group, often meeting up after the game.

Steve Bruce was a huge figure in David's career, the manager he played under the most. I met Bruce all the time, had many great conversations with him. The meetings tended to be at Hull's training ground; I didn't want to bother him on match day. An absolute gentleman.

Mike Phelan was assistant manager to Bruce for a while and then later became manager. Mike was mad interested in hurling, through his father being a Kilkenny native, and was always keen to meet and chat about that.

In September 2018, David got me involved in a charity match between

Liverpool and Celtic in Glasgow. My role for the day was assistant manager to Jurgen Klopp. A fascinating experience. I was Cork manager at the time and Klopp was really keen to ask questions about hurling. The speed of it, the tactics, the approach to matches. In return I got an insight into his work as a manager. It was brilliant, a lot of sportspeople are really genuine.

The high-profile characters in English soccer command the attention but there is a whole group of people fuelling the engine that drives the club. The staff at Hull were wonderful; the security guys dotted around the stadium on match day were so sound to deal with. They reminded me of the late Tommy Lynch, who was stadium caretaker of Páirc Uí Chaoimh and Páirc Uí Rinn for many years.

These are the people in the soul of a sports club or team who are hugely important to the players. The people in those roles at Hull and Sunderland were really important figures in David's life.

★★★

DAVID

IN THE SUMMER of 2014 a new wave of good lads came in. Michael Dawson, who had captained Spurs, and Robert Snodgrass. On deadline day the Uruguayan striker Abel Hernández and Senegalese midfielder Mo Diamé joined. Then we'd Harry and Andy.

I couldn't speak highly enough of Michael. He is up there with John O'Shea, Seamus Coleman and Jordan Henderson in terms of leaders I have encountered in my career. A breath of fresh air, an upbeat Yorkshire lad who had time for everyone. Snodgrass was a cheeky fella, a world-class moaner about everything but had a great personality. He fitted right into our squad.

Under Steve Bruce I was very settled at Hull, as I regularly played. There was one period later that some talk emerged of me going to Celtic. Nothing ever materialised. If it had become a concrete offer, I would have liked to give it a go.

I always had that affection for Celtic growing up. Got Larsson on the back of my first jersey, loved the team that he was the star of, and when I moved to England I'd regularly go up to Glasgow for matches with one of my mates. It was a good spin from Hull, over four hours, but I went to all the Champions League home games in 2012. The best was the night Tony Watt scored the famous goal to beat Barcelona. That stadium atmosphere would have been amazing to play in.

★★★

JOHN

THE TRAVEL WASN'T all glamour. I'll never forget a midweek night in 2008 in Morecambe, a Lancashire town on the west coast of England.

Sunderland were playing a reserve match against Everton, not long after David had signed for the club. Back then, the best way for me to travel over was on the boat from Dublin to Holyhead, something I often later did for midweek games.

When I landed that day, David rang to say the venue for the game had been changed from the Liverpool area. The only issue was they didn't know where it had been switched to. I was talking away to him and next thing I see the lights flashing behind me; the police pull me over on the motorway. I pleaded my case.

'I'm really sorry, but it's an emergency.'

'What's the emergency?'

'My son is playing a match for Sunderland and he's ringing, trying to tell me where it has been changed. Look, just let me off this time… I won't be on the phone again.'

'Well won't you have to be on phone when he rings to say where the match is on?' We got a good laugh out of that but I was let off, promising to pull in to take the call when David rang. Eventually the game was fixed for Morecambe, a three-hour drive north from Holyhead. I made it with five minutes to spare before kick-off to be greeted by a mixture of snow and rain blowing across the pitch.

Reserve matches started at 7pm; David would emerge out after by 9pm and, after a quick chat, I'd to dash back to make the boat sailing at half two in the morning. There was a McDonalds in North Wales which was my frequent pitstop; my goal always was to get there before closing time of 11pm to grab some dinner.

Travelling on winter nights meant you were at the mercy of the weather, waiting for the road closures that would send you off on a tour. I bought a Sat

Nav, my trusted companion for those journeys that helped me out when heading down small roads in Wales, keeping one eye on the clock and trying to make the boat home.

★★★

DAVID

WHEN YOU'RE IN a relegation scrap, you can't legislate for what other teams will do. Leicester were bottom at the start of April 2015 with just four wins all season, while we were 15th.

Then Leicester won seven of their last nine games, going on this amazing run to survive. We played a game less and only won twice in the same period.

Leicester caught everyone by surprise. Twelve months on they won the title. *Hard to get your head around that.* The game which cost us was the third last one, a 1-0 defeat to Burnley when Danny Ings scored. Our schedule that May saw us play Arsenal, Spurs and Man United. All top five teams. Burnley was the match to target for a win. They were fighting for their lives as well.

After that game, we knew we were in trouble.

The team pulled together that year and we fought until the end. When the threat of relegation grows, you feel the tension around a club increase. Training gets more intense. People are a bit edgier in the dressing-room. You have to live with that pressure and can't crumble. My form was hit-and-miss that year. Everyone had to look closely at themselves.

We needed to beat Man United on the last day, but Newcastle's win over West Ham took it out of our hands. Looking around the stadium after the final whistle was a horrible feeling. Everyone had taken a punch to the gut. Life in the Premier League was over. Back to the Championship and starting all over again.

Relegation has consequences.

Players automatically lose between 40% and 50% of their wages. It's unsustainable to remain at Premier League rates, even if the parachute payments soften the landing a little.There's cutbacks elsewhere in the club. As you get older you start to realise performances on the pitch will influence whether someone else keeps their job. Not just the manager and coaches, but the security team, the cleaners, the staff in the kitchen, all those people. If there are three laundry ladies working, that might be cut to two with relegation. You've cost that lady her job. I cared about that fact, others didn't.

It depends on the level you're invested in the club. A lot of lads kept their distance; all strictly business. At Hull I had more affection for the place, interacted with these people every day and that responsibility did get on top of me at times. My family got close to people at the club. After I retired, I would still go to games and could have 20 or 30 people coming up to me to ask after dad, and my wife and my kids.

It had been a long season. Despite losing the cup final, we still had the reward of European football as Arsenal had qualified for the Champions League. Instead of pre-season friendlies to feel our way back into action, we had Europa League qualifiers. I wasn't jaded, but didn't feel as fresh as I'd have liked.

We got past Trenčín from Slovakia in late-July; a 0-0 draw over there in a city called Žilina and then won 2-1 back in Hull. We couldn't get past the play-off to reach the group stage though. Lokeren from Belgium beat us on the away goals rule; Robbie Brady scored twice in a 2-1 home win but we missed chances for the third. Another month on, and we'd have won but we just weren't at the proper pace of the game.

Pre-season is critical in getting yourself up to speed. Any injury at that time means you're playing catch up. I missed a lot of those in my career. In 2014 I hurt my back and it took until early December for my first league start of the season when we played Everton. That was the beginning of 14 starts in-a-row in the league. I had cemented my place again.

Frustration always sets in when you're not playing regularly. The only time I accepted it was if the team was winning; you have to hold your hand up in that situation and respect what your teammates are doing.

We also met Arsenal in the FA Cup the following year, in the third round in 2015, and lost 2-0; And in 2016 we met them again and took them to a fifth round replay. That was three years in-a-row against The Gunners. In 2016, we also reached the quarter-finals of the League Cup before losing to Man City – in the previous round, I scored the last goal in a shoot-out to beat Leicester after I got subbed on in the 110th minute with penalties in mind.

I always enjoyed taking penalties; from underage days when dad would push me to take them to get on the scoresheet, to later assuming that responsibility for Hull. Penalties are an exercise in psychology. Placing the ball is important... don't have it elevated, set it properly. Have your mind blank.

Compose yourself. *Where am I hitting it?* Always pick a side and never change your mind. Wait for the referee's whistle... and strike.

I didn't overthink them but started to practice more when I became Hull's regular taker in 2017-18. I'd get one of the young goalkeepers the day before in training, hit five penalties and he'd get £20 for everyone he saved. That incentive ensured his focus.

★★★

JOHN

I FELT A savage pride at watching David play at Hull in a period where the club was really progressing. Over time, he became part of the fabric of the club and I could see the fans responding to that. Hull was where I got to know people best, as invariably I'd be sitting in the same section, week after week.

There was a game at Anfield when a Hull fan roared at him from the first minute to last. I never got involved in those situations. *Stay restrained, don't bite back.* The minute you open your mouth, the Irish accent is a giveaway and they'll make the family connection. It's not going to be a positive outcome. There were times when Stella and Sarah were with me; they got offended and found it harder to take.

But it drove me harder to do everything in my power to make sure David settled in England to his new way of life. It helped that David was driven. When he joined Sunderland, I told him that he should thank Roy for bringing him to England. He did, but Roy didn't want to receive any gratitude.

'I did nothing. You brought yourself to England. Now it's up to you to stay here.'

★★★

DAVID

WHEN RETURNING TO play any former club, there is an element of trying to prove a point. I had loved my time at Sunderland, only wishing I could have played more but for injuries. That Christmas in 2014 we headed to the Stadium of Light. A rare good day with our first win in 10 games; we conceded after 30 seconds but bounced back for a 3-1 victory.

Heading back to an old ground like the Stadium of Light, there's some polite applause when your name is called out before and then you get pelters all game. I lived by the sword when I played Sunderland; had constant run-ins with Lee Cattermole. We were both experts at winding each other up. Though Bruce used to warn me before games not to get dragged into a personal battle.

One time we played them, and I bumped into Cattermole when out that night. He had a go off me on the stairs of a nightclub; wasn't happy with some of the challenges that day. Once I crossed the white line, I meant business, it was nothing personal. I enjoyed those contests with Cattermole. Maybe he didn't expect it to get that heated. We'd got on well together at Sunderland, spent time together like going for a round of golf. We were similar characters in our style of play. Whatever ill-feeling existed was gone soon enough.

★★★

JOHN

LATER, THE TRAVEL was not just over to England. We were on the international stage, heading to Dublin and all over Europe as David started to nail down a place in the Ireland squad.

I still get goosebumps watching replays of the John O'Shea goal against Germany in 2014. Last kick of the game on his 100th cap to secure a draw and David had played the whole match after filling a gap at right-back. It was amazing to get your head around it.

The layout of the stadium at Gelsenkirchen had the dressing-rooms locked away. I rang him and he came back out onto the pitch to see myself and Stella up in the stand. We drove to Amsterdam after and were in a hotel for a few hours before the next morning's flight. I was wired with adrenaline after the game, and sat in the room at 3am with a can of Heineken to toast the result.

Cardiff in October 2017 was better again. That is my highlight of David's career. Without question. I didn't lack company that Monday night. Stella, Sarah and her partner Eugene were all on the flight over. David was captain of his country and a World Cup play-off spot was on the line. No one was going to miss it.

There was a huge sense of anticipation in the city during the day. Fans always have some nerves on match day but when your son is playing, there's that extra emotion. Over the years I learned to control that, not to get anxious and trusted that David was capable of performing.

I used to get asked what was my priority... *the team to win or David to play well?* I always said to get the win first and then we could rate his display. A team victory would always help cushion a personal blow, we both agreed on that. Even when he did his cruciate for the second time, we took consolation from Sunderland's 1-0 win that night.

The Cardiff City stadium was packed by kick-off. When they belted out the Welsh national anthem, *Land Of My Fathers* beforehand, the level of noise whipped up was absolutely frightening. The hairs were standing on the back of my neck as I looked around the stadium and I could feel this raw desperation in the air with everybody wanting so badly to go to Russia the following summer.

When James McClean scored in the second-half, we nearly lost our lives. Total bedlam. We were sitting in the middle, near the tunnel where the players come out. All the families of the Irish players were together, that was always the way. These were the people you celebrated and commiserated with; James' family were right in front of us, it was such a moment of pure joy for them.

Shane Long's mother was always there; the same for her when he scored against Germany in 2015. When Robbie Brady hit the winner against Italy in Euro 2016 in Lille, his dad Shay was roaring up at me after... 'That's my son there, John!'

We were all the same. Parents incredibly proud to see our children representing their country. South-East Radio in Wexford rang early the next morning; Alan

Corcoran had me on for a half hour as the proud father providing the eyewitness account from Ireland's win over Wales. A night I will never forget.

★★★

DAVID

EVERYONE WHO LINES out in the Premier League is a talented player.

Then there are levels which you discover as you play the best. I loved playing against the top six teams, to see these football icons up close. When I scored against Man United, Wayne Rooney hit this brilliant volley to draw the game.

Same when we beat Liverpool; Steven Gerrard tucked away a free-kick to level it. These players can change games in a matter of seconds with a moment of magic. David Silva was a genius for Man City in midfield. You just couldn't get near him. He would speed the play up or slow it down when he wanted... take two, three touches to pass the ball... suddenly switch to one-touch passes.

You feel fine and think you have Silva pinned down. Then he turns the heat up and the ball is flying around, or he makes a run and is gone out of reach. A game has accelerated out of your control. It's only when you're on the pitch playing against these players that you can understand that sense of powerlessness.

I scored against Silva once, when we were away to Man City in 2015. I gambled in following in an attack and after a Gastón Ramírez shot hit the post, I was there to fire in the rebound. It was great to go ahead, but then it was heartbreaking to see James Milner score a free-kick in the last minute to draw.

Still, a nice stat to complete the big three – Liverpool, Man United and Man City, and remember scoring against each of them in the league.

★★★

JOHN

THERE WERE TIMES I worried about David. Any parent, when their child moves abroad, you hope they'll get on okay. If they're a professional soccer player who destroys his knee twice, that concern is increased.

In those moments it was a comfort for us back in Cork to know there were people looking out for David in Sunderland.

Before the Euros started in 2021, Liverpool released a video on social media to commemorate Jordan Henderson's decade at the club. His dad Brian was talking about his son's career. That's the Brian Henderson I knew from the start, a terrific person, very good in looking out for people.

He gave David great help when he was making his way at Sunderland, always on the end of the phone if we needed him. If ever I wasn't sure how he was doing, I could ask Brian to check up on him. He'd come back to say they'd met up or all gone for dinner and everything was fine. Brian was a really genuine person.

Jordan's friends pitched in. Johnny Small was David's chauffeur, the staff at the Toby pub nearby kept him fed. He's blessed with the friends he's had; still close to that Sunderland crew and it's the same when he comes back to Cork. I still see him knocking around with the lads he grew up with.

I always believed he would recover from the injuries. I just wanted us to get a break, that's what I prayed for; a clear run for David where he was fit and could show everyone how he could perform.

In May 2014, we reached the type of day I'd dreamed about.

I grew up in an era when the FA Cup final was a huge sporting event, along with the Grand National and All-Ireland finals; those were the main occasions where we huddled around the TV in our home in Wexford.

The 1965 final is still clear in my mind when Liverpool beat Leeds United 2-1. Almost half a century later, I watched my son walk out from the Wembley tunnel to play in a game of that importance. The stadium was packed and the place felt alive. It was one of the best moments of my life.

★★★

DAVID

IN THE SUMMER of 2015, the hangover from relegation lingered. There was uncertainty, people got restless and the transfers rolled out. Chester and Jelavić left. The Irish crew were gone… Robbie, Paul and Quinny all moving.

Robbie got a route back to the Premier League with Norwich. After a couple of years at the top, adjusting to the Championship was hard. New faces came in… Sam Clucas, Moses Odubajo and Shaun Maloney played a lot. Everyone had to ask themselves the question… *Am I going to sulk or get promoted again?*

Amidst all that change, we turned it around. The lowest we were in the table that year was 7th; we were top in November, and again in February. The strong core of McGregor, Curtis, Huddlestone, Livermore, Dawson and Snodgrass remained. Abel Hernández was a goal-machine; he scored 22 that season. Andy Robertson nailed down the left-back spot, Harry Maguire came strong.

The start was positive. We went 11 games unbeaten for a time after September, hitting our stride with five wins in-a-row; I scored against Ipswich and Birmingham. We should really have won the Championship but just hit a really bad patch around March, winning once in eight games. That pushed us back from the automatic spots. We pumped both Burnley and Middlesbrough 3-0 before 2015 had ended, but they finished stronger to be in the top two.

In April, I was out with an injured hamstring and we were struggling. Steve Bruce called me into his office and asked would I play? I wasn't totally right but said I was good to go. I knew the risk and accepted it. I captained the teams in wins over Wolves and Reading but made my hamstring 10 times worse. The more I ran against Reading, the more I could feel it ripping.

Championship football can be a slog… 46 games in a season, not factoring in cup competitions. We had to go the extra mile with the play-offs. Midweek matches pile up… play Saturday, recover Sunday, light training Monday… play again Tuesday and start getting yourself right for the weekend again.

THERE WERE FOUR of us – Hull, Brighton, Derby and Sheffield Wednesday – in the play-offs and only one was going into the summer celebrating. Injury hit me at the worst time, I missed the last four games and the semi-final first-leg.

I watched in the stand as we beat Derby 3-0 at Pride Park. We blew them away. Hernández with the opener, then an own goal, and Robertson scored the third in the 98th minute. The next few days I was fighting to get fit and came on at home for the second-leg. Different story. Derby made a flying start and scored twice before half-time. I came on in the 52nd minute and we had to grind them down to go through.

Play-offs are mad games, there's this 100 miles an hour frenzy to them. The fans are all up for it, drama is guaranteed and previous form seems irrelevant. The final is termed the richest game in football; the prize of the Premier League means there's no escaping the importance.

Dad wasn't there, one of the few games he'd missed.

I didn't start; the timing of the injury was a killer and I couldn't get back into the team. I was not happy but had to accept it. After 30 minutes I got told to warm up. On four different occasions it looked like I was coming on for Diamé. Then, midway through the second-half, Diamé cracks one into the top corner. A wonder goal. Eventually I got on with five minutes to go. We won 1-0.

Afterwards I felt a bit detached from the celebrations, it was hard to enjoy it properly. Maybe it's selfish but I didn't feel I'd made a significant contribution. Part of my mood was due to the upcoming Euros and the worry Martin wouldn't pick me in the squad if I hadn't played recently for Hull.

That game was on a Saturday evening. Later we went back to the team hotel for the party, Cally and my buddies were all there. I did really enjoy that night. We'd won at Wembley and I'd got to walk up those steps to get my hands on a trophy.

Next morning, I flew over to Cork to meet up with the Ireland squad for a friendly against Belarus. It was a week of defining moments.

Havana Browns

Subway

Kelogs and Steven Gerrard

‘Sunderland ‘Til I Die’

Joyce Rome

Paulo de Silva and Cristian Riveros

Hungover on the Bench

★★★

DAVID

A FEW YEARS back I had some time off and made a quick trip home to Cork.

One of the nights I ended up out on the beer with the lads. We'd a good time and enjoyed ourselves. When you leave Havana Browns nightclub in the city centre, you come out to an alley.

I was full to the brim that night as I headed out the door, and went in the search of food.

There was a Subway open. *Perfect.*

Got my food, then sat down on the path on the side of the road to eat it. Normal enough late night scene of a lad swaying side to side but causing no one any harm.

A few young lads came over hassling me. I just tried to get rid of them. Someone took out their phone and recorded a video.

The problem was they put it somewhere the whole world could see. It was viewed over 100,000 times on Facebook. Nothing out of the ordinary; the footage just showed *David* after he's had a few too many.

But football meant I had a name and reputation and before all that, I had a family. My parents saw it; my mother got upset. The kid thought he was having a laugh throwing that video up on the internet but didn't realise the repercussions. He got in touch after to apologise and took the video down.

The damage was done though. It was too late.

FOOTBALL HAS OPENED doors for me to meet people I admired that I wouldn't otherwise come into contact with.

Jordan is a very private person, not too close with too many footballers. Steven Gerrard knew I was good mates with him, so put two and two together. I got accepted by association and we'd chat if I was at Liverpool's training ground with Jordan. It pains me as a Celtic fan that he's with Rangers now but I want to see him do well and take over Liverpool in the future. I'd speak to him every now and again.

He invited me over to play in a golf day he runs in Portugal at the Laranjal Course in Quinta do Lago. You get opportunities like that due to a *level of fame*, but I knew I wasn't a household name and at times got reminded of it.

Kelogs came with me for that trip; we got collected at the airport and brought to the complex of nice apartments where we were staying. We were eager to get a feel for the course, so went to play a few holes the day before and met a few people.

Max Rushden was there; he's a talkSPORT presenter and hosts *The Football Weekly* podcast, and introduced himself.

'Hi I'm Max. What's your name?'

'I'm David.'

'Oh, so what do you do?'

'I play football.'

'I should probably know that yeah. Who do you play for?'

'Hull and Ireland.'

'Yeah… clearly I'm not very good at my job!'

We started laughing about it. I heard him later joke I wasn't in kit and it was pre the Pardew headbutt, an incident which did make me known. Max hasn't forgotten me since anyway, so that's a good thing.

AS I GREW older, I felt I needed to be more careful in public. I was fully aware that I was in a position of privilege with the job and lifestyle I had but at times found it difficult when people didn't respect privacy and often felt they were entitled to something.

There are flashpoints, mainly when you're out at night and drink is added to the equation. Fellas sticking phones in your face trying to take photos. When I was home, I wanted to just catch up with my friends since school. Talking non-stop to strangers about the form of Man United or Liverpool was not high on my agenda. Fellas might have a pop off me if I didn't engage in full-blown conversation at 1am. To them you're rude and ignorant, but I wondered how often they walked up to random people they don't know in other situations and expected them to talk.

I always felt it reasonable to prioritise my friends on a night out. The money that a Premier League footballer earns will naturally make you a target.

A fella approached me one night in a bar in Cork.

'You're a f****ng asshole the way you go on, coming home here and buying loads of drinks.'

I painted a picture for him. *Only see these lads a few times a year... fortunate to have a good salary. Why not share that... take them all out for a night?*

Wouldn't you do the same for your friends... if you could?

'Ah yeah. I'm sorry Dave. You're actually alright, like.'

It didn't always work out as peacefully as that. Havana Browns was our usual spot. Paul Montgomery owned it; then you had the lads... Skinner, Sully and James Dullea running it. The boys were great in looking after us.

My mates used to save me in their phones as 'queue jumper'. We were well looked after and I met so many great people over the years. Back in your hometown and people genuinely wishing you well, congratulating you on a latest win, just treating me with respect. I really appreciated that.

But, unfortunately, the other side stays with you more.

So you learn to take yourself out of those situations. I got more mature and started going out less. If I was heading out in Cork, we had a clear plan in place for the night. The Havanas staff would be sound in letting us stay behind for 15 minutes after they closed up, so we weren't coming out early on a Sunday morning when Cork city is pouring onto the streets from the bars and clubs.

Then we'd run out, jump straight into a taxi and go home.

I got older and wiser and stayed out of trouble.

FANS ARE THE lifeblood of football clubs.

I understood that straight away in Sunderland and Hull. You play first-team in those areas and you're an important figure in their eyes. You will get stopped on the street. I'd always try to make time for people; catch me in a good mood and I could talk away for an hour.

Other situations were less ideal but you had to tolerate them. A Hull City fan in the park one day wanted a photo as I was trying to keep an eye on the kids running in the playground. He wasn't happy when I asked him to wait a few minutes, until Cally came to watch Alanna and Brody. But he did calm down; we took the photo and chatted away about Hull's form.

Hull is a big rugby league town so that competes for the sporting affections. In Sunderland there is only one show in town.

In recent years the *Sunderland 'Til I Die* documentary on Netflix has given people an insight into the area; the level of passion amongst the fans had hit me years before. My red card against Porstmouth in February 2010 had caused a wave of abuse but then a few weeks later I was getting hailed for playing well against Man City. I realised in their eyes, if you win you're right and if you lose you're wrong.

When you sign for a club like Sunderland, you have to buy into that. You go to Asda to do a food shop, and you'll have people coming up to you, questioning what you're buying.

My parents came over once and we went all out for a dinner. A fella came over and sat down unannounced at our table to talk about a recent game and point out where I'd gone wrong in my performance. They don't care if you think they're intruding. They work Monday to Friday to go and support Sunderland at the weekend.

That's what matters. It's almost Sunderland first and then your family, in that order. I loved that attitude.

I played at a positive time for Sunderland when they were in the Premier League. Got on well with the fans because I wasn't a show-pony type player, I got stuck in and worked hard. That is the minimum standard the fans demand.

Joyce Rome is one of the nicest people I've ever met in my life, the club chef that was one of the breakout stars of the Netflix series. Viewers warmed to her; she was genuine in front of the cameras with the level of emotion she invested in the club. When I played for Sunderland she was exactly that way, hurting when we lost... so happy when we won. She's been there a long time, a mother figure to players. If anyone needed anything food-wise, they got it; she would travel to all the away games on the team bus and look after us.

The club staff make these places special. If I go back to Hull games since I retired, the same security people are there to look after me and ask after my family. The same at Sunderland. They are the soul of a football club.

The documentary showed certain players didn't care about that. Sunderland signed some wrong characters, and others threw in the towel. It is the definition of a big club with the fanbase and stadium. It's heart-breaking to have seen them slip down through divisions.

I WAS FORTUNATE I settled and integrated so well into the areas when I played football. For others it was more difficult. At the 2010 World Cup, Paraguay had an excellent tournament, losing a quarter-final to eventual winners Spain.

Paulo da Silva already played for us, a defender who'd joined in 2009, and then the club signed another Paraguayan after that tournament in midfielder Cristian Riveros. He had been sensational that summer in South Africa but joining us was a nightmare for him. The style of football, the north-east weather and the language barrier all affected him. You head into training, it's freezing cold, you don't understand what lads are saying in the changing room and you can't get your football going on the pitch. It was a real struggle.

I wondered at the time, how hard would I have found it if I had to move to Russia or somewhere? The move to England is a challenge but more comfortable for Irish lads like me. It was no surprise in January 2011 when Paulo had gone to Spain and then Cristian moved to Turkey in June.

It's an issue with a lot of foreign players coming to England; they want the big city move. Their families can drive that, so life will be easier off the pitch. London, Manchester, Liverpool... these places are all attractive.

I played up north in Sunderland and Hull. London is a diverse place, but in Sunderland you've got mad Mackems everywhere. You have to immerse yourself in that atmosphere. I even saw some English players from down south struggling when they moved up.

You will help dictate the mood of a community. Walk down a street in London and you can step outside your life as a footballer, but not up here.

I HAD A good bond with Sunderland fans, but got a huge break in October 2011. The relationship could easily have been soured in a big way.

That summer I was in recovery mode from my second cruciate. My comeback was on the first of October, a last minute sub in a 2-2 draw with West Brom. I sat out the next few games and then the month ended at home to Aston Villa.

Trained on the Friday as usual and was told to be in Saturday morning for a light session. Frazier Campbell was in the same boat, as we were doing rehab on our knees together. He suggested we should mark the end of the week, head to Jesmond in Newcastle and have a few drinks. *Great shout.*

We'd do recovery in the morning, grab lunch and watch the match.

The plan was to head home about six that Friday. By 11pm we were both still out and well on our way. Eventually, jumped in a taxi and I crashed in Frazier's house. We'd often do that, make sure we were together if we were going to be late for training the next morning.

We woke up on the Saturday and felt rough but got through the training work, had food and rocked down to the stadium. Went to the match day sponsors event, usual meet and greet with people.

Then Nadia who was running the event for the club, came up to me.

'David, you're wanted downstairs by the manager.'

My mind was racing as I went down

'Get your gear on... you're involved today!'

I sat in the changing room with all these fears running through my head. My preparation consisted of a day on the beer, a training session that morning and a full dinner an hour before. I was in no fit state to play.

Phil Bardsley was next to me and clocked straight away I'd been out. Soon other players did too.

The saving grace was being on the bench, surely just there to make up the numbers. Never coming on. But in the second-half, the shout came to warm up and in the 81st minute, I'm brought on.

Running onto the pitch, I was petrified how it was going to go. Shay Given took a goal-kick for Villa. Our back four were playing high but then retreated and roared at the midfield.

'DROP... DROP!'

I heard the instructions, jogged back... and tripped over my own feet... left sprawled on the pitch.

Richard Dunne put Villa up 2-1 a few minutes later but Stéphane Sessègnon saved the day with an 89th minute header for the draw. I'd survived.

There was just one problem. On the Friday night I'd met a Sunderland season ticket holder in the pub; a lovely fella and we chatted away. Obviously he's at the game on the Saturday and sees me playing near the end.

He got in touch with the club to complain about me being on the drink. *Perfectly fair.* Monday morning, I report for training and get summoned straight to Steve Bruce's office.

A long walk upstairs. *Could be game over here, Dave.*

You'll do well to explain your way out of this one.

The beauty of Steve Bruce's management was that he could draw on his playing experiences. He told me a story about playing for Man United, when he was out for a few games as he was due an operation. He went wine-tasting with his wife one day and ended up having a lash of pints after. Turned up at the match and there was a defender ruled out late on, so Bruce was thrown in to start.

'But don't you ever go drinking the night before a game again… even if you are injured!'

It was just a freak incident. I had genuinely been told I wouldn't be in the first-team, then I got dragged in last minute and end up playing a Premier League match hungover. No one ripped into me, they appreciated the confusion. But it was only okay because I hadn't made some mistake that cost the team a goal and a result.

I was a lucky lad.

Fired!

Wexford Player Power

Dual Players

Darren Stamp

Tommy, JJ, Hogan and Hickey

★★★

JOHN

THERE ARE TWO types of managers in sport... those that have been fired and those that are going to be fired.

You should never be deluded into thinking everyone wants you to stay in charge or wanted you appointed in the first place. Sometimes there's no point in codding yourself that you've left on your own terms.

And in October 2008 there was no mistake about how I left as Wexford senior hurling manager.

I was fired.

AFTER THE 2008 championship ended, I wanted to start preparing for '09 straight away, the third and last year of my term. We met the Wexford players in Gorey on the Friday week after losing the All-Ireland quarter-final to Waterford. It was a review of the season with different topics raised. Several players felt our fitness had dropped; the loss of Padraig Murphy as trainer that year was raised. The County Board wasn't happy with team costs after 2007 and looked for cuts. As much as I desperately wanted to keep Padraig, I wasn't able to.

I still felt the meeting was positive.

If the players thought I had shortcomings as a manager, I was happy to discuss them in that setting. Afterwards, I started planning. Looked for a new hurling coach. Contacted Niall Moyna in DCU to recommend a strength and conditioning coach. Sorted an improvement in our stats and analysis. Lined up people to come on board. Then the Wexford chairman Ger Doyle rang in early October. He said we needed to talk and pushed to meet in person. We arranged to go to the Park Hotel in Dungarvan, with the secretary Margaret Doyle also there.

There wasn't huge rapport between myself and Ger. The previous chairman Seán Quirke had appointed me; we'd got on well, but he was gone a few weeks after I took over. I didn't have any sense of impending trouble when I drove to Dungarvan that Tuesday morning. But when I walked into the hotel, Ger got straight to it. They had met four players representing the squad, and they weren't happy with me staying on as manager

I was stunned. *Where was this coming from?* The group had met the previous week and that hadn't been raised. The problems that were identified, I was in the process of addressing. Ger was adamant that I wasn't wanted.

'That's totally wrong!' I replied.

'Not one of them stood up in the room in Gorey and said that,' I told him.

He didn't identify the four players. But subsequently they were happy to stand up... David O'Connor, Diarmuid Lyng, Rory Jacob and Eoin Quigley.

I wanted to go to Wexford to meet the players. If someone had a problem with me, don't let the issue fester and let's sort it. But I was fighting a losing battle.

I haven't spoken to three of them since and will not. I felt annoyed at not being told in person by the players that they weren't satisfied. *Could I have done things better over the two years?* Of course, that goes for every job.

ON THE SUNDAY night of the 2006 All-Ireland quarter-final weekend, I headed up to the pub in Garryduff in Cork. The usual crew having a few pints... Seán Cullinane, Padraig O'Sullivan, Paddy Hayes... talking about the weekend's hurling. When *The Sunday Game* highlights came on, the bar-stool analysis was scathing. A weekend when Cork won and Wexford lost wasn't going to pass without comment.

'John, why don't you go back down there and do something about Wexford hurling?' An off-the-cuff remark but it planted a seed in my mind. I've lived in Cork for over 40 years but my desire to see Wexford win has never waned.

Seamus Murphy had stepped down as manager, so I decided to throw my hat in the ring. I rang the Wexford secretary Mick Kinsella about it. Some would view that as a blunt approach but I figured I'd nothing to lose. He told me to send them down a plan as a candidate. I emailed a three-page document with my background, my analysis of Wexford and my future strategy.

Mick got back to me about coming down for an interview with the five-man committee. Both sides had questions but I felt it went really well, and a few days later the offer came to become the new Wexford manager. By October I was in.

Heading to Wexford, the place where I grew up, felt like a personal homecoming.

IT WAS 10 years since Liam Griffin's team had won the All-Ireland. In 2006, Wexford had been blown away by Kilkenny and Clare. They were struggling.

I was an outsider and needed to make an impression on the players. Willie Sunderland from Oulart and Nick Byrne from Bunclody joined as selectors; they knew the club scene really well. Nick organised everything; we went on a four-day training camp to St Helen's Bay early on and he mapped the whole thing out to perfection.

I researched the players in depth, not just those who'd hurled in 2006 but those on the outside. Travelled all over Wexford to see games, not just the traditional senior clubs, but looked at junior and intermediate to unearth talent. I packed as much in as I could, doing four games one day... two in Curracloe... two in Cushenstown.

After we picked the panel, we'd a meeting and a meal in Griffin's Ferrycarrig Hotel; presented the gear to the players after. We wanted a gathering to hammer home the point this was a clean slate, but the bar had to be raised.

Padraig Murphy from Castlebridge was recommended as fitness trainer. He presented the RTÉ show *The Health Squad*, had been an Irish kickboxer and trained the Wexford under-21s.

Padraig was absolutely brilliant. He tidied up the gym at Wexford Park and got in new equipment. We trained anywhere with floodlights... Cranford, Bunclody, St Patrick's Park in Enniscorthy. Then to the beach in Curracloe on Sunday mornings at 9am, where Padraig would test the lads on punishing five-mile runs and order them all to jump into the sea after.

He was really good at the individual needs of players, at a time when more inter-county hurlers were employed in construction. Darren Stamp's work was in laying concrete, he was strong as a horse. A great committed character.

'Darren, I want you in at six on Thursday for training.'

'Listen, I've a load of concrete coming in at five that needs to be levelled, so leave me alone now until I get that done.'

Finding the balance was difficult but Padraig managed it. He got on brilliantly with the players and created an elite environment. Then I lost him after the first year. A sickener. We were back to square one.

IN THE TWO years with Wexford, one theme jumps out… facing the Kilkenny machine that we just could not stop.

We reached the 2007 league semi-final after a good quarter-final win over Ger Loughnane's Galway. The team was resilient, as we had crashed by 11 points to Waterford on the first day out. That game was an eye-opener.

There were a lot of question marks then; my aim to resurrect Wexford hurling looked to be in bother after day one. But we redoubled our efforts and got to that semi-final. Then we collided with Kilkenny. Henry Shefflin wasn't available but they still scored 2-22 and beat us by 15 points.

The start of an established pattern. In 2007 they beat us in the Leinster final 2-24 to 1-12, and the All-Ireland semi-final 0-23 to 1-10. In 2008 we lost 0-23 to 1-5 in the league, and 5-21 to 0-17 in the Leinster final. The only time we got close was the 2007 Walsh Cup final, but Kilkenny still won by six.

That was my introduction as a sideline eyewitness, viewing what Brian Cody had built. Try to stop Tommy Walsh in defence, then JJ Delaney turns up. Tackle a forward line where Henry Shefflin, Eoin Larkin and Eddie Brennan are on fire. Then brace yourself for the firepower coming off the bench. A collection of some of the best hurlers ever to play the game, who all happened to be in the same dressing-room.

It was our misfortune to constantly run into them. Our best win came against Tipperary in 2007, but the reward was Kilkenny in the All-Ireland semi-final. *No escape.* I always felt we could match them; you have to adopt that frame of mind. But now, there is an acceptance that Kilkenny's brilliance created a gap at that time that we were never going to close.

At half-time in the 2008 Leinster final I felt we were in with a right chance at only two points down. Simple message in the dressing-room… *keep this game tight for the second half and hang in there.*

But with Kilkenny, there was always a sense of danger lurking around the corner. A row broke out early in the second-half; that got their temper going and they hit us with 2-3 in five minutes. *Game over, and our heads left spinning.*

On the sideline, you feel you've lost control as a manager. Your mind is racing for solutions to the problems you see but Kilkenny always had the ability to kill a team in a short space of time. We sought to remain positive but it's a serious challenge to convince a group of players that they can beat a team, when the evidence is piling up to say different.

Nobody can convince me that they weren't the greatest team of all time. In that period, there was nothing to match them in athleticism, strength and hurling. They could play the game whatever way they wanted. Tommy and JJ epitomised their greatness. Shefflin and the other forwards got all the acclaim, but Kilkenny hurling was based on sheer guts and heart; it was the lads in the trenches like Tommy, JJ, Brian Hogan and Noel Hickey who made them so hard to wear down.

Their hunger to win would make you think they had no medals between the lot of them. The moment a game finished, they were looking at what was next.

FOR THOSE GAMES, I would leave Cork on a Sunday at 6am, meet the team at the Ferrycarrig Hotel and get the bus to Croke Park. I always felt it was important to travel with the players. Afterwards, it was a quiet bus journey back to Wexford and then a long drive home after that disappointment.

Wake up on the Monday morning, turn on RTÉ Radio and the news would greet you of Wexford taking another hammering from Kilkenny. That word would drive me mad. *Hammered.* Everyone else seemed to be beaten by Kilkenny. But Wexford were... *hammered.* Walking around Cork after losing heavily and people asking what was I doing at all with those lads down in Wexford?

Brian Cody drives the whole Kilkenny operation brilliantly.

I've the height of respect for what he's done. On match days he was always very courteous; that continued when I was Cork manager and Kilkenny beat us in my last game in charge. Your spirits could have sunk low by full-time but Cody wasn't going to be jumping around in celebration to rub your face in it. A handshake, a quiet word and he was off thinking of the next challenge.

I don't think Mick Dempsey got enough credit for his work as trainer. He often rang me in CIT when we had Kilkenny players like Fennelly, Taggy and Jackie, and would ask did I mind if they worked on fitness programmes he would draw up. It was a sign of the hands-on role he had in developing these players.

AMIDST ALL THE pain Kilkenny inflicted, we had one truly great day in Croke Park. The 2007 All-Ireland quarter-final, when we knocked Tipperary out.

Babs Keating was in charge and that summer was full of rumour of upheaval in Tipperary. Brendan Cummins and Eoin Kelly weren't starting. They'd three games against Limerick before losing in Munster.

I was wary of Tipperary. *Was all this talk just a smokescreen?* I'd enough of a job to get our heads right after losing the Leinster final by 15 points.

We played really well that day. The breaks fell for us with the timing of a good goal from Barry Lambert and the impact of Doc O'Connor, when he came on wing-forward. By the last minute, we were two points down, one of those championship endings when your pulse is racing and everything seems frantic. Then we got a bit of luck.

The referee James McGrath judged a Tipperary defender had interfered with the ball as Lambert lined up a free right of goal. He moved it into the centre... 20 yards out. I'd wanted Barry to pop over a point but now the angle was different and we sent the rescue call to the opposite end of the pitch. Damien Fitzhenry made the long run up and didn't give the five Tipp men on the line a chance, burying a shot to the net. We added another point and, suddenly, it was over. We'd won 3-10 to 1-14.

The buzz from a result like that, especially when it's secured so late, is just magic. I just went around hugging people; Babs in commiseration, and the Wexford lads in celebration.

Fitzhenry was the hero, another chapter in the story of one of the all-time greats. *What a super goalkeeper.* He kept us in so many games, stopping bullets that looked destined for the net. You'd see his saves with your own eyes but were left unsure as to how they were even possible. In 2007 against Galway, he made a stop from Kevin Broderick that I couldn't get my head around. It was described as a golden age for hurling goalkeepers but he was the best.

And a lovely person to manage, a rock-solid character. Nothing was ever a problem. Rory McCarthy was similar. The two of them were the last left that had started in 1996 but there was a humility there; you wouldn't have known they'd reached such heights.

THE TRAVEL AS Wexford manager never bothered me. Wherever we trained meant a round trip of over 200 miles, but I always arrived well in advance. A manager's car becomes their office; get on the phone and use your time on the road effectively.

Sometimes I had company. The journalist Enda McEvoy joined the spin one day for an article he was writing for *The Sunday Tribune*. He came down from Kilkenny; we'd lunch in the Tennis Village in Cork, then away to Wexford and did the interview in the car. A gas man.

Eanna Martin was a young player from New Ross who joined the panel at the end of 2006. He was in college in UCC and that first year I used to bring him down from Cork for training. A brilliant fella who played everywhere for Wexford; in goal, defence and attack. He'd do any job asked of him.

In the 2007 Leinster intermediate final, we were losing to Kilkenny when I put him on corner-forward and told him to get a score. He hit 1-1 and we won the game. In 2019 he was sub goalkeeper and got a Leinster senior medal after years of trying. I was delighted for him.

That Wexford intermediate team was a good news story in 2007; we'd beaten Waterford in the All-Ireland final. It was a nice boost as we looked to develop players for the seniors.

Dual players were a hot topic in Wexford then. The footballers went on an incredible run in 2008 before losing to Tyrone in the All-Ireland semi-final. Three of the footballers started when we won the intermediate. Brian Malone, a commanding centre-back. Redmond Barry, a wing-forward with a great engine. Ciaran Lyng, the forward who could sniff out a score. They wanted to play football, I wanted them for hurling.

The dual option was teased out a little but it wasn't workable.

Before the Tyrone match, a journalist rang me for an interview about Wexford's hurling year. The progress of the footballers came up and I wished them well. I mentioned in passing the three lads I'd worked with and that I'd loved if they were in the hurling squad.

The article was published with the headline... MEYLER TO ENTICE

DUAL PLAYERS BACK TO HURLING. It was portrayed that I was trying to undermine the football set-up and poach their prized assets. I'd walked myself into it, but in no way did I want to unsettle the footballers. I was simply praising the hurling abilities of the three lads.

The backlash came anyway. I got a load of phone calls from Wexford, asking me what the hell was I thinking? The whole of Wexford had gone football-mad and some thought the hurling manager was trying to wreck that.

But it blew over and there was no lasting bad blood. I thought I'd win them over but they stayed with the football.

SECOND SEASON SYNDROME.

It often happens. We started 2008 away to Waterford in the league and won by a point. The TG4 producer grabbed me after to come over for an interview.

'Jesus, that was brilliant hurling, really exciting,' he said.

I was wondering if we'd been at the same match. What I had seen was an absolute slog on a heavy pitch. Sometimes people get confused between excitement and quality. I knew there were problems in our hurling and over the next month our form went to pieces. We faced Antrim; they brought us right up to the north of the county, the first time that the Dunloy club had hosted a National League match. We helped them mark the occasion as they completely dominated us. It finished 3-11 to 1-10.

I made a big mistake for the match. Fitzhenry had missed the Waterford game; he was away in America. I should have played him, but I left Dermot Flynn in and a ball went through his hands to the net early on. Antrim got the momentum after. The whole day was a total disaster.

When we got back to Dublin, I tore into the lads; got off the bus and drove home to Cork, my annoyance growing with every passing mile. By the Tuesday night, my rage hit the roof. The chairman said two players had been out on the Saturday night when we'd stayed in a hotel in the north. I asked for the proof, but none was forthcoming and the uncertainty of the whole episode left a stain.

The wheels started to come off. We got relegated; Dublin survived as they had a better scoring difference. We lost our last game against Cork by two points and that became a real issue.

That spring the Cork hurlers had gone on strike and gave walkovers for their first two games. The GAA handled it all terribly. Kilkenny and Waterford got full points, but Cork were not docked points for not fulfilling their fixtures. *Where was the fairness?* I came under pressure not to play that last game; urged that week to pull the team.

That wasn't my style, even though I found it nonsensical Cork had home advantage for such a critical game. We didn't perform but were left sore at how the whole issue played out.

The summer road ended at the quarter-final against Waterford. Stephen Doyle, who I couldn't get in 2007, made a big impression and scored 2-1. For all the good things in our game, they outscored us in the last five minutes. We got a penalty late on but this time Fitzy's rocket flew over the bar. Fine margins.

AND THAT PROVED to be my last match. One point short of Waterford, where a win would have put us in an All-Ireland semi-final against Tipperary, a county we'd beaten the year before. I felt there were clear signs of improvement as 2008 had progressed but three months later, it was all over.

When I left Dungarvan after that fateful meeting with the Wexford chairman, I knew in my heart and soul that I had conducted myself properly. That helped put me at peace, even if the outcome didn't make me happy.

I rang Willie Sunderland at home to tell him we were sacked; he was pretty shocked. Same with Fitzhenry.

There are no trophies to show from my time with Wexford but I felt we competed and improved. If we took bad beatings from Kilkenny, then that was the same for every other team in Ireland.

I enjoyed the experience and the way it ended didn't leave me feeling bitter towards the county. I was more than happy to return to Wexford and work with St Martin's subsequently. David has taught me the value in sport of looking ahead, not dwelling on the past. His life in English soccer, which is so fast moving with the constant turnover of players and managers, conditioned him to think like that.

Quinny, McShane and Robbie

Slutsky

The Liverpool Net

Coleman and Henderson

Zlatan and Me

Swapping Shirts

Cesc

Cally

★★★

DAVID

TWELVE DAYS AFTER Steve Bruce left as Hull City manager in 2016, we flew to Austria for a pre-season tour. The club was in chaos. Keith Bertschin, the first-team coach, turned up with his luggage only to be told he wasn't needed. Diamé had just moved to Newcastle. Dawson, Odubajo, McGregor, Alex Bruce and Maguire all stayed home as they nursed injuries.

We had made no signings. Mick Phelan was caretaker manager. There were only 13 senior players on the plane with a group of under-23s.

We played a Turkish team in a friendly in Kufstein, a few miles from the German border. Beautiful place surrounded by snow-capped mountains. The day after that 3-1 win, a group of us took a cable car to the Asitz mountain station. Up there, 1,800m above sea level with this stunning scenic backdrop, I suggested we take a photo.

Back row... Robertson, Snodgrass, Huddlestone, Clucas and Diomande.

Front row... myself, Livermore, Curtis and Elmo.

All the lads wearing the club gear. Curtis put it on social media first with the caption... *Hull City squad photo 2016–17*. Then a few more did; it was a joke but we were making the point how small our squad was.

We'd that day off as we headed up to the mountains but were told not to go drinking. Livermore is an eccentric character, a superb teammate. Snodgrass is a born comedian, so quick-witted. The time the police phoned me over the

Pardew headbutt, I suspected it was Snodgrass winding me up. The form was good amongst the lads.

There was a debate… *Would we have a drink?* Snodgrass made a valid point. *If we all had one, how bad could the fallout be?*

The club didn't have many players, they couldn't drop us all.

So we started with a couple of pints and it turned into a day on the beer. We went tobogganing for a while, down a slide of a few hundred yards. Eventually we came down off the mountain, bumped into the physios and they could see we were all full up. Then Mick called a training session for 6pm. He said we'd taken the piss going drinking.

We'd to do six runs between the penalty boxes… 20 seconds to go over and back. We were all moaning, Snodgrass was cracking jokes but we just got through it.

Then every first-team player beat the youngsters in the running. Mick went absolutely berserk at them, he made all those lads do another six runs.

NIGHTS OUT WERE a staple part of pre-season tours. If there was an unplanned one when Steve Bruce was in charge, he got over it if the whole team was together. If the group splintered into twos and threes, there was a problem.

On one trip to Portugal, he ordered us to stay in. By the end of the week we were getting restless. Dawson organised a bus to come collect us. We'd a 22-man squad; two lads were Muslims who don't drink.

The bus Dawson ordered had 19 seats. I volunteered to make my own way in, went to the hotel reception and ordered a taxi. Turned away and walked straight into Steve Bruce, Steve Agnew, Steve Clemence and Gary Walsh.

'Where are you going?' asked Agnew.

'Nowhere!'

'Come on, don't forget we all played,' said Clemence.

Bruce looked at me.

'How many of ye are going?'

'20.'

'Okay, make sure everyone's home at a reasonable time… and ye don't leave anyone behind. Go and enjoy yourself!' Couldn't argue with that. I headed in to meet the lads, walked into a bar and told them the gaffer had given us the green light. A massive cheer went up.

Leonid Slutsky also took us to Portugal.

Dawson was captain and I was vice-captain. We figured one of us needed to get permission for the night out so I went to Slutsky. There was no problem but put a cap on it of five drinks. That was never going to be adhered to.

We'd a bus to the airport the next morning.

Dawson is an early bird, so myself and Allan McGregor stayed near him and gave him room keys. Told him not to forget to wake us. Greggsy was brilliant fun on a night out, we got back around 6am. Dawson came in the next day and chucked buckets of water over the two of us.

We were pushing time but we'd packed the night before and made the bus. A goalkeeper, Jon McLaughlin had come on trial; he'd done really well but kept the bus waiting that morning. When we got back to England, he was never seen in Hull again.

WHEN WE GOT back from Austria before the 2016-17 season, there was still mayhem at the club. The players were united. We finally made some new signings like Ryan Mason, Markus Henriksen and David Marshall. From the outset we were written off as relegation favourites.

Then we made this amazing start. Played the champions Leicester City in the opening game of the new Premier League season, and beat them 2-1.

Won 2-0 away to Swansea, scoring twice in the last 11 minutes.

Lost to Man United, but only after a 92nd minute Marcus Rashford goal.

Then grabbed a draw with Burnley, when Snodgrass scored in the 95th minute. Our fight and spirit dragged us through. Mick Phelan had us so well drilled and organised. You always believe you can sustain that momentum but it's a fairytale.

We didn't have enough first-team players. Reality started to intrude.

We only won once in the next 18 games, right up until the middle of January. If we had strengthened the squad a bit more it would have helped; but the depth wasn't there. It goes back to Steve Bruce's exit the previous summer, he knew what was coming.

We suffered some bad defeats.

Arsenal 4-1... Liverpool 5-1... Bournemouth 6-1.

That last one was a real concern; losing to the big teams is one thing but a thrashing like that makes everyone – manager, players, owner – start to question things. There was a personal consolation in the Liverpool game, scoring a goal at Anfield. It was my last one in the Premier League. Snodgrass swung in a corner, it broke and I caught it cleanly to lash in a shot.

A rare cause for cheer that day. We were down to 10 men after half an hour. I was brought on to play right-back after Elmo got sent-off. It's the worst feeling as a footballer, coming on when your team is getting pumped. Subs are meant to make an impact but when everything is in disarray, you're not going to turn it around.

When I scored we were down 3-1 but I didn't celebrate, just sprinted back to our half. Roy recalled the incident later at an Ireland camp. 'Why did you run back so quickly??

I pointed out that's what teams do in that situation; they try to get the game going again in the hope of a comeback.

'Yeah, but ye were 3-1 down, ye weren't getting back into that game. You might as well have taken your time and enjoyed it.'

He had a point.

Liverpool ripped us apart that day. In the second-half, the ball went out for a throw. The home fans were heckling me as I went to take it.

'Come on man, hurry up!'

'We're 4-1 down and have 10 men! I'm not rushing for anyone.'

A big group of the crowd actually start laughing.

After that game, myself, Jordan, Adam Lallana and James Milner were all due to go out. Our wives had arranged it; we were all going to Manchester for dinner. I'd got to know the lads through Jordan, we'd often meet up. I'd always tell Cally… Don't plan anything after games, the result would dictate my mood. *If I've played and we've got a result, then let's do whatever you want afterwards.*

This night was long arranged. Cally's mother was looking after Alanna and we'd booked a hotel. Then Hull got hammered. The only reason I went out was that scoring the goal at least helped me. The Liverpool lads only went out because they had got a good result. When we'd beaten them 3-1 in 2013, there'd been plans to meet after but that got binned once they lost as Jordan was raging.

Football is a small world that sparks plenty of relationships.

I'm very good friends with Seamus Coleman and with Jordan Henderson. One's the Everton captain, the other's the Liverpool captain. They hated one another for years. Openly hammered each other when talking to me. I used to laugh and tell them they were both so similar. Their drive and desire, their family values, their no-nonsense attitude to drinking!

When Seamus broke his leg in the Wales game, there was a Merseyside derby soon after. Jordan wrote a piece on him in the match programme. Wished Seamus well; with such a massive rivalry, you want the best players involved in derbies and it was a shame Everton had lost their captain.

Seamus rang me after.

'Your mate is actually alright.'

I rang Jordan later to tell him and now I would say, they're not friends, but there's a mutual respect there. It's funny how it evolved over time.

WE WERE FORTUNATE that Mick Phelan took over as caretaker, someone we knew. The strange thing was why it took him so long to get the Hull job full-time? He was eventually appointed in October but the results piled the pressure on and by January he was gone.

After four years of Steve Bruce, we saw a lot of change. In my last two years at the club, I had four managers… Mick, Marco Silva, Leonid Slutsky and Nigel Adkins.

Marco was a leftfield appointment. He'd managed in Portugal and Greece. Paul Merson famously wasn't too impressed on *Soccer Saturday* on Sky Sports.

'Why's it always got to be a foreign manager?'

I'd a more open mind. He was my new manager and I'd to get on board. It wasn't like I had 10 clubs knocking on the door looking to take me.

Marco changed the philosophy and freshened it up. If we had Marco from the start of that season, we would have stayed up. The first day he took over, we trained for three hours. I've never trained so long for one session in my life. Everyone was blown away by the attention to detail. It wasn't hard, but Marco walked us through everything he wanted from us. Did that every day for weeks.

The tough thing for Marco was, in 2017 it felt there was a constant flow of big names exiting Hull. It started with Snodgrass and Livermore moving in January. Five players joined, but all on loan, and building cohesion wasn't easy. By the end of May, Marco himself had departed. Then Harry, Andy, Tom, Elmo and Curtis all left over the course of June and July.

It felt surreal. I was looking around wondering who would stay?

When I moved in 2018, someone mentioned it was time to turn off the lights on my way out. A sledgehammer had been taken to the squad that had won promotions and reached the FA Cup final. There was nothing left.

WHEN LEONID SLUTSKY came, that lack of togetherness was the same problem. We played Derby.

Fikayo Tomori had joined on loan from Chelsea.

The first time I met him properly was in the tunnel before the game. *How can you strike up a relationship like that?* All these loan moves didn't help. When we had days off, those boys were from London and went home to see their families. Of course I'd no problem with that but we couldn't build a culture in the club. The first time I'd signed for Hull, everyone lived in the general area. When you sign for a club, you need to buy into it and the area where the fanbase are from.

I did that and felt more at home as a result.

WE PLAYED MAN United three times in early 2017.

Lost the first-leg of the League Cup semi-final 2-0, won the second-leg 2-1 and then drew 0-0 in the league. I started right-back in all three games. There was a good buzz to those cup semi-finals on January midweek nights. We pushed them all the way in the second-leg. Huddlestone opened the scoring, Pogba equalised and then I crossed for Oumar Niasse to score with five minutes left. That was the only time I beat United in my career, albeit we lost on aggregate and missed out on Wembley so it felt a hollow success.

Myself, Harry Maguire and Sam Clucas were talking before that trio of Man United games. We all wanted the same shirts… Pogba, Rooney and Zlatan.

So we made a pact, rotated through the fixtures so we could get them all. Plenty of players don't care about swapping shirts. I like to get them as mementos and a reminder of happy times.

In the second-leg, United get a corner near the end. Zlatan is walking backwards, I'm minding the front post.

He stands on my foot and turns.

'Woah, sorry big man!' he says.

'You're a bit bigger than me,' I tell him.

He just laughed and after the game I asked for his shirt.

'No problem my friend… I'll give it to you inside.'

So we go into the tunnel and swap. I always kept a Sharpie marker in my washbag. The shirts are great, if you can get them signed they're even better. Later I walked out and Zlatan was leaving at the same time. He's this iconic figure who has played for Ajax, Juventus, Inter, Barcelona, AC Milan and PSG. It's unlikely we'll cross paths again.

One chance. You don't get anything if you don't ask.

'Zlatan! Have you got a second to sign the shirt?'

'No problem, my friend. Can you sign your shirt?'

'Yes Zlatan, absolutely I can!'

I have that shirt framed and hanging on the wall in my house. I haven't yet seen 'Meyler 7' in the Zlatan Hall of Fame. I liked his larger than life persona as he backed it up on the pitch and found him just really respectful that time.

Some don't approve of swapping. Roy hates it.

What probably frustrated him more was people asking him for his shirt. Jordan has never asked anyone for a shirt in his life. Seamus would only swap if he's playing against Ireland lads. But it doesn't bother me. I grew up a football fan and I'm still one; the memorabilia is cool.

I always did it off the pitch, away from cameras and the eyes of the world. You think of the criticism when André Santos got Robin Van Persie's shirt in 2012 in front of the whole stadium. *Got to be smart, don't give people a chance to slate you.*

I've a nice collection. Under Trapattoni, Ireland played Spain at Yankee Stadium in New York in 2013. The final whistle was about to blow as I asked Cesc Fàbregas for his shirt.

Then he wanted mine.

No problem Cesc!!

It was the alternate black jersey that had been brought out. He collected shirts from every country he played against and hadn't got an Ireland one after Euro 2012.

MARCO SILVA ALMOST engineered the great escape. Seventeen points from his first 11 games, but we only got four from his last seven. Finished the season getting walloped 7-1 by Spurs as Harry Kane scored a hat-trick. That game was on a Sunday, Marco resigned on the Thursday and by the Saturday he was announced as the new Watford manager. That's football, it's a mad business.

That year was my last taste of the Premier League. I'd reached the point of no return and anyway I was distracted. The struggles with my knees had returned.

In April we were at the end of a training session, when I went through one-on-one. David Marshall came flying out from goal and collided with my knee. I heard a click in my left knee. It was the right I had damaged twice before, but waiting for the physio to come over felt like an eternity. He instantly said my medial was gone. I told him to check my cruciate, so he performed the test. Lying on the pitch, I'm thinking if this is my third cruciate... *I am done. Game over.*

It wasn't. I still needed a scan to confirm it but the signs were good. The diagnosis was a Grade 4 MCL tear, which is still horrible and required another operation. The surgeon felt this was a good time to clean up my other knee as well. I wish I hadn't got that second knee surgery done, it didn't help me in the long run. The physio Rob Price and the doctor Mark Waller at Hull, two people I respect, felt it was best for me at the time. I don't blame them, I'd always have taken their advice.

The club sent me down to a specialist in London to get it done. Every surgery I've had, I've wanted to start the journey back on my own. Didn't want people at my bedside. When I woke after that surgery, I was high on the pain medication and not sure what I was raving about. Next thing the door opened... and Cally was there.

Hull gave me two options for the trip home – get the train or they'd send a car down. I wasn't sitting in a car from London to Hull. I preferred the train, felt I could get up to move if I needed, but the journey was still a disaster.

Reaching Platform 6 at King's Cross Station usually requires a few minutes' walk from the entrance. It took me an hour and 15 minutes on crutches. Cally was in tears. I nearly passed out three times, sweating and exhausted. She bought Lucozade to give me an energy boost. Got on the train eventually and sat at an angle, flopping my leg up on the table.

For the first three weeks at home, I slept on the couch. Didn't have the strength to go upstairs; needed help to go to the toilet and to shower.

One night, I'm lying in the living room and needed to go to the toilet. Wanted to do it myself... took me 45 minutes to muster the energy to lift my legs off the couch, the sweat pouring off me. I'd accepted at one stage I was going to have to piss myself. Then one of my crutches fell and made a loud bang. Cally is a light sleeper and she ran downstairs worried. I told her I was just trying to get to the bathroom. She broke down at that sight, my inability to stand up and hobble over a few yards.

I was stubborn, clinging to my independence.

We weren't going out when I had twice done my cruciate. Seeing me in this helpless state with my knees in bits, that was a proper eye-opener for Cally. A severe injury will generate bad days. You have to accept them, when the pain in your knee can flood your mind with negative thoughts. *Just have to ride them out.*

I retired at the age of 30 and they still crop up, the mornings when you wake up… feel that knee pain and know it'll bother me during the day.

To see me like that in 2017 was hard for Cally. We both have traditional values. Husband and father is the alpha male character. There I was at my weakest and most vulnerable. When tearing my cruciates, I was young and fearless, and could focus on myself. Now there were others to consider. Cally had to deal with a 28-year-old limping about… and look after our 15-month-old daughter Alanna.

It'd be a shock to anyone's system.

The knee injury did cause me to relocate to the Portuguese sun that summer. Six weeks in the Algarve. I first booked a family break for a fortnight and then Hull wanted me to extend it because one of the physios was out there on holidays. So I'd work with him at 10am while our wives, who are really good friends, went off to the beach. After that, Hull were coming out for pre-season, so they just told me to stay on. Cally loved it, she didn't go home.

For those first few weeks I was stuck in a dark tunnel with no flickers of light appearing. But you just keep going. There is no choice and gradually it improves.

Then six months after needing guidance to get to the toilet, I captained Ireland to beat Wales in Cardiff.

XIII

Under-15s
Shoulder To The Wheel
Sciath na Scol
Patrick Horgan
Mark Keane
Under-21s
Limerick

★★★

JOHN

FOR A FEW years, Cork hurling was placed under a microscope and what people saw up close was not positive. The senior battle to win the All-Ireland was one thing; it was the lack of underage trophies that attracted the most heat. Every hurling stakeholder in the county was getting hammered.

Over 2014 and '15, I remember seeing Donal Óg Cusack on *The Sunday Game* giving out about Cork's underage record. He put up a screenshot of Cork's results to compare them to the rest of Munster. That drove me mad to see how poor that record had become.

My response was to look at myself. *What was I doing to address the problem?* I hadn't been involved for years with Cork underage teams. In 1997 I helped with an under-15 team, moved up through the grades with them and was a selector when they won the 2001 minor All-Ireland.

I always felt I had something to contribute but hadn't been asked. It was time to be proactive, so I put the word out that I was interested in helping. Pat Horgan, the County Board development officer, rang me about taking over the Cork under-15s for 2015.

That upset a few people who had been involved the previous year at under-14, but I was determined to drive on.

I studied the Cork underage hurling landscape, the previous results, the players available and the coaching options. It was time to get to work.

I'VE SPENT YEARS coaching adult teams but there is a pure enjoyment in working with youngsters. When David was in primary school at Beaumont, I collected him one day and Liam Weir, a teacher there, grabbed me for a word.

Would I do some hurling coaching with the school team?

I was happy to help. The plan was one afternoon a week, but after we finished the first session the young lads asked, 'Are we going again tomorrow?'

Suddenly we were training most afternoons, using the Avondale soccer pitch nearby. The enthusiasm of the kids was up-lifting. They were mad keen to play hurling, and it was easy for me to facilitate that. They became really successful in the local Sciath na Scol competitions. Later, David and Simon Zebo became best known in sport, but a lot stayed to play GAA for Blackrock and St Michael's. A superb group.

Around that time I started an indoor hurling tournament in CIT, inviting out the schools in Beaumont, Douglas, St Anthony's and Mahon. It turned out to be a huge success and I handed it over to Sciath na Scol to run as it got bigger. Any initiative to promote GAA at the grassroots level in Cork was worthwhile in my eyes.

Liam Weir also brought me into the Cork Primary Game set-up. There were brilliant people involved like Marty Fleming, Eamonn Kelly, Christy Twomey and John Boylan. We'd contact teachers in schools to nominate players. Giving young lads the opportunity to play in Thurles before a Munster Senior Championship game in front of 40,000 people was a wonderful moment.

The match programmes are all still stored in a box at home. I kept an eye on the development of players… our 2001 forward line of Patrick Horgan, Colm O'Neill and Paudie O'Sullivan all pushed on with Cork.

I saw first-hand with David in 2002 the level of excitement the Primary Game generated. The matches only lasted 10 minutes but the memories remained for years.

KIERAN 'FRAGGY' MURPHY and Seánie Barry joined me for the Cork under-15 projects. I knew Fraggy going back to his Cork minor and CIT playing days. He stuck a hat-trick past Kilkenny in the second-half of an All-Ireland minor semi-final. His intelligence as a player was replicated as a coach.

Seánie was involved with the Barrs then, but I'd known him since he was young. In the early 80s, we lived in Ballincollig and his father John ran a petrol station near us. When I became Kerry manager in 1992, that was my pitstop on the road down. Others like Niall O'Halloran, Seán Cremin, Donal Hurley and Padraig O'Sullivan came on board. From the winter of 2014, we worked our socks off. The first thing to be done was to throw the rule book out the window. The guideline was to only train once a fortnight but that was a non-runner.

Every Sunday night we went to the Na Piarsaigh indoor hall or to the third pitch in Éire Óg. We weren't flogging the players with mad running sessions. It was all ball work, focusing on skills improvement. That was key.

I insisted we weren't training, they were coaching sessions. The players were instructed to describe it like that if anyone asked. The Sunday night timing worked as it didn't interfere with their clubs and we tested them in challenges against minor teams. There was no backlash from parents over the schedule.

I never got criticised for that, instead the criticism would come when fellas were left off the team. Starting out in coaching, I'd made a rule to not deal with parents and focus on the players. But my thinking had evolved and I knew I needed to make them feel involved, so they were happy with what we were doing.

WE WERE SUCCESSFUL, which kept the show motoring on. In 2015 we won the Carrigdhoun Munster Tournament and in 2016 we won the All-Ireland competition up in Tipperary in a final against Galway. We treated it like a proper occasion. Mindful of the distances players would have to travel on the Saturday morning, we made the trip up the night before and stayed in the Abbey Court Hotel in Nenagh.

We handed them over at under-17 to John Considine and they won the All-Ireland against Dublin. I'd slag Considine that we gift-wrapped a team for him; he only made two changes to it. The day they won in Croke Park, I'd my Hogan Stand ticket sorted and was able to shake hands with every one of them before they collected the cup. Considine continued the work, then Pat Ryan and Donal O'Mahony pushed it on with that team at under-20 level.

We put in a fierce effort and went to every match under the sun to find players. Every Wednesday there were schools hurling games where we could judge players in a different setting. The schools system is crucial; look at how Kilkenny and Limerick have tailored it correctly.

I went to Carrigadrohid one day, a few miles off the Killarney road, to see an under-16 C schools game. There was a centre-back playing and I was immediately struck by him. Conor O'Callaghan is from Dromtarriffe, football country in the north-west of Cork near the Kerry border. But there was something in his hurling I liked, so we brought him in.

In July 2021, he captained Cork to win the All-Ireland under-20 hurling final.

I wasn't there that night in Nowlan Park, with the restrictions on fans attending, but watching the game on TG4 didn't diminish my pride at seeing familiar faces do so well.

Conor... the Roche twins Eoin and Brian... Aaron Walsh-Barry... Daire Connery... Tommy O'Connell... Seán Twomey... Shane O'Regan. They had all been with us in those under-15 and under-16 teams.

Not every player stuck with hurling. We were dealing with teenagers who faced that sporting dilemma... *What am I going to concentrate on?*

I would never pressurise young fellas but I wouldn't shy away either from the fact that a call has to be made at some stage. I'd witnessed it with David when he'd to choose between GAA and soccer.

We had four young hurlers... Mark Keane (Ballygiblin), Blake Murphy (Na Piarsaigh), Charlie Lyons (Valley Rovers) and Conor Russell (Douglas)... that I really wanted to keep working with. They all went elsewhere.

Charlie played soccer; he signed for Preston and then came home to join Cobh Ramblers. Blake and Conor went after gaelic football, they both played under-20 for Cork, and Blake made the senior squad.

Then there was Mark Keane, who at the age of 18 moved to the other side of the world to play Aussie Rules in Melbourne. Then he came home in November 2020 to score the famous goal for the Cork footballers as they dumped Kerry out of the senior championship.

Mark was always a highly-rated footballer but had great potential as a hurling wing-forward. Big presence, strong in the air and aggressive.

His dad Eamonn was brilliant to deal with and we kept in touch. When Mark moved to the AFL, I drew on my experience of David moving abroad to play professional sport, to help his parents and pass on any advice that we had learned as a family. When he made his AFL debut for Collingwood in 2020, I was in touch straight away, absolutely thrilled for him.

We lost those lads in hurling but I'd no problem with the decision they made. They made a choice to travel their own sporting roads and I just wished them well. We put a fierce effort into those two years but the pay-off was the huge enjoyment we got. Often I felt happier and more at ease working at that level than senior inter-county. There's pressure to win trophies and develop players, but less politics and sideshows.

I get a massive kick out of seeing what all those have gone on to do, those in other sports and those that have climbed the Cork hurling ladder; how they've grown on and off the pitch. I can ring them to catch up and they'll take time to chat. I treasure the relationships. I may only have had a small input in their development but I know they have gratitude and respect for the work that was put in. All the lads in that management team would feel the same.

There was unbelievable work put into those players and they gave us so much in return.

AFTER WE WON that under-16 tournament in 2016, the question was where to go next. Denis Ring was already settled as minor manager and had his team in place.

Then Frank Murphy rang and asked me to take over the Cork under-21s.

I'm not a fan of voting for manager positions. I prefer to get a phone call from a club chairman or county secretary for a chat about the role, and an offer. Committees can be formed to make the managerial choice and then if asked, I'm willing to do it as long as there's no interference. The guarantee of support from the start is crucial, creating division is of no benefit.

I had no reluctance becoming Cork under-21 manager. People may have thought it was messy after the fallout when I was senior selector in 2002 but I've never carried any baggage. I'm straight with myself and others. If people wanted to label me, that was grand. I hadn't been asked to do anything with Cork for a long time but I was happy to now. A few weeks later, Frank rang with another proposal. Doubling up as senior selector. It was felt it'd bring continuity and help with the emphasis on bringing young players through to the seniors.

There was a new breed coming in Cork. Shane Kingston, Mark Coleman, Darragh Fitzgibbon and Luke Meade were all youngsters with huge potential. And 2017 was when they started to make their mark.

Kieran Kingston was senior manager and we met a few times in the Mount Oval Bar to sketch out how he saw my role. He wanted that link to the under-21 team as well and having been with other county squads, I had experience to offer.

My own under-21 management weren't too happy. Fraggy and Seánie Barry had come up from the under-16s with me; the notion that I would double-job wasn't something they were too keen on. I felt I could manage both, even if it meant being on the road every night. If we played a National League game at 3pm on a Sunday, there'd be an under-21 challenge at 7pm. It was hectic but I loved it.

The arrangement worked fine. Kieran never said he was unhappy. Pat Ryan was really good at the senior coaching and always open to input. Diarmuid O'Sullivan had been full-back in 2002 when it all ended badly for that management, but I had no beef with Sully. Pat Hartnett was the other selector; I knew him from games against Midleton in the 80s.

2016 had ended with Wexford's first championship win over Cork in 60 years. We were starting from rock bottom. When I first met Kieran, we spoke of the importance of winning matches straight away.

We won the Munster pre-season competition that January in a final against Limerick and they reversed that result in a league quarter-final. If expectations were low, the Munster Championship proved a brilliant experience. A flying start against Tipperary, further momentum against Waterford, and then rounded off with a win over Clare.

In the last few minutes of a tight game I like to spend it behind our own goal, shouting instructions. Clare put our defence under siege late on in the Munster final but we held out. We laughed about it after when Kingston said he didn't see me for the group hug. The four members of the management team jumping around by the dugout... and I was down behind the goal. It was a great win.

We were in the All-Ireland semi-final and had a rematch against Waterford.

Two points up with 15 minutes to go that day, and a place in the final was within reach. We should have closed it out but couldn't hold on. Damien Cahalane's red card was the big talking point. Damien is an old-fashioned sort of defender; incredibly honest, wears his heart on his sleeve. A big figure in the squad, he was just rash in his decision making for the second yellow and his devastation afterwards was plain to see.

The roof fell in on us as Waterford hit three second-half goals; we couldn't hold them out. We knew how far away the team had been in the couple of years before, but also the size of the opportunity that had been missed.

ALL SUMMER, I had been combining senior responsibilities with the under-21. Four days after the Munster senior final, we'd our first under-21 game down in Walsh Park against Waterford on a windy night.

We won but it was daylight robbery really. Declan Dalton rocketed home a penalty with the last puck of the game. Dalton was the third-choice goalkeeper for the seniors that year; he'd played there at minor.

There was an under-21 challenge against Limerick up in Martinstown earlier in summer. I was away with the seniors but told the lads to put Dalton in the forwards if they were stuck. I'd seen him play there for his club Fr O'Neills, a brilliant striker of the ball.

We'd a meeting every Monday night in the River Lee Hotel on the Western Road. At our next gathering all the lads were raving about Dalton as a forward. So we played him there against Waterford and he scored 1-12 to win us the match.

I lost the run of myself in the TG4 interview after. Being Cork manager carries a lot of pressure and huge expectations surrounded that team with the senior players involved. Darragh Fitzgibbon had been sent-off, then we were awarded a penalty… and snatched a win in the 65th minute. All pent-up emotion came out, I was nearly in tears trying to answer the questions on TV.

For the Munster final we were down three big players. Luke Meade injured his hand playing for the seniors. Billy Hennessy put out his shoulder in training. We were in Croke Park a few days before to appeal Fitzy's red card but that failed and he was suspended. Those missing lads would have made a difference. We lost to Limerick by two points; the free count was 20-4 against us.

That game was a critical turning point in the Limerick-Cork hurling rivalry. Those Limerick players won the All-Ireland under-21 that year and have added senior medals since. Cork were left waiting for the breakthrough.

That defeat will always be a huge regret.

Seamus

The Pennant

Wales 0, Ireland 1

James McClean

Wes

Tórshavn to Paris

Martin and Roy

Set-pieces

Ireland 1, Denmark 5

★★★

DAVID

AFTER THE FINAL whistle sounded at the Cardiff City Stadium in October 2017, one of the first people over to congratulate me was Seamus Coleman. I had captained Ireland to beat Wales 1-0 and keep our World Cup qualifying hopes alive.

The greatest night of my football life. The importance of it was rooted in my personal long-term journey, but also my short-term one, recovering from the double knee surgery six months previously.

I was fortunate my injury hadn't kept me out for long, mindful of the struggles of others. In March we drew 0-0 with Wales in Dublin – the game was overshadowed by Seamus breaking his leg.

Captaining my country in those 2017 qualifiers is my fondest football memory but that only happened because Seamus got injured. After the final whistle, my main thought was for his well-being.

I visited him the next day in a Dublin hospital and after talking to him, I didn't worry about his ability to recover. With his strength of character, I was certain he would be back.

Two months beforehand, Hull played Chelsea and early in the first-half I came on for Ryan Mason. He had been treated after suffering a clash of heads. As he came off on a stretcher, I ran past and said, 'You'll be alright Mase!'

Later, myself, Tom Huddlestone and Michael Dawson went to the hospital.

It was a short 15-minute visit, it was horrible to see him like that. It was an awful accident which had such severe consequences. Ryan had fractured his skull and a year later was forced to retire from football on medical advice.

Witnessing two incidents like that on the pitch was unsettling.

You wonder... *Why them and not me?* I have a scar under my right eye from a game against Arsenal in 2015. Rose for a header with Laurent Koscielny and whatever way we landed, his boot hit me and slit my face. A couple of inches higher and I was in trouble. The Hull doctor said I was lucky I hadn't lost my eye.

It must have been frustrating for Seamus to watch that Wales game but his attitude after, in going around to everyone, summed him up.

It was a measure of the man. Reaching the play-offs brought us one step closer to the World Cup finals and I was desperate to qualify for Russia so that Seamus could play there.

THE PENNANT NEXT to my jersey was the giveaway.

I arrived into the dressing-room 90 minutes before kick-off against Moldova, on a Friday night in October 2017. The Irish kit lads had all our gear laid out as usual. When I saw the extra item next to mine, the realisation hit me. *I'm captain tonight.*

Jon Walters had been deputising for Seamus, but he was out injured.

It was a stroke of genius not to let me know in advance. Instead, I had no time to become distracted about being Irish captain for a World Cup qualifier. Martin was good at that, in keeping everyone focused on the game. His tactic of delaying team announcements was criticised but it gave everybody a chance to stake a claim to start and helped keep players switched on.

I'd got back into the Ireland team in September against Serbia. After drawing with Georgia, the midfield was changed with myself and Wes coming in. It was a game where the midfield area became a proper scrap. Nemanja Matić was a big powerful opponent but there is a mutual respect from that type of physical confrontation.

We lost 1-0, Aleksandar Kolarov scored a bullet. So in October we were very focused when facing Moldova. I was really glad for Daryl Murphy, he was clinical in scoring his two goals. We were there to win and once it was finished, all eyes turned to Wales.

IN THE FIRST-HALF in Cardiff, myself and James sandwiched Joe Allen in a challenge for the ball. It reflected our mentality – we had to win and would have run through him to do so. Joe was a brilliant link-man for Wales. But he had to go off; they were already without Gareth Bale, and then Aaron Ramsey had to drop deeper. Their challenge was weakened.

I'd played against Ramsey many times for Hull against Arsenal. A nice, slick passer who you had to watch. I met his agent at the launch of the Fifa 20 video game; he also looks after James Maddison who we were doing some work with. His agent said Ramsey used to hate playing against me. He knew he'd get lumps kicked out of him.

There were times when Ramsey was miles ahead of me, and others when I frustrated the life out of him. There's a great photo of when we played Wales in Dublin. I won the ball back, Ramsey falls as he comes after me and he's pulling at my shorts to hold on. My attitude was to bring Ramsey to my level. Though the best players don't come down!

The atmosphere in the stadium that night was highly-charged with emotion. Wearing the armband sharpened my focus, but you couldn't help be taken in by the national anthems. The Welsh one was seriously impressive.

In the team huddle before, I kept reiterating that we would not lose the game. The winning goal was about Jeff Hendrick's control. No matter how many times I've watched it back, I'm still not sure how he didn't let the ball slip out of play. When he put in the cross, James McClean met it brilliantly with his right foot.

Near the end I saw my name in lights as the ball bounced, just me against Wayne Hennessey racing from the Wales goal. *If I win it, I've got a tap in to an empty net in front of the Irish fans.* But I'd nothing left in the tank, lunged in too late on Hennessey and got a yellow card. Martin O'Neill went mad at me privately after because I got suspended for the play-off first-leg.

After the game, I went back to Hull and came back down to earth, getting sent-off against Norwich. From the best feeling in the world to a reminder about the day job.

But the Monday night memories of Cardiff will never fade.

JAMES MCCLEAN SIGNED for Sunderland in August 2011. He was the same then as he is now – a nice, quiet fella, who's a bit dangerous when he has a phone in his hand. He likes a tight circle. His wife and children, his brothers and his parents; he holds them all close. A good fella with a kind heart.

We got on well from the start. He's a month older than me but I was three years ahead of him in English football experience. At the start he was constantly going home to Derry but he settled well.

He's had a challenging time. In February 2021, he made the point that with the focus on racist discrimination against footballers, he had never got the same support when suffering abuse.

He mentioned former teammates not standing up for him. Privately he clarified he wasn't taking aim at me, as I had helped him, but the reality was I could have done more. I distanced myself when he was subjected to horrendous stuff.

Why? The simple truth was it was a world that I didn't want to get drawn into, potentially making myself and my family a target. My attitude was a bit selfish but I was fearful of getting involved.

I don't view James as a political person, more someone who is shaped by what he and his family have gone through. We've never really talked in depth about it but there are sensitive issues at play for them. When at Wigan, he explained his decision not to wear the poppy. I felt it was reasonable and if people didn't agree with it, they could at least accept it.

He is the hardest working footballer I've met; fanatical about this fitness. When we lost to France in Euro 2016, the squad went out to drown our sorrows. James rarely drinks; he didn't that night and early the following morning he was in the hotel gym on a treadmill. He refuses to switch off.

Myself, Cally and Alanna were on holiday in Portugal one time, when we met James, his wife Erin and children as they were staying nearby. Later, Erin drove Cally back so they could get changed for dinner. I thought we'd relax by the pool but James decided this was a chance to fit in a gym session, headed off and left me minding all the kids.

Before he scored the winner against Austria in November 2016, he got an epidural in his back. He wasn't supposed to play, could barely walk a couple days before, but was so determined. James and the doctor figured out how to get him through it.

He was the hero that night but he'd earned all the praise.

THE OTHER KEY man in Vienna was Wes Hoolahan.

When we started playing with Wes, we really got to appreciate the talent he possesses. He was the type of fella who would go training with a woolly hat, a big jacket, a pair of gloves and a pair of pants on. You never knew what mood he was in.

But in games he could prove how gifted he was. Running around, closing people down... that wasn't part of his game. He just wanted the ball and then he had the vision to pick off these stunning passes. I used to say to Wes... 'If you see me with the ball and I turn, I'm looking for you, no one else'.

It was a freezing night when we played Austria at the Ernst Happel Stadium. I was wrapped up in layers on the bench, when Glenn Whelan hurt his hamstring in the first-half. Suddenly Martin is shouting and I'm running on without having warmed up. It took me a few minutes to adjust to the pace of the game and the conditions. But I grew into it, shielding the back four and in the second-half, our confidence soared.

Kevin Wimmer tried to play the ball to David Alaba on the wing for Austria, when I went in to tackle. He felt he'd been fouled, but no whistle came and I played on. I was thinking of firing it down the line and, then I saw Wes out of the corner of my eye. Got the ball to him and he split the defence with this perfectly-weighted pass into the path of James, who shot to the net.

Players can be reluctant to admit it but the ball should always be given to the better player. I knew what Wes was capable of; my job was to supply him and that would help us win matches.

It is a real shame he didn't play more for Ireland. The breakthrough came too late in his career but he showed what he could do, as he still does at club level for Cambridge. A remarkable player.

INTERNATIONAL FOOTBALL TRAVEL is not glamorous. You're there to do a job. Fly in... get the right result... home!

My first away trip was in October 2012.

A World Cup qualifier in Tórshavn, home of the Faroe Islands. I was brought on in the last minute for my second cap. We stayed at this hotel on a big hill, surrounded by sheep in the middle of the North Atlantic. You wonder how your job has taken you to places like that. Same with some other trips, cities like Chisinău and Tbilisi in Eastern Europe.

Airport... hotel... pitch... stadium.

That's your itinerary. You might go for a half-hour walk on the morning of a game for couple of miles, but that's all you see. The flying can take its toll but a win lifts everyone's spirits on the plane home.

The tournament experience was different; flying around France for Euro 2016 to play in Paris, Bordeaux, Lille and Lyon. Based in Versailles, we had downtime some afternoons. Myself and Ciaran Clark googled 'Things to do in Paris'... then ticked the list off one day.

The Champs-Élysées, Arc De Triomphe, the Eiffel Tower... we'd take photos of each other at these landmarks. Paris was full of Irish fans, so you're going to run into people. They were great though, no hassle and seemed surprised to see us out sightseeing. Boredom can easily set in on away trips. It depends on your personality.

Video games, darts, pool, cards, and I love watching TV series and films. I always had enough to keep me going.

Clarky was my usual roommate; we'd been friends a long time. If one of us wasn't in the squad, no one else came into the room to take that spot. That was the system. The Ireland management were clever in pairing people up.

Robbie Brady and Jeff Hendrick.

The St Kevin's Boys players.

Shane Long and Kevin Doyle, they'd the Reading connection.

Robbie Keane and Shay Given, the long-serving lads.

Seamus Coleman and James McCarthy have been roommates since 2010.

On the bus, we'd start with Martin and Roy up top, then work our way through the team staff, with the players all further back. The more experience you have, you can push further to the back of the bus. Robbie always sat on the back left of the bus.

He could demand that seat, he had the CV to back it up.

Callum Robinson came into the squad after Robbie left. A bubbly, lively character and first day he sat in Robbie's seat. Jon Walters called him on it, just messing, but Callum smiled away, oblivious to it

My wife knew what it meant to me to be involved with Ireland. When I was still playing, I was lucky enough that Alanna was young so she didn't know any different. Of course you'd miss them; an Ireland camp could mean eight to 11 days away from the family but we'd FaceTime often.

It was always nice to go see the Ireland lads. We'd a tight-knit bunch around my age – Seamus, McClean, myself, Clarky and James Mc. We were friends, there were no egos involved and that was reflected on the pitch.

IF I WON with Ireland, I came back to Hull on a high.

After the Wales game, I had my chest out. Seb Larsson was in the play-offs as well with Sweden. We watched the draw together; they got Italy, we got Denmark. He'd said before that Denmark were one to avoid, a good team.

A month later we lose to Denmark; Sweden qualify after putting Italy out.

I come back to Hull and he's got his chest out; he's the one going to the World Cup. As much as managers might say it is great to see you play for your country, the focus quickly moves to Hull. The fans don't care about my experiences in Cardiff or Vienna.

Steve Bruce was asked once for his thoughts on me captaining Ireland? He was in a press conference, and he'd been unaware of it. The Hull job was what consumed him. Steve never had a problem with you going but he would go mad if you came back injured. Marco Silva used to message me the best of luck and tell me he'd be watching the games.

When I was with Reading, Paul Clement didn't want me to go to one Ireland trip. It was September 2018, when we got hammered 4-1 by Wales. He wanted extra training sessions as our results hadn't been great. The only way I wasn't going was if Martin didn't pick me.

He did and then I had a massive argument with Clement about it. A sign that things wouldn't work out with Reading.

WHEN YOU JOIN a national squad, you wonder how the older stars will take to you. Meeting someone as iconic as Robbie Keane in Irish football was a big deal, but Robbie was always very good to me.

I'm not sure Ireland will ever produce a striker like him. Robbie had a street-footballer mentality. He thrived in tight spaces with his skill. Obsessed with goals, if it was a five-a-side in training, he'd run off and celebrate with a cartwheel if he scored. He prided himself on his finishing.

We played Gibraltar in 2014, the week before the Germany draw. Robbie got a hat-trick early on. He could smell blood in the water against teams. If a manager took him off when he was on two goals, there'd be uproar as he chased a hat-trick.

People said he scored loads of tap-ins but that was down to how good his positioning and awareness were. Some said a lot of his goals were penalties. But that showed how cool and calm he was under pressure.

I've wondered did Robbie really get the appreciation he deserved when he played... 68 goals is an unbelievable tally and that's enough proof of how incredible a striker he was.

IT WAS FRUSTRATING to hear during Martin's time in charge that Ireland never played football the right way. Our midfielders were regularly in the spotlight for that. I was probably lucky that I didn't get as much criticism as Jeff Hendrick, Glenn Whelan or James McCarthy. My job was to win the ball back and get it to a better player.

Martin would always encourage us to pass; he'd have a go off me the whole time, saying he needed more. Fans and media want to see attractive football but results are the number one aim. It's a balancing act. Take the Slovakia game that Ireland lost on penalties in October 2020 in the Euro play-off. It might have been ugly, but Martin's teams would have found a way to win that game

Some of the biggest and best moments you'll remember as an Irish fan were not games of beautiful football. But we still talk about them, how they made us feel emotionally. The Shane Long and Robbie Brady goals on teams I played on will be remembered as fondly as Ray Houghton in 1994 and Jason McAteer in 2001.

When those debates raged, I needed to learn to block out the noise. I played one game for Ireland where I got a 5 out of 10 rating in a newspaper the next day. But in our camp afterwards, Martin and Roy were ecstatic about my performance. You have to step back and realise their views are most important.

It would bug me when suggestions were made that there was a lack of thorough analysis in the Ireland set-up. Martin looked back at Ireland games all the time; he'd be getting onto Ger Dunne, the lead analyst, for the footage straight away if we lost and for away games he'd watch them on the flight home. Same after training in Castleknock; the players headed for lunch and Martin to his office to watch videos of the session, see if he could spot anything.

The Ireland analysis team made three I-Pads available for the players. We used

Hudl, the performance analysis app; everyone had a login and if you wanted to watch games or any opponent, there were specific clips available. We did collective team analysis but that extra individual stuff was up to each player.

I preferred to focus on myself, make sure I felt mentally right and fit, that my sleep and diet had been good. Seamus would watch wingers that he would be facing. Figure out their traits like if they drop the shoulder to come inside. He found it very beneficial.

Defending set-pieces was at the core of Martin's philosophy.

We played Poland in November 2015, just after beating Germany. Their midfielder Grzegroz Krychowiak scored a goal after a corner came to him at the edge of the box and he fired it in through a crowd. That drove Martin insane. We must have watched that goal back 50 times. Same story with the Shaun Maloney goal for Scotland in 2014; lazy defending, someone not switched on and the team reacts too late.

Martin was adamant that games are won or lost with set-pieces. He went into them in so much detail but the players were also involved in the planning. He would throw it out to the floor on areas like positioning… and who would be comfortable on the posts? He took great pride in getting it right.

We had some great moments with Ireland and supporters wanted that all the time. It's not that simple, however.

'It's easy to get to Manchester United. It's hard to stay there!' was a regular saying from Dwight Yorke at Sunderland.

That sums it up. Consistency is what everyone in football is striving for.

TUESDAY NOVEMBER 14, 2017.

The Aviva Stadium is packed and full of anticipation. Three days before, we drew 0-0 with Denmark. I watch on in Copenhagen as I was suspended but the lads put in a brilliant resolute performance. For the game in Dublin, I get back in the starting team and I'm captain. A place in the World Cup within our grasp.

And then at half-time, I'm done!

Martin calls out the changes. Myself and Harry Arter are off.

Aiden and Wes in.

We're losing 2-1 after a perfect start with Shane Duffy's goal. I wished the lads around me well, got changed and back out to the stand to watch the second-half. Denmark battered us 5-1. Christian Eriksen got a hat-trick, destroying our dreams of going to Russia.

Martin got it wrong at half-time.

If you want to take me off, that's fine.

Same with Harry. But don't take off your two holding midfielders. Get Wes or Aiden on for more creativity and then pin a player on Eriksen for the rest of the game. Instead, there was no protection for the defence and Eriksen has a field day.

My suggestion is different but I don't have Martin's experience. When he left Ireland, we chatted and went back over the years. He didn't apologise for that half-time decision but he did acknowledge that change could have been better.

We needed to hang in there at the start of the second-half. Then throw the kitchen sink at it late on, if we were still losing 2-1. Think about the crowd roaring us on, willing the ball to go into the Danish net. In September 2019 I was on radio co-commentary for *Off The Ball* as Ireland chased Switzerland. David McGoldrick equalised and that night I felt the energy in the stands pushing the team on.

Denmark could have been put under pressure but they didn't need to worry as the goals were flying in. They started planning for Russia early.

I WAS IN a bullish mood before the game.

Seamus pulled me over an interview, where I'd said that Denmark didn't have the character and heart that we had. Seamus would have been more reserved; I was declaring what I felt in my heart.

I had full belief in our team. Watching the second-half was devastating. I wanted to get to the World Cup, not just for myself, but to give Seamus the chance to lead Ireland out. I was conscious I was a stand-in captain and always pointed out he was our leader. After what he'd been through with his leg break and people doubting him, imagine if he could have come back to that? I felt powerless as that hope slipped away.

How long did it take me to come to terms with that night? I'm still not sure I have. The hurt lingers and I don't know will it ever completely go away. The end of my dream of playing at the World Cup.

We went up to the players' lounge in the stadium after. All my family were there. Cally had flown over, it was the first Ireland game she was at. Dad had been joking that she was never coming again after that result. He'd warned her that my mood wouldn't be great but she knew that already.

All my buddies who I grew up with were at the game; they were going out in Dublin, I said we'd go meet them. Then Cally told me to go out and blow off some steam; she'd have an early night and head back to the hotel. It was really thoughtful of her.

I went out with the lads, drinking around Dublin. That group had been there for magical moments in my career but they also shared in the disappointments. They were gutted that we lost but not as invested as I was.

'Ah look Dave, get over it… will ya?'

'Do you want a pint or what?'

That sort of talk pulls you back to reality. My last memory of the night is of the lads… one of them talking about his little boy growing up, and showing me photos.

It's a few hours after the biggest sporting heartbreak I've suffered. The pain of the loss and my performance is still raw, and I'm listening to how a toddler is growing.

And in a way it's nice, it gives me some perspective.

Life rolls on.

Carlow

Mount Leinster Rangers

Eddie Coady

Waterford

Ireland vs Scotland

Bonnar Maher

Tommy Walsh

★★★

JOHN

IN MAY 2014, my two sporting lives intersected on the same weekend.

That spring, David went on this brilliant journey with Hull City through the rounds of the FA Cup and they went all the way to the final. Meanwhile, in a different universe, the Carlow senior hurlers were stuck in the Leinster Championship in a new round-robin qualifying group.

I was the supporter of one team, the manager of the other and trying to juggle everything was challenging.

It all came to a head when Hull faced Arsenal in the final at Wembley on Saturday 17. Carlow were meeting Westmeath in our fourth, and last game, on Sunday 18 at Dr Cullen Park.

Missing either game wasn't an option. Hull lost the final after extra-time and afterwards David was delayed as he was selected for drug testing. It took a while; he was drained after such an exhausting game. We ended up not meeting that night in the team hotel until nearly midnight. He was like a bull with the way the day had gone after losing the match and the long wait afterwards on his own, when all he wanted was the company of family or teammates to help ease the pain of defeat.

We didn't really get a chance to talk through the game, something we always did. I could only stay with him for an hour and then I'd to head to Heathrow at 1am to check in at a hotel at the airport. I only spent a few hours there... my flight was at 6am.

Landed in Cork at half seven, went to Mass on Popes Quay at eight, home before nine and into bed for two hours. Back up at 11, drove to Carlow... met the players at 1pm.

Throw-in for the match was 2pm.

We won by two points, our first win of the group but not enough to get us a Leinster quarter-final against the big boys. I got home at 11 o'clock that night, completely wiped out after such an emotionally charged weekend.

That was my last game as Carlow senior hurling manager.

IN THE AUTUMN of 2012 I took a phone call from Michael Meaney, the Carlow chairman. He was sounding me out to see if I was interested in the senior manager job, so I went up to Bagenalstown to meet him and five of the players. It felt a positive fit, so I went for it.

Carlow has some fantastic hurling places. They're on the border with Kilkenny, they're close to Wexford as well, just surrounded by strongholds of the game. Their clubs were playing in the Kilkenny leagues, which struck me as a really progressive move. They had that mix of enthusiasm and passion; the job then really appealed to me.

When I was driving up there from Cork, I used to go through Kilkenny city, passing big senior clubs like James Stephens, Dicksboro and O'Loughlin Gaels. Then a half hour drive out the road, as you go by Clara... Gowran, the home of DJ Carey, and Paulstown... then you hit the Carlow hurling catchment area.

From a place that was eating up All-Ireland titles under Brian Cody to one that was trying to climb up from a low base. I'd wonder why such a gap existed between two counties only a few miles apart?

IT MAY ONLY be a hop across the border but they're in different hurling worlds. In Kilkenny it's the only show in town; that's reflected in the tradition and importance they place on it. Football is a competing interest in Carlow and there isn't a similar number of clubs. There were only five competing in the 2020 Carlow Senior Hurling Championship.

In 2013, we finished bottom of Division 1B in the hurling league. We'd been very competitive but suffered some cruel losses in our first three games... five points to Wexford, three to Limerick... two to Offaly. That was the year Limerick won Munster; my old Barrs teammate John Allen was in charge.

It was the same old story for a weaker county, so near but still so far away. You're only short a few points on the scoreboard but bridging that gap and getting over the line to actually win is the really difficult task. The defeats got heavier and we lost the relegation play-off to Antrim.

That theme continued in the championship. We beat London and lost to Laois in Leinster before heading down to Wexford to play them in a qualifier at the end of June.

The crucial moment of that game is still burned in my mind.

James Doyle was on as a substitute. He got the ball out the far wing, cut inside and went for goal... but struck the post. If it had hit the net, we would have been five points up with less than 15 minutes to go.

Instead, Wexford got out of jail. They went down the field a minute later and David Redmond scored their second goal. We levelled near full-time but they hit two late points and won 2-16 to 0-20.

The performance was superb but the result was a sickener. I couldn't fault the application of the players but it hadn't materialised into the victory we craved against a top team. The dressing-room afterwards was full of grief, fellas crying on benches as they realised how close they were to taking down the hot favourites for a win that would have been remembered for years.

How big a boost would that have been for Carlow hurling? The next day Wexford lost to Clare after extra-time in Thurles. Clare went on to win the All-Ireland in September. Of course, it doesn't automatically pan out like that but considering the potential impact if we'd beaten Wexford, it weighed on my mind for some time.

IN A WEAKER hurling county, it's a constant struggle for numbers. You don't always have the best players available. Some fella decides to go travelling for a year, another might be out injured long-term. In a stronger county, you simply turn around and see who's next up to slot in. In a county like Carlow, the depth in the player pool is shallow. You can't cope if key players are absent.

Take our preparations for the 2014 season.

That winter and spring, Mount Leinster Rangers travelled all the way to the All-Ireland club final. It was a magical success story, not just for Carlow hurling, but for the whole county. It caught the wider imagination. They upset Ballyboden St-Enda's from Dublin and Oulart-The Ballagh from Wexford to win the Leinster title.

The day that final was played in November 2013, I was over in Hull to see David score his first Premier League goal in a 3-1 win over Liverpool. It was my *Super Sporting Sunday*, watching this win unfold at the KC Stadium and getting texts with the score updates as something historic was happening back in Nowlan Park.

Mount Leinster went on to win the All-Ireland semi-final the following February, by a point up in Newry after a real battle against Antrim's Loughgiel Shamrocks. We were all there in Croke Park to cheer them on, on St Patrick's Day, but the final was a step too far against Portumna with the class they had in the Cannings and the Hayes brothers.

I wasn't surprised by their progress. If you knew the Coady brothers for instance, particularly Eddie, you knew they'd go far. Eddie was just an outstanding hurler, a wing-back who wore his heart on his sleeve, and an absolutely lovely person. I'd great time for him and his brothers Richie and Paul. Then Denis Murphy was a brilliant forward and free-taker.

But all the while, I was trying to run the Carlow senior side. Mount Leinster Rangers supplied seven players to our squad. The Nolan brothers from Myshall were out injured. I was absolutely delighted for Mount Leinster Rangers but it disrupted our progress. We could have done with all of them as we were trying to get out of Division 2A.

Now, the rest of the lads drove it on brilliantly and the only round-robin game we lost was down in Tralee against Kerry, the day before the club final in March.

That put us in a league final against Kerry again in Thurles in April. The tricky thing was whether or not to bring the Mount Leinster lads back into the team. We did start them but lost 3-16 to 3-13. That was a really important play-off and then we didn't get out of the Leinster Championship group either.

If 2013 had seen us take a couple of steps forward, 2014 drove us back five or six paces and we were struggling once more. The classic story of life in the hurling lower ranks.

I had argued strongly at the end of 2013 with the GAA hierarchy not to relegate us from Division 1 of the league. I begged them to leave us for a second year to help us develop rather than being stuck in a yo-yo state. If we hadn't performed in that second year, then make that call to send us down.

I made my case to the top people in the GAA at the time but it hadn't made a difference. By July 2014 I was gone from Carlow, finished up after the two-year cycle. We all just agreed it was time to move on.

SOME MANAGERIAL JOBS never got going for me. Speculation always lights up when someone leaves a county and there's a vacancy to be filled.

In September 2011, Davy Fitzgerald stepped down in Waterford and they were looking for a new man. The County Board rang and asked me to come down for a chat. I drove to Dungarvan; the interview was in one of the holiday homes at the back of the Park Hotel, next to Fraher Field.

I was very interested in it. They were a strong championship team with a couple of legends like Tony Browne and John Mullane still there, and a load of young prospects. I don't generally go for interviews but the chairman was very courteous to me in the first phone call, so I was happy to talk to them.

But from the start of that interview, I was really disappointed in the conduct of one person on the committee. He was more concerned about the manner in which I'd left Wexford than what I could bring to the Waterford job. His line of questioning was very negative. I couldn't figure him out and he was the only one that kept returning to that topic.

It also seemed a fait accompli that another candidate had a management team in place and ready to go. I made the point at the meeting that I wasn't going to approach people and ask them to commit as part of a management team unless I could guarantee them I had the job.

On the drive home, I rang the secretary Timmy O'Keeffe and just said it wasn't for me. The questioning from that individual wasn't right and I reckoned someone else was in pole position. Afterwards when Michael Ryan got the job, it added up that he was the number one contender from the start.

It would have been an interesting role to get stuck into. But I didn't get it, so I didn't dwell on it and quickly moved on.

THE GAA IS local and tribal, club and county; those are the battles you become obsessed with fighting.

The one truly different management job I did get, away from all that, was with the Ireland team that played Scotland in the Shinty hurling series. The games were two-legs played every year, home and away.

Myself and Michael Walsh from Kilkenny were asked by Paudie Butler and Pat Daly in Croke Park to take the under-21 team first. I had won three All-Ireland under-21 B titles with Kerry, so they felt I'd have the insight. Then after doing the under-21s, they gave us the senior job for a couple of years.

Hurling is a small community, so myself and Walsh knew each other from over the years. We got on like a house on fire and we loved the Shinty experience.

It was a chance to manage an Ireland team so we got stuck into it. It was mainly players from second-tier counties; at senior you were allowed four players from the Liam MacCarthy Cup counties.

We organised trials for Ratoath in Meath. At least one player from each county had to be picked, so I rang all the under-21 managers around the country to pick their brains.

The trials were tricky to judge players. The very first one, the Laois goalkeeper Eoin O'Reilly came up halfway through and started giving out he hadn't even touched the ball. *Fair point.* We switched him around for the second-half; he stopped bullets and made the team. We tried to pick players who were proficient at soloing and playing through the lines. Every year we got better and we never lost to the Scots in the senior matches.

After the squad was picked, there was a month to prepare so we squeezed in a couple of training sessions in Laois, as it was the most central location. We'd play the home game in Ireland and then head to Belfast Airport on a Friday night to get the flight to Inverness.

On the Saturdays at Bught Park in the city, it was a festival-like atmosphere with the game as the centrepiece. There'd be a meal that night, a few pints in the hotel, breakfast on the Sunday morning and catch the flight home.

I was really grateful to be asked to do something completely novel and get out of my comfort zone as a manager.

Getting to know the players was superb, like Neil McManus from Antrim and Richie Hogan in Kilkenny. The Carlow lads Des Shaw and Shane Kavanagh, I got on well with and that paved the way for me later managing them. Other times you were getting to work with people again, like Jackie Tyrrell and Darragh O'Connell.

Choosing the senior hurlers took a bit of thinking. We looked at the type of player that would suit the game, not just the biggest stars. Bonner Maher from Tipperary was a prime example. He could pick, turn and go with the ball better than most; he'd pop it off then. We'd Seamus Callanan and Patrick Horgan as finishers inside, and stick hurlers in defence like Tommy Walsh and Shane O'Neill.

Managing Tommy Walsh was a real honour; an outstanding hurler and person. Michael was very friendly with Tommy, said he was mad to play it.

One year the three of us met at Dublin Airport, then took one car together up to Belfast before flying out.

We got in early that Friday and decided we'd go for a puck-around in the afternoon. First fella out on the pitch was Tommy, getting himself psyched for this light training session. He'd all the All-Irelands and accolades in the hurling world but there he was in the Scottish Highlands, more up for a few pucks than anyone else.

It summed up his drive and enthusiasm, and in a wider sense captured the essence of Kilkenny hurling. Tommy was bursting for road, running around the pitch like a spring lamb. On the Saturday he got welded by the Scots but the harder the hits, the more he threw himself into it. He had to head back early after the game as he'd committed to attending an awards ceremony where he was being honoured in Dublin that Saturday night, but he was still happy to make the trip over.

In 2020, when everyone in Ireland was having their summer holidays at home after lockdown, I was in Lahinch in Clare one day walking down to the beach. I saw this couple running up towards their car, a couple of kids racing behind them. Tommy Walsh and the family.

'Well John, how's the form boy? Must run off there... we've to get back home for camogie training tonight.'

He was shouting at me as he sprinted to the car, the same whirlwind of energy as he was on the pitch.

One of the greatest people I've met through sport and not an ounce of ego in him.

XVI

Goodbye Hull

Hello Cork

Reading and Coventry

All-Ireland or Bust

Poland

Doug Howlett

Martin and Roy

Cally

2018 Munster Championship

Alanna and Brody

July 31, 2019

★★★

DAVID

IN THE SUMMER of 2018, I left Hull City.

It was March when I found out the end was in sight. At breakfast before training, the Hull press officer Luke Cash came up to me.

'Dave, I'm sorry… the club aren't extending your contract.'

'What do you mean?'

'Oh s**t, do you not know?'

'No.'

I was confused. Later, the club would make their contract offer with a substantial 40% cut. I knew they were trying to get wages under control. The first year we got promoted with Hull, the average player wage was £10-12,000 per week. The second time we got promoted it had gone up to £25-30,000. Finances were a tricky thing to navigate.

I played 191 times for Hull and if I hit the 200 mark, I got a bonus. It was notable at the end of my last season, I didn't play much. I understood decisions had to be made but I deserved more respect and to be told in a civilised way, not to discover through the media officer that I was heading for the exit.

AT THE HULL Player of the Year awards, the lads would all go to the director's box beforehand to meet the club owners, the Allem family. Ehab Allem was heavily involved but his father Assem had started everything and we met that night at the end of the season.

'David, I've heard that you're leaving!' said Assem. 'You need to come see me... we can sort this out.' It was an awkward moment with someone I'd so much time for. Assem didn't seem to know what was going on. I didn't end up chasing him for that conversation; in my mind I was gone.

Aseem was born in Egypt and famously came to England in the 60s with £20 in his back pocket. Joined a company, Tempest Diesels, worked his way up and then bought it, renaming it Allam Marine. They manufacture generators.

He lives 15 minutes away from me now, a multi-millionaire in a modest sized house. Assem took over as Hull City chairman in 2010. He's done so much good for the club that all the recent upheaval is sad. Plans to change the name to Hull Tigers, to further develop the club's image, caused so much anger amongst fans. I played in the most successful Hull team of all time and have fond memories of the place. But they had so much player and managerial turnover, that we lost stability.

The Russian coach Leonid Slutsky took over from Marco Silva in June 2017, lasted six months and then Nigel Adkins came in. Nigel was my last manager at Hull. The most positive man I've ever met in my life. Every morning he'd bounce into the training ground. You'd wonder did he ever have an off day.

Hull were far from promotion that season, we finished 18th. I played my last game in April, a 2-0 defeat to Cardiff City. It was good of Nigel to play me, the last home game of the season is a traditional farewell to the fans. I got to walk around after to say goodbye and had Alanna with me. It was sad. After six seasons and plenty of highs... but the end had come.

★★★

JOHN

I WAS STANDING outside the Madejski Stadium in Reading when my phone rang. It was a Saturday afternoon, September 23, 2017, as I waited for the Hull City bus to arrive to get my match ticket off David.

Kieran Kingston was on the line; six weeks had passed since the All-Ireland semi-final defeat to Waterford.

'John, I'm just ringing you to let you know I'm stepping down as Cork manager.'

'Ah Kieran, why?'

'Look, I have my reasons, I'm stepping down.'

He caught me completely on the hop. Reading and Hull fans walking past and I'm trying to process this big moment for Cork hurling. I tried to talk him out of it. Pointed out that it was only September and if he was feeling jaded, why not take a break? Myself and Pat Ryan could have run the pre-season between us.

But Kieran's mind was made up and he wasn't for turning.

I wanted him to stay. I felt there should be continuity. We'd had a progressive year. Now we needed to build and go again, learn from our mistakes. It sums up Cork hurling for the last 20 years. Too many managers only there for short periods. I get you need to see improvement every year but the constant changing uproots the whole structure.

Kieran's decision surprised me. I went in to watch David play for Hull in a 1-1 draw where Reading grabbed a late equaliser.

Shortly after full-time, the County Board had released a statement back home and everyone knew Cork needed a new hurling manager.

The question then moved on to who would replace him?

★

DAVID

PLAYERS RARELY LEAVE a club without another offer. After the revelation in March, my agent Neil Fewings got to work. Steven Gerrard wanted to sign me for Rangers. I turned that down; would have caused too much hassle with the Ireland connection.

There was talk of Nottingham Forest, and I nearly signed for Leeds but the money wasn't good enough. Reading looked like the best option.

Their manager Paul Clement flew to Dublin to meet me in June, when I was studying for my B coaching licence. We chatted for an hour over coffee, and I was impressed by him and excited by the challenge.

The four-year contract offer was a good deal at the age of 29. But the medical raised concerns over my knee and the offer was cut to two years, with a possible option of another year. I resented that change while also understanding it. Reading had to rely on proper advice.

WHEN JOINING SUNDERLAND and Hull, I just had to pack my bags and go. Signing for Reading, I had more to consider with a wife, a daughter and another child on the way. Cally was settled in Hull but there's no time to debate, you have to leave.

They moved to Reading after pre-season and we rented a house. Thankfully, we didn't buy and kept our place in Hull. Maybe that was a sign we didn't commit fully to the change. It was a four-hour drive for Cally's family from Manchester, more convenient for mine as we were close to Heathrow Airport.

Dad would fly over every Saturday; Alanna waiting with her toy bricks to build towers with grandad.

Do I regret moving to Reading? Not a bit.

Cally had three miscarriages before our son Brody was born in April 2019. Being in Reading allowed us access to a specialist nearby in London and he resolved a blood clotting problem that she had.

The football side to our Reading story was difficult, but the move helped our family in the most important way.

PAUL MCSHANE AND John O'Shea were familiar faces when I joined Reading. Paul was there a while and warned me there were a few bad eggs in the squad. Straight away, I realised the problems with the club's culture... the time players showed up, how they trained, their demeanour. That stuff needs to be rooted out because it can ruin a team.

The season began against Derby; Frank Lampard's first league game in charge of them. We took the lead in the second-half but Mason Mount equalised and then Tom Lawrence scored an injury-time winner. A week of sporting heartbreak. The previous Sunday, dad was manager when Cork lost an extra-time epic to Limerick in the All-Ireland semi-final.

I'd flown back after the game in Croke Park, devastated for him.

Results didn't improve for Reading. No wins in our first six games left us second from bottom. On September 1, 2018, I started at home against Sheffield

Wednesday and got taken off after an hour. That was the end of my Reading career. I never played for the club again after that Saturday afternoon.

I got slaughtered by Reading fans for my displays, starting with the Derby match. Early defeats soured the mood at the club, their frustration grew as the season progressed and Reading finished 20th, just clear of relegation.

I tried my best to break into the squad, and had plenty of conversations with Paul Clement but got nowhere. I'd fallen out of favour, and experiencing that rejection was all new to me

There were two away games in November against Wigan and Leeds. Clement wanted me to travel as we were staying up north for a few days.

I was desperate to get back on the bench and figured I would when he brought me on that trip.

I didn't make the squad for either game. Clement wanted me around to help raise the spirits but I wasn't there to be an entertainer.

Hard times like that cause you to fall out of love with the game. It's never been about the money for me. It's great to earn a salary at that level and it has set me up for life, but I wanted to play. People said at least I was getting paid at Reading but I shouldn't have been because my job is to play football and I wasn't doing that.

You try not to take it home with you but I imagine for Cally, I was a nightmare to live with. At the club to make up the numbers... soul-destroying. I always wonder what I could have done differently but the whole move was just a disaster from the start.

In early December, Clement was sacked and before Christmas the new boss arrived. José Gomes from Portugal.

ON HIS FIRST day, Gomes asked to see me.

Eight players were brought in one by one. All told we could leave. Gomes apologised but said he had too many players. Happy Christmas.

Now, there's the door!

I wondered were the shots being called above the manager. I left the room that day in a blur of emotion. Then I saw the kitman packing up my locker. I couldn't change with the first-team anymore, train or eat with them... or speak to the manager again. I'd never had problems with any club I'd been at before; this was a bleak end to 2018.

★★★

JOHN

I'M LIVING IN Cork since 1974, the best part of 50 years and I've a fierce grá for Cork hurling. But I don't consider myself a Cork man. I'm a Wexford man. Even if I wanted to say I was a Cork man, locals wouldn't let me class myself as that. Bishop John Buckley said to me once that in Cork there are only two types of people… Cork people and those who think they are Cork people.

There's some truth to that. I've never pretended to be a Cork person. I've given 100% to any role I've had in the county in hurling and coaching. I live and work here. I've two children and a wife that are madly passionate about Cork hurling.

I'm still an outsider though. That's not a glib remark. I'm a Wexford man here and I should never think any different.

THE SPECULATION TURNED to Kieran Kingston's replacement.

I'm not in the business of getting onto the local paper or putting out something on Twitter to declare my intentions. I kept my counsel and waited to see how it would play out. A selection committee was formed to find a manager and then Frank Murphy rang me. 'Come down to Páirc Uí Chaoimh for a chat.' We met and went through for an hour the various issues to do with the role. But you know the main topic going in the door! It's not about doing this for the good of my health, it's about winning the All-Ireland for Cork.

Can you do that? That's the job spec in a nutshell.

I was concerned about the level of upheaval across the board. I felt the 2017 system of Kieran Kingston with the seniors, myself at under-21 and Denis Ring at minor had been positive. None of us had won All-Irelands, but we had all made improvements. If I took the senior position, that created a vacancy elsewhere.

I'm fortunate that Stella, Sarah and David have always supported me taking on roles in hurling. Never a barrier put in place.

There was one problem I needed to sort through. Stella had booked a holiday for us in 2018. Three weeks in South America. The trip of a lifetime but it was smack bang in the middle of the hurling championship.

I needed help and made a call.

'Sarah, I need a favour.'

'Yeah, go on dad.'

'I want you to go to South America with your mother next summer.'

'That's grand, dad... no problem!'

So I told Stella then that I was thinking of taking the Cork job and Sarah was going to take my place on the South America trip. The two of them went and had a brilliant time; they loved it all.

David was very keen for me to take it. Ultimately I didn't want it at the time. Sometimes you get jobs when you're not ready. I felt if I did the under-21s for another two years, I'd be better suited to step up to senior with those players.

But you can't turn down the chance to become Cork senior manager because it doesn't fit your schedule. I was 61 years old and it wasn't an opportunity that would come around again if I let it slip by. In October 2019, 10 days after watching David captain Ireland to beat Wales in Cardiff, I became the new Cork manager.

I had to take it.

AS A SENIOR manager in my sixties, the tag of old school fitted easily on me in some people's eyes. The modern way is to look at older people and dismiss their ability to evolve.

In the last 10 years, I've become absorbed in reading to help me improve as a manager. It's given me more awareness to take a more holistic view than a narrow picture. Now, I'd often be raging that I wasn't properly reading and searching for this stuff 30 years ago. I was never a reader. My wife would go through a book every few days. My brother used to read all the time as a child. John Allen, my old St Finbarr's teammate, was a fella who was constantly reading.

I find myself often returning to *Legacy* by James Kerr for advice; his focus on the All Blacks and what their rugby success can reveal about leadership. I look for books that contain lessons rather than just reading for enjoyment. I found that in *Legacy*. How they changed their culture and became the machine that won the Rugby World Cups in 2011 and '15.

I watch all sports religiously, searching for any new ideas I could pick up. Look at successful sportspeople and what could be learned from them? Jim Gavin's Dublin side always impressed. The way Gavin got good people around him, trained the team hard and created the proper environment for the players to prosper.

★★★

DAVID

MY IRELAND CAREER petered out after the Denmark play-off in 2017. I only got three more caps afterwards, coming on as a sub in 2018 against Turkey, France and Poland.

The Polish match in Wroclaw on Tuesday September 11, 2018, was my last game for Ireland. Five days earlier we lost 4-1 to Wales in the Nations League. I hadn't played. We trained the next day in Cardiff. The worst session is the day after a game when you've not played. You're annoyed and if the team has got pumped, you know the coaches are going to make you work twice as hard. My head wasn't in it at all.

Martin came up after and said, 'What the f**k is wrong with you?'

'I'm f****ng annoyed.'

'It's the worst I've ever seen you train.'

'Well I'm pissed off we got hammered and I haven't played!'

That wasn't the main argument that got people talking.

BEFORE THE POLAND game, a voice message surfaced on social media. Stephen Ward detailing an argument Roy had with Harry Arter and Jon Walters a couple months before. It spread like wildfire.

I felt it was blown out of proportion.

I've seen Roy go mad... Martin go mad... loads of people losing the plot. But everyone found out about this one as they listened to what Wardy had to say.

I was brought along to the pre-match Poland press conference, where Martin pointed out we'd had an argument in Cardiff and it was normal.

They happen all the time in football.

Paul McShane punched me in the changing room at half-time during a Hull game, a proper hit to the jaw. I've had more arguments with Paul than my own family; he'd fight with his own shadow in order to win. In training, if his team started losing, he'd be screaming and if you were on the other team it was pretty funny. That row happened on a Saturday during a defeat as Hull chased promotion at the end of the season.

Paul called me as we were going out to training on the Monday.

I just turned and said, 'Don't say what you're going to say. It's fine, move on.'

'Fair play!' I knew Paul was so desperate to win and I was the same. Some fellas take it to heart, I'd no grudges.

Move on. Once I get in my car to go home, it's forgotten about.

THE WALES MATCH was Wardy's last appearance for Ireland. I don't know if there was a way back for him. I know Roy rang Wardy.

Look, these things happen. You just need to be careful in what you share with friends when you're in football.

I didn't think too much about that Ireland controversy. Footballers are selfish, my concern was not playing in that Wales match. Whatever dispute existed between Roy and Jon Walters, was their issue. I get on really well with Jon, I get on with Roy. Football is a small world; focus on your own relationships rather than taking sides.

Alan Pardew was linked one time with taking over as Hull manager. *How would that have played out for me?* It didn't materialise but it would have been a challenge I'd have had to face.

★★★

JOHN

I JOINED TOO late to influence picking the Cork panel for 2017, but it was different for '18. I would have been slow to release the older lads. You can get rid of too much experience. Some leave of their own choice but you must be conscious of the void in the dressing-room.

The Bishopstown players Patrick Cronin and Shane O'Neill, both former Cork captains, were let go in 2016.

I came across Shane through the Ireland Shinty teams. A really good hurler, and an intelligent figure with the character to influence younger players. I regret not properly going after Shane and pushing to get him back.

I did approach Patrick Cronin; met him at the start of 2018 and asked him in. He thought about it and turned us down. I liked what he offered as a half-forward, remembering his 0-5 from play against Waterford in the 2015 Munster semi-final. He had *something*.

I also went after the footballers. Eoin Cadogan joined in 2018, Aidan Walsh the year after. They had their All-Ireland football medals, they were two winners. They wouldn't be everyone's cup of tea but they'd stand up to anyone; you see Cads against Peter Duggan in 2018, Welshy against Limerick in 2019.

They brought a presence on the pitch, two physically stronger figures. Cads had a big decision to make, he was in Australia that winter. He'd been under-21 fitness coach with me in 2017 and the footballers wanted him. I'd to make the pitch as to why I needed him.

We also kept bringing through new players. Seán O'Donoghue, Tim O'Mahony, Robbie O'Flynn and Jack O'Connor made their championship debuts in 2018, then Robert Downey, Declan Dalton and Niall O'Leary came on in '19.

I WENT INTO the job with my eyes open as to the demands it would make on me. The Cork senior job is a 24-7 position. Hurling only takes up a fraction of that. The pitch is your sanctuary, the 90 minutes of training is what I loved.

It's everything else that wears a manager down and eats up their time. The phone is glued to your ear... talking to players, selectors, coaches, physios, S&C team, logistics, the analysis team, the County Board, club managers, the media.

You leave training at Páirc Uí Rinn at 9.30pm and your night is only starting. There's someone in the car park to chat. Then a few calls to make in the car heading home. At the kitchen table until late at night, with the diary and laptop out, reviewing and planning. Get up in the morning and it starts all over again

I had good people alongside me. Fraggy came in to coach the team. He wasn't long finished playing with Sarsfields; he was busy working for PwC, and had a young family, but made the commitment. He was fresh and knew the game. Donal O'Mahony had been goalkeeping coach and became selector. Vice-principal with Christians, a shrewd hurling man, well-respected and knew the underage talent. The management team was small but we were tight and had the same purpose.

Then there were the key characters in the backroom.

Seánie Barry did logistics, Pat Keane was the kitman, Dr Con and his son

Colm on the medical side. Declan O'Sullivan did the physical training. Richie Mooney and Mark O'Donnell stayed on as masseurs. Dave Nolan and Stephen Tabb looked after the analysis and video. All really good operators.

These are people the players trust, and they act as the grapevine where issues can filter to us. I floated that team with a few players and the feedback was good.

We got to work.

★★★

DAVID

THE MONTH OF January 2019 was spent training with the Reading under-23s, isolated away from the football spotlight. We'd change in a Portakabin, often sharing it with the groundsmen. We were in exile; we called ourselves… 'The Bomb Squad'. You find out who your friends are in those situations. Paul and John were brilliant, they'd come down to see us. Sam Baldock, who I'm still friends with, was in the same scenario but he was determined to outlast Gomes, which he did.

We used to joke about who would crack first. I was tipped to be last but I folded early; told the coaches I wasn't training one day and they could tear up my contract. *I was gone.* The club asked me to take time to think about it.

I rang dad on the way home; he told me to slow down and not do anything stupid. Cally was similar; she was panicking as I was being an idiot. I slept on it, went back in the next day, told Reading I was staying and told them they would pay every pound they owed me.

It started to take a toll but then Reading brought in Seb Ewen, a transfer fixer, and it was his job to find us all clubs. He said Coventry in League One were interested in a loan move. My head was all over the place. At Christmas, Cally and Alanna had moved back to Hull. It made sense as she was pregnant and felt more settled there; we didn't know what my future was with Reading.

Seb just asked me to speak to Mark Robins, the Coventry manager who'd famously won the FA Cup in 1990 for Man United under Alex Ferguson. Within two minutes of speaking to Mark, I had my mind made up. I joined until the end of the season, packed the car and drove up to the West Midlands.

I only played five games for Coventry; injury struck again, but I loved my time at the club. Mark was great, said not to worry about my fitness and he made me feel wanted. It was a refreshing situation. A squad of young, hungry players. Michael Doyle had been at the club a long time but moved on. I was now the veteran Irish midfielder.

Mark gave me free rein to improve the squad culture. I didn't want the mistakes of Reading repeated. The dressing-room should be a sanctuary and a place to build chemistry. I got speakers in so there'd be music on, set up a table to play Uno cards and we got players into the habit of coming in early before training.

I had no family in Coventry, so I'd stay at the ground every day until 3.30-4pm. No rush to leave. We'd do gym sessions, play cards and just hang out. The young lads would be picking my brains on training techniques, or different Premier League experiences. We kept them disciplined; Mark would fine them for using phones in the dressing-room. I'd fine them if they were late to the gym.

The club provided me with an apartment in Coventry and then on days off I'd head home to Hull to the family. It seemed a strange existence, living on my own but I'd a nice network of players from the club... go out for dinner, watch a Champions League match or head to a pub quiz. Ways to pass the time.

My hamstring injury slowly came right; then in April I came on against Bristol Rovers and 13 minutes later was heading off after busting my left shoulder in a challenge for the ball. I snapped my AC joint, Grade 5. The pain was severe. I had surgery to repair the damage and nine days later Brody was born.

I couldn't even hold him. Cally was after a C-section and my arm was in a sling, so it was a bit chaotic in our house for those few weeks. We got a nanny in to help and we got by.

I wish I'd played more at Coventry but I did feel I helped galvanise the squad. It was just a shame we ran out of steam and missed the play-offs; finished eighth, but the following year they went up as champions. I had been in such a bad place at Reading, that Coventry got my buzz back for playing football.

MICK MCCARTHY CAME in as the new Ireland manager in November 2018.

I never got to play for him. We spoke on the phone a few times; he brought up that I wasn't playing much that season for Reading and Coventry. He said he needed lads playing regularly. I fully respected that. It didn't finish the way I wanted on the pitch with Ireland but after I retired I was invited back to Dublin in September 2019.

Ireland played Bulgaria in a friendly and I got presented to the crowd that night with Cally, Alanna and Brody by my side. To get recognised like that was really nice. Mick was in charge during a tough, damaging time for Irish football with the constant revelations during 2019 about the finances of the FAI.

I was taken aback like everyone else by all the stories that emerged. People would ask how was I so oblivious to it all? When we met up for Ireland duty, our focus was on the pitch for training and the match that followed.

No idea what was going on in the boardrooms and offices.

I met John Delaney plenty of times during my Ireland career. But the interactions were always brief. He'd say well done after a game and if we made small talk, it usually revolved around hurling... how Cork and Waterford were going, or he'd ask how my Dad was keeping. As players our focus was on getting results for Ireland and that's what we cared about.

At that time what John Delaney or any FAI official was doing, wasn't something I was concerned about.

I came across a lot of good people in the FAI, like Peter Sherrard and Lisa Bergin, who looked after the players. The security team of Bobby, Martin and Drew. The physio Ciaran. The chef Dave. Our doctor Alan Byrne. The kitmen Dick and Mick.

To later hear all the stories that emerged about the FAI, of course it was wrong. I did get a copy of *Champagne Football*, the book that details everything. It is people in the background that suffer.

But I've spent many years in football and nothing surprises me.

MARTIN O'NEILL'S TIME with Ireland didn't end well.

There became this hostility towards him, the mood turned sour. It was tough as I had huge time for the man. I don't think Martin helped himself at times. The interviews with Tony O'Donoghue made for uncomfortable viewing.

People were harping on about the unattractive football being played. Martin got results though; we qualified for the Euros and were 90 minutes away from reaching the World Cup. That was forgotten about near the finish. Didn't help that a few lads came out to put the sword in but that's football, lads who don't play always have more to say.

There's always been great pride and passion in Ireland's performances for years. I want to retain those core values and if you can add a possession-based style, that's brilliant. We can't lose the grit that makes us hard to break down.

My biggest concern for Stephen Kenny when he took over, was when would he get that opportunity to work on an expansive style of football? International windows are narrow; it's difficult to implement something complex.

Stephen has done brilliantly in bringing through young players but getting results is not easy. Martin was able to dig out games. The day Martin left Ireland, I had finished training with Reading when someone told me the news. Rather than text him, I'd more respect and rang him. We spoke on the phone for an hour as I drove home, reminiscing about different times.

I chatted with Roy later; I knew he didn't want sympathy then. But I felt it was right to talk to Martin. He was the manager when I'd had my best moments for Ireland. I can't say a bad word about him.

★★★

JOHN

A COUNTY MANAGER must keep an eye on several areas. Take the education demands facing players. Exams clash with the Munster round-robin series. I didn't want interferences with the players' ability to perform. When they arrived on the pitch, we wanted them tuned in and free of worries.

If a player has an exam the following morning or is behind in study, that can be a problem. We got help. Gary Wade, who founded the Cork School of Economics, does tuition for university students. He organised grinds if we had a player who had to repeat a college exam and needed help during the summer.

Conor Kelleher, a lecturer in CIT, was my education manager for the squad. He dealt with the 15 or 16 fellas who were in third-level. Checked in with them regularly, found out where they were at with exams and assignments? Then, if a player was doing well but stuck for a summer job, we used business contacts to help them. It was all designed to get the best out of their hurling so they were not weighed down by pressures.

THERE WAS EXPERT input as well. Gary Keegan was with Cork for two years, a highly-rated performance coach who has been so successful with teams like Irish boxing and Dublin football.

Kieran Kingston had brought Keegan in first, when the morale in the squad had been wiped out after a couple of hard years. I'd always felt Cork hurling carried a great sense of self-belief but defeats had proved damaging and knocked them back. Keegan worked at building that up.

I really wanted him to stay for 2018.

We had weekend camps down in Clonakilty, staying in the Quality Hotel and training in Ardfield at the St James club. A Friday afternoon would involve hurling training, a bite to eat and then work with Keegan from 5-7pm that evening. On Saturday morning he'd meet the players for an hour; we'd train, and back to Keegan for the afternoon.

He conducted group and individual sessions, working separately with players and management. Challenging us all, getting us thinking. He took on a bigger role in 2018 working more with the players.

Patrick Horgan was a prime example of the influence Gary Keegan had.

I never had to worry about Hoggy. He just went from strength to strength. At the start of 2017 he was 28 years of age, had one All Star and a Munster medal. Over the next three seasons he won three All Stars, two Munster senior medals and was a Hurler of the Year nominee in 2019.

His scoring returns were incredible. In 2019 he scored 7-62 over six games. Hitting 3-10 against Kilkenny was ridiculous, scoring a goal off his knees that day.

JBM is still the greatest Cork forward I've seen but Hoggy is one of the best Cork have produced. In my two years in charge of Cork, I couldn't fault him any day. I fault myself for not creating an All-Ireland winning side around him.

He didn't let me down, I let him down.

Hoggy is obsessive over the game. He arrived every evening for training by 5.30pm. Pottered out onto the pitch, got five sliotars, went over to the 21-yard line and put them down in a semi-circle. Starts shooting on goals, goes in to pick them up... back out, and sets it again from a different angle or distance.

He had a great influence on other players. Alan Cadogan and Shane Kingston would get to training early as well, start falling in on those shooting drills with Hoggy. In a weekend game Hoggy will fire a point over his shoulder but during that week, he will have practiced that shot 100 times.

When Doug Howlett worked with Cork in 2019, he talked about his routine as a rugby player. Every Thursday in training he would make sure to catch 100 balls. Then by Saturday, he felt ready to catch any ball pumped down on top of him.

Hoggy was similar.

I'D WORKED WITH Anthony Nash in the Cork minors in 2001 and in CIT. Knowing each other created an element of trust when I came in as Cork manager. He was one of the fellas I used as a sounding board.

You'd get the vibes from the dressing-room off the older fellas like him, Cadogan and Hoggy. It was a two-way conversation; if there was a problem the players wanted sorted, they'd approach me. I was happy to get that feedback.

Nash was a great example of a hurler who patiently waited for his chance and grabbed it when it came at the age of 27. He established himself as a modern quarterback in goal, calling the shots with his puck-outs. Penalty-taking was another area of innovation that he perfected to such a level that the GAA stopped it on safety grounds.

But it showed how he thought about the game and would push things to new levels.

CERTAIN PLAYERS REALLY prospered over the couple of years. Daniel Kearney was one. I loved working with him. He wasn't a Cork minor, played one year under-21 and plenty thought he was too small for the senior game.

He was seriously intelligent and there was a narky streak to him that was invaluable. He'd question everything. During the video analysis, he wanted every base covered before a game. You had to be ready with your answers and one step ahead of him. *What is Danny going to ask today?* He would throw a load of 'What if' scenarios at us, he really thought about the game and we wanted players to take ownership.

I coached him the way I'd have learned from Donal O'Grady and from his father Jimmy. Look at the two choices you have in a match and ask yourself...

Which should I focus on? Take his shooting style, we broke it down that from distance his right-hand side was a better bet than his left-hand.

The points flew over in 2018 as he worked up and down the wing.

Conor Lehane was an enigma of a hurler. Some of the tricks he would perform at training would defy logic. He would glide around and make it look so easy. There were times Lehane was really on it. In 2017 against Tipperary, he got 0-10, five from play. In the 2018 All-Ireland semi-final against Limerick, he hit 2-3.

We just couldn't get it out of him often enough.

I often thought with Lehane, Horgan and Cadogan, the talent was there to win an All-Ireland with that trio, but getting them all clicking on the pitch together at the same time was a challenge.

★★★

DAVID

I MET CALLY when I was 25. The best thing that ever happened to me.

She helped slow me down and mature. Alex Bruce introduced us. I was one of the few Hull lads who was single. Alex and Cally had a mutual friend, and he set us up. I got her number, started messaging, and the rest is history.

When we started going out, she lived in Manchester and I was in Hull. We were back and forth all the time. I put down the marker about football early on. For our third date, we went to see Liverpool play an FA Cup fourth round replay. A Wednesday night in Bolton, very romantic setting.

Cally only lived about 40 minutes from the ground. I was going to see Jordan play, so picked her up, we went for dinner before and then to the game.

Cally's family are all Man City supporters, old school fans from the Maine Road days. Her grandmother has an unbelievable match programme collection. Her mum is from the city, her dad is Scottish but he's settled in Manchester a long time. Cally's football knowledge has got better over the years.

She knows how much I'm into it and takes interest. If there's a big Champions League match on, we'll watch it together.

When our kids arrived, it grounded me. Alanna was born in January 2016,

Brody in April 2019. After Cally first became pregnant, the goalposts were shifted. She made me realise that my life couldn't be training, matches and nights out.

Cally would have worked in her family's clothing supply business, but she moved down before Alanna was born, to Cottingham, where I had bought my first house outside Hull. We're still there, well settled.

We got married on February 15, 2018. We'd initially planned a big wedding but decided to postpone it as Cally was pregnant, and then she sadly had a miscarriage.

We were going to New York, just the two of us later in 2017, and I tried to arrange another wedding over there. I'd seen Shane Lowry got married over there, had met him a few times; he's just a massive Irish sports fan.

So I spoke to Shane about where they went, photographer they booked and everything like that. But then Cally wasn't as big a fan of a New York wedding with no family present. It dragged, until we were arguing over the date one night and then she just booked a registry office in Beverley near us. We set a date, our families came over… and we got married.

I trained that Thursday morning with Hull as we were away to Chelsea in the FA Cup on the Saturday. Then the game was changed to Friday night because of TV coverage. I explained the whole situation to Nigel Adkins and he was brilliant. He told me… get married, stay for few hours for dinner and get the last train down to London.

After training, the rest of the players were getting ready to go to the train station. Frazier Campbell asked me for a lift to the hotel where we were meeting first.

'I can't.'

'Why?'

'I've got something on.'

'What could you have on?'

'I'm actually getting married.'

He started laughing, he couldn't believe it. I'd kept it quiet, just didn't want to jinx it after the other postponements… and Frazier started telling the other lads.

It was a strange experience in a way, particularly the train journey that night, but still special and we'd a great time. I want to do something when we're married five years. A big party to mark it with all our family and friends. Cally isn't religious but my dad is and I would like to get a Catholic blessing.

I started in the game at Stamford Bridge. We lost 4-0, conceding all the goals in the first-half… and I missed a penalty in the second-half.

A couple of days I'll never forget.

★★★

JOHN

DID I ENJOY my two years as Cork manager? I only truly enjoyed winning games. The experiences can be exhilarating. The draw against Limerick in Munster in 2018 before a full Páirc Uí Chaoimh was an amazing night of hurling to be involved in. There was always pressure hanging over us and I knew the goal that had to be realised for the job to be deemed successful. The way we fell short in 2018 was incredibly hard to take.

Six points up with eight minutes left in an All-Ireland semi-final. You question every decision you made in that game. *Why didn't I go a different way?* I found it tough to come to terms with. We simply should have shut up shop.

I still feel a few incidents went against us. Eoin Cadogan came out with the ball, was held up and referee Paud O'Dwyer gave a free against him. Seán O'Donoghue wasn't awarded a free at another stage. In the first-half Cian Lynch scored a goal but I thought Daniel Kearney was fouled first

We were inches away from killing the game off. Robbie O'Flynn made a brilliant run but his pass was slightly off. Seamus Harnedy controlled with his hurley instead of catching and Nickie Quaid had the chance to make that famous stop.

We got hammered after for our substitutions. The dressing-room at full-time was like a war-zone with fellas on the floor. It was the first year of extra-time in the All-Ireland semi-finals. I wish we could have all got on the bus and headed back to Cork to get set for a replay.

Instead we'd to go to the well again. Kearney and Harnedy had been two outstanding warriors for us all year. I asked them were they good to go; they nodded they were okay and in that split-second, I trusted it was right to stick with them.

No time for long deliberation. It backfired and we'd to take them off in extra-time. I accept responsibility for that; you make a snap decision and then live or die by it. The margins were so fine between two brilliant teams that day. Fair play to Limerick, they took the opportunity and won the All-Ireland. But it was a killer for us to be looking on.

Alan Cadogan was the missing link.

We made a stupid mistake with him. He was on the way back from injury and the thinking was he'd be fully fit for the final if we got there. He wore No. 27 against Limerick and did the warm-up but we should have put him in the 26-man squad. It cost us. We wanted to bring him on for extra-time but couldn't as he wasn't in the original squad.

I try not to dwell on past games. Watching them back isn't helpful now but the disappointment doesn't fade away.

THE HANGOVER FROM 2018 never fully went away.

There was always a cloud hanging over us in 2019. Aidan Walsh came back into the squad and we got some more young fellas. Aidan was going well, then he nearly cut his finger off in a workplace accident before the Westmeath game and missed the end of the championship.

Our performances against Tipperary and Limerick, two games in the space of seven days, at the start in Munster were miles apart.

Liam Sheedy going back to Tipperary really fired them up. They laid down a marker against us in the league, winning 1-29 to 1-16. Then we lost Bill Cooper down in the Páirc just before the championship game. His back gave way and it threw us off completely. Bill tore into teams on match days, he had horsed into Limerick in 2018. A brilliant competitor, a tough physical man. He set the tone in a match.

We were superb against Limerick, beating the reigning All-Ireland champions 1-26 to 1-19 in their backyard. We bullied them in the second-half but it was the last great game we played that summer.

We were consistently inconsistent, that was the problem. Beat Waterford, lost to Clare… on a day with sheets of rain coming down mixed with flashes of lightning in the middle of June in Ennis. Beat Westmeath… lost to Kilkenny.

Searching for the answer was incredibly frustrating.

As a management, we wrecked our heads trying to figure out why we couldn't extract it from the group more regularly. We hadn't bared our souls to each other after the Tipperary loss or done anything unusual before then beating Limerick. We looked at every aspect of our preparation. But the more we looked, the further we were from finding the reason for our loss of form.

Keegan had left after doing his two years. We talked about him staying for 2019 but he came back to say he was starting up a new business.

The search began for someone else. I used to talk obsessively about the All Blacks rugby culture, so Fraggy suggested we should get on to Doug Howlett.

Donal O'Mahony mentioned he was up in Christians one day a week doing some coaching. He had a word. Howlett came in with us. He was brilliant, fully immersed in it. His humility, honesty and personality shone through. The first night Howlett drove into training, Nash spotted him and asked what he was doing here?

'He's coming in to work with us.'

I could see straight away by his reaction that there would be a buy-in from the squad. Hoggy spent a lot of time with him, that relationship worked well.

Doug moved back to New Zealand later in 2019 with his family. Before he left, he asked to meet me and we'd a cup of coffee in the Rochestown Park Hotel. Then he gave me a parting gift, pulling a New Zealand jersey out of his bag, with the writing on the sleeve… *NZ v Samoa, June 16, 2001.* It felt emotional, an All Blacks legend giving me one of his jerseys.

I'll always treasure that item

If there is a theory that our struggles in 2019 were down to Keegan's exit and the team was lost without him, I'd reject that. When you lose, it's easy to point to an individual reason. Keegan was really good, but so was Howlett.

Everyone in our set-up, myself included, had to accept personal responsibility for how 2019 went.

★★★

DAVID

IN THOSE FIRST few years after moving to England, I acted like an idiot at times. You're a professional footballer, you get excited... you become too big for your boots.

I was young and earning too much money.

Coming back to Cork, I'd go out and pay for all my buddies. If I wanted to go on holidays and the lads couldn't afford it, I'd pay and then they'd have no excuse for not going. I had a brilliant upbringing from great parents but the money and fame made me get a bit ahead of myself.

When I was 19, there were three cars I really liked.

An Audi A3.

A classic BMW M3.

And an Mk2 Golf GTi.

I couldn't decide which one I wanted, so I ended up buying them all.

I've no idea what I was thinking. Eventually I was just looking at the three of them in the garage. Dad rightly pointed out I could only drive one at a time. I sold two of them quick enough.

I had some fantastic times as well.

The summer of 2013 started by going to Marbella straight after we got promoted with Hull. I came home, went out in Leeds that night... next day flew to Ibiza. Back for two days, then a trip to New York and Las Vegas. Finished off with time at home in Cork and then back for pre-season.

Different lads came for different trips, Kelogs was there for them all. A brilliant, mad couple of months. We were young, no responsibilities and living the dream. It took me a while to figure out this way of life.

I wouldn't say I thought I was better than people but I got drawn into arguments, especially back home in Cork when there was drink involved. Looking back, I think I needed those experiences; they served as a wake-up call and I matured.

And ultimately, what 23-year-old wouldn't be affected by earning tens of thousands of pounds a week?

WHEN I STARTED playing for Hull, we'd get a few kids coming up after games for autographs and pictures. After a couple of years, the crowd had grown to 100. The increase wasn't to do with my performances for Hull, it was all to do with video gaming and Fifa.

My dad would be looking on and trying to get his head around it.

I was always into video games growing up like everyone else. Around 2015 I got really into Fifa and one of the lads suggested I should start online streams when I played. Then a young fella asked me could I upload the streams to YouTube, so he could watch them back as he had missed one.

I looked into it, set up my own YouTube channel and it became a hobby. It's grown to over 340,000 subscribers, people watching on when I play. It's something I enjoy. When I played football, the Fifa gaming was a way to switch off.

It was never a problem when I played for Hull but at Reading there was a perception I was more interested in video gaming than being a footballer. Fans had a pop off me over it but it honestly never affected my performances. It helped me relax.

I'd play in a hotel room before Ireland games or the big matches with Hull.

My biggest downfall was I publicised the fact I was gaming but loads of footballers do it, bringing a PlayStation or an Xbox for away trips. It's a way to unwind and kill time. Apparently Martin and Roy were intrigued about the YouTube videos, so they watched them one day.

'Ah, they're very good David!' said Martin.

Not sure if they later became subscribers.

People tune into the streams for the personality of the gamer and the content, how good they are at it. Esports is a different world but it's growing massively. Look at Logan Paul; he started uploading videos and ended up fighting Floyd Mayweather. On the outside it may strange but there is an enormous market for the industry. When I retired, people assumed I might go at it full-time. But you would have devote all your time and the big money if you're professional is in other games like Fortnite or CS:GO.

Family is my priority.

I like football coaching and punditry. I want to get my golf handicap down; Dad got to four and that's the aim. Gaming is a hobby, something to play online with my friends when we all catch up and have a few drinks on a Friday night.

★★★

JOHN

AFTER 2019, I had a meeting with board chairperson Tracey Kennedy and CEO Kevin O'Donovan down in Páirc Uí Chaoimh. A standard post-season review with the County Board.

I was wiped out after we lost to Kilkenny. I had to reflect on everything and chatted to David. We'd be straight with each other.

He said it was time to go.

I figured if I was to go again, I'd need to reshape the whole set-up. *Had I the energy and the drive to do that?* I wasn't sure.

I'd done two years manager and a year as selector.

I never had a problem with resources, we got all the support we needed from the County Board. But there had been so much stuff going on outside of the hurling when it came to our preparation, that I hadn't the fuel left in the tank to keep going. At that meeting with Tracey and Kevin, they felt like the relationship had gone as far as it could.

I agreed and I was out the exit door.

THE ONE THING I am proud of is winning the 2018 Munster Championship. I know it's not the All-Ireland title that Cork people craved, but I was the first manager to win Munster after the round-robin format.

We were unbeaten in our four games and then came from eight points down to win the Munster final. The game changer was before half-time. Seamus caught the puck-out and Luke was on his shoulder to run in for a goal.

We went in at the break four down. We spent 18 and a half minutes in the dressing-room; kept everyone calm, regained composure and went out to show the character to win the match. The hour after the final whistle was brilliant. Fans and players on the pitch. All my family there... photos with the trophy. One of the better days.

★★★

DAVID

AS A FAMILY, the year of 2017 tested us in ways we could have never imagined. Cally had three miscarriages.

Devastating moments. One happened the day Ireland played Wales in March.

Cally rang, traumatised by the experience. There were ambulances outside my house in Hull and I was in a hotel room in Dublin preparing for a match. Martin O'Neill and dad both said to go be with my family. The next flight was a few hours later to Manchester and it would take another couple of hours to get to Hull.

Cally's family had arrived to look after her. I weighed everything up, decided to play the game and head home the next day.

In September 2019, I did a radio interview with Joe Molloy on *Off The Ball* on radio. I shared my story of that time. He pointed out that fans could have hammered my performance, not realising the trauma of that day. No one really knows what's going on behind it all with a player.

For the first two miscarriages, I focused on supporting Cally but the third hit me the hardest. I thought I wasn't going to have another child and I was desperate for Alanna to have a sibling.

I didn't know how to cope.

Bad moods.

Drinking at home. It was around then I was back in Cork and had that video recorded of me drunk, which was later uploaded to Facebook. I lost my way. I didn't confide in anyone and soon hit rock bottom.

The Hull physio Alan Peacham asked Brian Lenihan one day was I alright. Brian had sensed I wasn't. The club doctor Mark Waller called me in and I told him everything. They set me up to speak to someone. That process was hard. It helped a little but I sort of resolved it myself, found a way to get going again.

Something as simple as getting out of bed early on a day off, and planning something to do.

Brian is five years younger than me. Another Cork lad who started off at Corinthians and later signed for Hull. He made his first-team debut in April 2016. I was in Paris that weekend but Steve Bruce gave me the heads up, so I arranged for Brian's family to be flown over to see Hull's game.

Brian used to come around to our house all the time. Cally would cook dinner or we'd play some pool. A great fella.

WHEN I DAMAGED my shoulder in April 2019, I was facing 12-to-16 weeks out. I saw it as a prime opportunity to rest my right knee and get ready for pre-season. Coventry were good at helping, but I ended up finishing my rehab at home and hired my own physio, Stuart Leake who'd been with Hull City before.

But the lack of exercise saw my knee deteriorate. It faded away.

The clock was ticking.

As that summer progressed, I started doing some running but my knee was in so much pain. My physio recommended seeing a surgeon in Leeds in June and he sketched out the three options.

1. Tidy up the knee with a minor procedure, get four or five weeks relief but soon you'll be back to square one.

2. Drill four holes in my kneecap on either side, to relieve pressure. A very specialised surgery costing £50-60k. A 10-15% chance of getting back playing and it would require at least 18 months rehab. Needed to fund all that myself.

3. Call it a day.

Take your pick.

There was talk of a knee replacement. I was 30. The shock of that was like getting a punch to the jaw.

I left Leeds that day, and rang dad and Cally. I think my family felt it was all in my head at times but I knew how much pain I was in. Even now my knee is riddled with arthritis and on a cold morning when I wake up, it is painful as I walk down the stairs.

The decision weighed on my mind over the coming weeks. There was an obvious choice to make but I couldn't bring myself to say those words... *I'm going to have to retire from football.* Part of me refused to accept it.

I was only 30; if I'd got to 35 I'd have been content.

I had to sort out my Reading situation. Even if I wasn't playing, my contract wasn't up. I'd started to make peace with the fact that I was going to retire but it was about my children now and I wanted to get paid.

My agent was clever; he'd put a contract clause in that if I was fit for a certain number of games, I got an extra year. Dad had written down every game I was available, including when I was at Coventry as that was Reading's choice not to select me. I did some of the negotiations myself. Mark Bowen, a former Welsh player, was handling it for Reading.

It was a game of poker. We eventually struck a deal. I got paid 70% of what I was owed and moved on. Soccer began as a sport for me. Later, I realised it was a job in a cut-throat industry and by the end it was a ruthless business where everyone had to look out for themselves.

★★★

JOHN

I TRY NOT to have regrets. Reflecting we could have gone harder at the league both years and built momentum. It was a balancing act. Trying to keep players fresh and get everyone flying come the summer.

The way 2019 ended left me down at times.

Bishop John Buckley had always been very good to me when I was with Cork teams. He rang one day to meet me. Gave me a set of rosary beads that he'd got in Rome off the Pope. A gesture of thanks for everything I'd done for Cork hurling. That meant a lot.

Results dictate everything in how people rate managers.

The phone rings with well wishes if you win… and you get told to go back to Wexford if you lose. That's the cold reality but I always knew that.

I'd love to have won an All-Ireland with Cork. That always was what I'd be judged on. I know if I had achieved it, I'd have parked it quickly and looked for what was coming next. In sport I always look forward.

★★★

DAVID

MYSELF AND CALLY have two great children.

When Alanna arrived, it was a shock to the system like it is with any first child. Cally's mum was a huge help, I probably should have done more. After Brody was born, I was aware and involved from the start.

My daughter knows that Daddy played football, but Brody is too young. I retired seven months after he was born. It's a shame I couldn't go on longer so he could have some recollection of me playing. But you can't have it all your own way.

Everyone had to adjust to the changes Covid caused in 2020. I was home more often and it turned out to be the best thing that happened to me as a father, spending so much quality time with my kids. As tough as the lockdowns was for so many, it brought us closer together as a family.

Initially the lack of routine after I retired was hard to deal with. Football had come first for so long and everything else worked around that. I needed direction and I was lucky that I got two phone calls.

One was for a job interview for *Uncut*, a series the Premier League filmed, and they asked me down to London to screen test for a presenting role. It went well and I got the position to interview Premier League players.

The second was from Colin O'Brien to get involved with coaching the Ireland under-17s as I was completing my UEFA A Licence.

They were great opportunities but the Covid-19 pandemic stalled a lot of my plans. I enjoyed doing punditry work with *Off The Ball* but co-commentating on games had to stop.

I'm at the point now where I'm wondering what I want to pursue? The next 12 months will tell a lot.

I was 30 when I retired, entitled to feel my football career had been cut short. My wife and my father always thought I was going to have a breakdown at some stage. I kept watching games, went to the Champions League final in Madrid to see Jordan lift the trophy, saw my former teammates in action and did punditry work.

It was as if they feared all that exposure to football would overwhelm me.

Gradually, I just learned to make peace with it though. I'm happy for all the lads still playing. This is their moment. I had my mine.

I did what I set out to do as a kid and I'm thankful for that.

ROY PUT IT best, when he rang me after I retired.

'Don't look back with regrets.

'Look at what you've achieved.

'You've had an incredible career.'

I was taken aback by him saying that. It doesn't stack up at all next to his. But he put it into perspective, that medals and trophies are not the only measure. Football is so competitive and so global, that for an Irish player to make it for a time in the Premier League is a real achievement.

ON WEDNESDAY JULY 31, 2019, it was officially announced that my contract with Reading had been terminated by mutual consent. By coincidence it was the same afternoon that dad left as Cork manager. A day of departures.

The decision on my future was dragging on. On Friday August 30, I put it up on Instagram and let the whole world know I was retiring.

The picture I chose for that post was from that night in Cardiff in 2017, when I grabbed the crest on the white Ireland jersey and felt that rush of joy from succeeding with my country.

At the end of the statement, I paid tribute to Cally, dad, mum and Sarah for their support. The final two lines summed up the journey.

You've helped a young boy live out his dreams.

Thank you for everything.

A Father's Life in Hurling

John has faced, and won and lost, against the very best hurling managers in the game, including Limerick's John Kiely (above), Kilkenny legend Brian Cody (right), and (below) Tipperary's Liam Sheedy and Waterford's Derek McGrath.

Although he vested the largest portion of his managerial career in building up Cork underage hurling structures and seeking to guide the senior team to All-Ireland glory, John also brought his knowledge of the game to many clubs and other counties such as Kerry (left) and Carlow (bottom of page).

He also took charge of the Ireland team in the Shinty International Series against Scotland in 2012 when amongst others, he worked (above) with Kilkenny's iconic defender Tommy Walsh.

Celebrating with Wexford's brilliant goalkeeper Damien Fitzhenry after defeating Tipperary in the All-Ireland quarter-final in 2007 and (right) commiserating with Babs Keating after the same game.

John at work on the Wexford sideline during the 2008 Leinster final.

Working with some great people, like Cork's under-21 and senior management teams, allowed John to strengthen his hand as a manager. It also afforded him time for all the other duties a manager has to take on board, like meeting with the media (below).

Hard at work on the sideline during the 2018 Munster Championship final victory over Clare.

Anthony Nash talks to the Cork players before the game begins against Clare in 2018, and (left) Seamus Harnedy and Eoin Cadogan raise the winning trophy after one of the most rewarding days of John Meyler's managerial life.

Early family fun days with John and David and Sarah (top left) and a few years later (above) they're all together during John's early managerial days. A family enjoying Munster glory (left).

David (right) with John's sister Carmel, Sarah, Cally and Alanna, and Stella supporting Cork in the Munster Championship, and (below) John and Carmel celebrate victory together. John's brother Gerry (below), who passed away at the beginning of 2021, stands outside the family pub in Wexford.

Father and son, John and David, shared the good times and the tough times together on the playing fields of Ireland and England, but cherish a victorious moment after Cork were crowned Munster champions in 2018.

EPILOGUE

⋆★⋆

SARAH MEYLER

SPORT WAS ALWAYS huge in our family.

As kids, we were always going to matches, and so much of what we did revolved around sport. Mom and dad never pushed us into anything, they wanted us to do well and gave us every opportunity. I was big into swimming; that was mom's background.

David couldn't handle the early mornings for the pool, he liked his sleep.

There was never a problem with our parents in getting up early to take me to the pool, or driving David to training or a match. When I went to college in Limerick, to Mary Immaculate to study teaching, I was trying to keep swimming going in the 50-metre pool in UL.

I'd swam for Ireland when I was younger and to a high level, but it just wasn't working for me. I gave it up in the end and when I told mom and dad, they were so supportive.

They'd always back our decisions.

***

PETER 'KELOGS' KELLEHER

DAVID AND MYSELF grew up 100 metres from each other. I'm from Lissadell and he's Rochestown Rise in Cork, a short walkway between the two estates.

From the age of six, we just became best friends.

Dave was the fella that was talented at every sport. We'd play soccer constantly on the green, or spend summers in Douglas Golf Club as we got older. He was big into GAA; I always thought he was a brilliant hurler.

We'd slag him when he was younger... 'You'll go off to soccer trials in England and come back with a Dublin accent from hanging out with those lads'.

***

SARAH

WHATEVER SPORTING ROAD David went down, he'd have excelled at it.

He has such a driven mentality.

When he dropped out of school, I thought at first it was ridiculous but the opinion of his older sister wasn't going to matter.

When he moved to England, he vowed he would make it.

When he tore his cruciate, he vowed to get back.

If he puts his mind to something, he'll achieve it. He wasn't the flashiest footballer; he was a workhorse and would do whatever a manager asked him to do for the team.

David's core group of friends always stayed supporting him. They'd all travel to games and I thought that was a special part of it... seeing them all at the FA Cup final with Hull jerseys and Meyler written on the back. Kelogs was constantly heading over to him... he's like the fifth member of our family, and always there for David.

Dad put so much time into travelling the length and breadth of England. I don't know how he did it. It was great for David to have him there.

★★★

KELOGS

WE WENT TO different schools in Cork. I went to Pres and he went to Christians.

Rugby was the big sport in both. In 2007, I was playing as Pres won the Munster Senior Cup… and Dave was the Christians cheerleader in the stand.

We were both so into sport growing up. I was playing rugby to a high level… Munster and Ireland under-18s. Dave was excelling at everything.

I played for Cork Con in the All-Ireland league for a few years, went to Newcastle in Australia to play for a year, came back to play a bit in Cork, and then in Dublin when I moved there for work. Dave was a great supporter.

He'd come to games with John when I was in Cork. I'd a Fiat Stilo car at the time. Dave used to borrow it if he was home at weekends. The other rugby lads reckoned he was the only Premier League player driving around in a Fiat. He'd always return it with a tank full of petrol.

★★★

SARAH

I LOVED SUPPORTING dad when he managed teams.

Kilmoyley has been the big long-term involvement… I went down to Kerry with dad a lot. He's such a part of that community… he's not viewed as an outsider.

I used to become really immersed in it when I was at dad or David's matches; probably took it all too personally when I'd be watching in the stand.

When dad was Carlow manager, I drove to Laois to see them play one day. And sat next to two old men watching the game, who were giving out that this new manager had brought in a chef. I started explaining that at least the players were getting fed properly. They ended up agreeing that it made sense… we'd a great chat.

When David was playing for Hull, if fans were abusing him, there were times

I'd shout back. One man at a Hull kept on giving out and calling him… 'Mailer'.

I turned around.

'If you're going to make fun of him, at least say his name right.'

Mom was similar. There was an Ireland game where a fella kept on saying how bad Ireland were and she just asked… 'Why did you bother paying for the ticket?'

★★★

KELOGS

HE WAS SO driven in everything he did. We used to play Rugby 06 on the PlayStation… I was better than him. His grandmother then bought him the game. I didn't see him for weeks, and then called down to his house one day and he started hammering me. So competitive… such a hard worker. That's why he got so far in England and was able to bounce back from injuries. I never doubted him. I went over a lot to him after he got injured… I was in college and had plenty of spare time. He was working hard in rehab but it was tough for him.

Joining Sunderland was a big deal for all of us. The first summer he drove home in a lovely new Audi A5, and we were all like… 'He's actually made it!'

I went over to a lot of games; the big highlights were following him at Hull. I was at the Hull-Cardiff game with John that decided promotion in 2013… and Dave jumped into the stand with us after the game.

The two of them bawling in each other's arms. It was a class moment.

★★★

SARAH

I FOUND PARTS of the Cork job hard when dad was in charge.

Part of the problem was I'd read social media… some of the stuff was horrible, same when David was with Ireland. The two of them would be giving out to me… telling me not to read it. It all affected me more than the two of them.

But we had some great days. The Munster final win in 2018 with Cork was magical. And myself, mom and dad had a brilliant time following Ireland around France for Euro 2016.

It's funny, sport provided days when the four of us could be together. On Christmas Day we mightn't all be in the one place. Mom could be working; she'd be in Ireland with me. Then David and dad could be in England.

But matches were occasions to all be present.

When dad won the county title with Courcey Rovers in 2011, we were all there as David was home. We got a photo after the match in Páirc Uí Rinn... David has it blown up and on the wall in his house in England.

***

KELOGS

OFTEN, WE WENT to support Dave as a group... the seven or eight lads from Cork. The Denmark play-off... and Hull's FA Cup final in 2014 were unreal occasions. When the team lost, we tried to be there for him... take him out for a few drinks.

Ask any of our buddies,and they'll all say Dave is extremely generous. He was on good money through soccer but he always wanted to look after us... just enjoy himself with his friends. Dave hangs out with the exact same crew now that he did when we were all teenagers. He hasn't lost touch.

***

SARAH

LOOKING BACK, I probably wish I went over to see David play more. Those were trips that were amazing when David played... or scored. The other side was if he wasn't playing or the club had signed another midfielder... that'd be a challenge to face.

The Ireland games were huge experiences.

We'd have the wait to hear the team named before the game to find out if he was starting. If David was a sub, I'd be more interested in watching the sideline to see if Martin O'Neill was going to call him at any stage.

The Wales game in Cardiff was the best night. Myself, mom, dad and my partner Eugene were all there; it was fantastic from start to finish. It was the first away Ireland match I was at. Walking across the car park before with mom to get a cup of coffee, and hearing he was in the team... so exciting.

★★★

KELOGS

I WAS VERY lucky... he included me in a lot of amazing experiences. He got invited to Steven Gerrard's Golf Classic in the Algarve. We flew out and played golf the day before. We were about to tee off and four lads came down at the same time.

Meyler is saying hello... we all shake hands.

I whispered to Meyler... 'Who are they?'

'That's Gerrard and his buddies.'

'What?!'

I didn't recognise Gerrard at all... he was smaller in real life than I thought he'd be.

Before I hit my drive, Gerrard shouts out in his Scouse accent... 'Right big lad... let's see what you've got!'

★★★

SARAH

WHEN DAVID WALKED out before a match, I'd nearly well up... nearly praying that that game would go well for my younger brother. You'd want the team to win, but I almost wanted David to play well first. Maybe that was because I was aware of the criticism if he didn't have a good game.

I think it's remarkable what he achieved given his injuries. He had to battle back on his own, motivate himself and stick at it to recover. That's something in his character that a lot of people don't have... an ability to never stop.

★★★

KELOGS

I'D A RUGBY match with Cork Con on a Saturday, but David was home and headed out on the Friday night. He texted me at 11.30pm.

'Any chance of a lift home?'

'Ah no, Dave. I've a game tomorrow.'

'I'm just out with Roy here.'

'Oh right... yeah I'm on my way.'

So that was the first time I met Roy Keane. Any fella in Cork would drop what they're doing to pick him up.

I met Roy a few times after that. In 2014, Ireland were playing Portugal in New York... Dave told me to come over, we were going on holidays after. I got a taxi to the team hotel and was waiting in the lobby for him.

Roy walked into the hotel and sort of did a double take when he saw me. I wasn't going to bother him, but he came back 10 minutes later... asked was I alright waiting, to go to the bar or reception if I needed anything. Very sound of him.

All those Irish lads that I got to know were good fellas At one Ireland camp, Daryl Murphy asked Dave, 'Is Kelogs coming to the game tomorrow night?'

Then someone else shouted, 'Oh yeah... how is Kelogs?'

Roy was listening in.

'How does everybody know this Coco Pops fella?!'

***

SARAH

IT'S FUNNY THE way it's worked out, that I'm settled in Wexford now... not too far from where dad grew up. I live in Ballymitty and work in Wexford Town... principal of St Iberius NS.

Dad comes down regularly, goes for a swim nearby and comes in for a coffee after. He's just a great help with everything... when I was building my house, or if I needed help in school.

I went all over the country to watch matches when he was a manager, just my way of supporting him.

Sport made dad and David well known.

When I started working in the school where I am now, the kids there didn't know that I was David's sister. The chat started one day about the Premier League... and I mentioned that my brother had played in it.

'Stop Ms Meyler... your brother did not play soccer!'

'He did... Google it now when you go home!'

They came in the next day; they couldn't believe it and just wanted to hear stories about David's soccer career.

To me, they will always be David and dad.

We're so proud of them both.

★★★

KELOGS

I FOUND ALL the footballers that I came across were great... Jordan Henderson, Ciaran Clark, Robbie Brady... I got to know all Dave's buddies. Once you were introduced to that circle, they couldn't be nicer to you.

I'd be good friends with Peter O'Mahony as well... we started playing rugby together as eight-year-olds in Cork Con and later in school in Pres.

Between Dave and Peter, I'd always tell people that these professional sports stars that you see on TV, they are still grounded and just normal fellas. Whether it's Dave playing video games or Peter doing his gardening... they're happy out of the spotlight, spending time with their families or hanging out with their friends.

They have their sporting fame, and they're not looking for extra attention.

His family were central to it in driving Dave... his dad in particular. Dave idolised John when he was growing up, and what he'd achieved in sport.

And we're all very proud of Dave with everything he has now achieved.

Watching the two of them, best friends... it's what every father and son would wish for!